AQUITAINE

Arthur Eperon is one of the most experienced and best-known travel writers in Europe. Since leaving the RAF in 1945 he has worked as a journalist in various capacities, often involving travel. He has concentrated on travel writing for the past twenty-five years and contributed to many publications including *The Times*, *Daily Telegraph*, *New York Times*, and was Travel Editor of the *Sunday Times* magazine. He has also appeared on radio and television and for five years was closely involved in Thames Television's programme *Wish You Were Here*. He has been wine writer to the RAC publications and a number of magazines.

He has an intimate and extensive knowledge of France and its food and wine as a result of innumerable visits there over the last forty years. In 1974 he won the *Prix des Provinces de France*, the annual French award for travel writing. The French Government has now awarded him the *Médaille du Merite Touristique*. His *Travellers' France* topped the paperback bestseller list for eleven weeks.

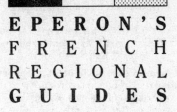

EPERON'S FRENCH REGIONAL GUIDES

AQUITAINE

ARTHUR EPERON

PAN BOOKS
LONDON, SYDNEY AND AUCKLAND

First published 1991 by Pan Books Ltd,
Cavaye Place, London SW10 9PG

1 3 5 7 9 8 6 4 2

© Arthur Eperon 1991
Illustrations © Mary Smith 1991
Maps © Ken Smith 1991

The right of Arthur Eperon to be identified as author of this
work has been asserted by him in accordance with the Copyright
Designs and Patents Act 1988.

ISBN 0 330 31221 9

Photoset by Parker Typesetting Service Leicester
Printed in England by Clays Ltd, St Ives plc

CONTENTS

KEY TO PRICES

ROOMS A = Under 100F   MEALS A = Under 75F
          B = 100–150F   B = 75–90F
          C = 150–200F   C = 90–125F
          D = 200–250F   D = 125–150F
          E = 250–350F   E = 150–175F
          F = 350–450F   F = 175–225F
          G = over 450F   G = over 225F

Room prices per night for double room without breakfast.
Meal prices include tax and service.

1   *Departments of France*

INTRODUCTION

Aquitaine is a land shaped by water, war and wine. The Romans named it Aquitania (Land of Water) for its sparkling rivers, which they used for watering their crops, for trade and transport, and for protective barriers against their enemies. But it was the sea meeting these rivers which made Bordeaux one of the great ports of Europe. And it was man's fight to hold back the ravages of sand and sea which turned Les Landes into a great brooding pine forest, which then brought riches to what had previously been poor, wild moorland.

War came with one invasion after another as tribes and countries fought for a land which controlled the Pyrenean passes, had a vast coastline and also rivers with connections deep into much of what is now southern France. The Germanic Visigoths came through Spain, the Franks came south and the Moors of North Africa came right through Spain and onward to Poitiers, seeking to spread their Mohammedan faith through all Europe. The English came through a royal marriage and stayed for 300 years, fighting off the French and the Spaniards. The French won it by war around 1453 and are still there.

So too is wine, which the Romans brought with them from Italy. Wine in the end made Aquitaine wealthy and great, gradually shaping its trade, its land, its way of life and even its philosophy.

Aquitaine is rather like Camelot – a legendary land of troubadours and fair ladies, of gallant and dastardly knights, of love affairs, political intrigue, flashing swords and brave men. Yet, technically, the name Aquitaine did not exist for hundreds of years and was only reborn in 1986 when the area became one of the new economic and development regions of the New France.

While the name always remained in the hearts of the French, to the English it was Gascony, called after the people

who lived there and their language. It was under the English
crown from 1152 to 1453 – England's first Empire. In 1152
Eleanor, who had been left the Duchy of Aquitaine when her
father Duke William X died on a pilgrimage, married young
Henri Plantagenet, Count of Anjou and Duke of Normandy,
who promptly became King Henry II of England. He ruled
from the Scottish borders to the Pyrenees. But after he and his
son Richard the Lionheart died, the French gradually won
lumps of this English Empire, so that for most of the time that
England ruled, Aquitaine stretched only from Bordeaux to the
Pyrenees. That is the area covered in this book, together with
the inland country to Auch and Toulouse, to Pau, Tarbes and
Lourdes, and the Pyrenees to the Spanish border. In modern
terms, we cover the departments of Gironde, Landes, Gers,
Pyrénées-Atlantiques and Hautes-Pyrénées, plus a small part of
Haute-Garonne to include Toulouse, which is in a different new
region called Midi-Pyrénées. Toulouse is so much the centre of
south-west France that it cannot be left out of a book either on
Aquitaine or on Languedoc-Roussillon. Like the French, I cannot find a better name than Aquitaine for this part of France.

The department of Gironde is the land of Bordeaux wine.
Bordeaux has dominated it for centuries, for here the Garonne
and Dordogne rivers run into the wide Gironde to the sea, and
these were the main trade routes until the railways came. Most
of the vineyards lie between the Dordogne and Garonne rivers
and on both banks of the Gironde – Médoc, Bourg and Blaye.

The beaches of the coast are of fine sand with dunes washed
by powerful Atlantic rollers, which are fierce and dangerous in
the wind, better for surfing than swimming. Behind the coast
are shallow lakes of silver water, *étangs* made of old water
courses, now a delight to holiday-makers for watersports.

The boundary between the departments of Gironde and
Landes is artificial and strictly for administrative purposes. For
150 miles from the little resort of Montalivet, with a vast beach
beloved by campers and nudists, to Hossegor (just north of
Bayonne) with its little watersports lake, it is really all Les Landes
– a big, sandy coastal plain which was a desert until the late
eighteenth century, unable to support even a meagre existence.
The sands were blown by Atlantic gales until they threatened

even the vineyards around Bordeaux. Nothing would grow to bind them. Then in 1788 a road- and bridge-engineer called Brémontier discovered how to hold the sand by planting a palissade of stakes 8 to 10 metres high, which built up rough walls of the sand itself 12 metres high. These were kept in place by fast growing grasses called *gourbet*. These sand walls protected from the sea the land further back, which was then planted with shrubs. When they reached a height of 2 metres in four years, pines were planted under their protection. By 1867 the work was complete, and as the pines grew, their fallen needles formed a topsoil.

Another problem arose. Further inland there was a layer of rock (*alios*) a few inches beneath the sand stopping water drainage, so the sand became a bog in winter. Herdsmen moved around it on stilts, as they did in East Anglia before the marshes were drained.

Under Napoleon III's empire an engineer named Chambrelent found a way to break up the rock. The bogs were drained, the land planted with cork oaks and evergreen trees, and Les Landes found prosperity from its forests, providing wood for pit props in France and England, for furniture, and for paper-making. The bark of the oaks was made into corks, resins were tapped from the pines for glue, sheep grazed on the tough grass of the dunes which over the years became finer.

More recently, a new threat has come with tourists and more motor cars coming to the area. Forest fires can undo in a few hours the work and growth of centuries. But the forests are still delightful – shading you from the fierce sun and surrounding you with a perfume of pine. To the south of the forest area is rich agricultural land, and from here come the duck, geese and chickens which have helped to make Gascony renowned for food.

The superb beaches right down the coast are a magnet for tens of thousands of campers in summer, with Mimizan the most popular camping resort. Arcachon, on the edge of a great basin almost enclosed by a long finger of sand, is a family resort with many hotels and villas, and loved especially by dinghy sailors and all watersportsmen. Development of villas and apartments is being very strictly controlled on the coast, and nothing over three storeys high may be built.

The queen of resorts on this whole south-west coast is Biarritz, no longer so fashionable and expensive as it was from the days when Napoleon III built a palace there until the 1930s, but still elegant and almost out of place in its surroundings. Nowadays this is part of the department called Pyrénées-Atlantiques, but to the world it is the Basque country.

The Basques are a mysterious people, hardworking,

friendly, but very independent indeed. They speak their own language, the Eskuara, and only about fifteen per cent of them live in France. The others live across the Pyrenees in the Spanish provinces Guipuzcoa and Vizcaya on the coast and in the inland provinces of Navarra and Alava.

No one knows where they came from and their language bears little resemblance to any other tongue, though it has over the centuries taken words from Latin, French, Spanish and Languedoc. The guessing game of their origins has been played by scholars through the centuries and there are few countries in the world that have not been suggested. Even Japan has been mentioned. The strangest theory was that they were Scots transplanted here by the Romans – possibly because they play bagpipes. But they were certainly here long before Roman times. The most popular and most logical suggestion is that they were an Iberian tribe driven north. Their own folklore suggests that they were a tribe of nomads who wandered the steppes of Europe with their herds thousands of years before Christ. One of their ancient folk tales tells of them losing their tribal fire and having no way of cooking or keeping warm until they found the fire again in the Pyrenees after a lightning storm had struck trees, so there they settled.

They survived, perhaps, because the Romans left them to run their own affairs. They evaded the attentions of the conquering Visigoths and of the Franks who followed them. Then for 300 years they were allowed to run their own affairs by the English. In fact, they got along so well with the English that the great Basque sailors fought alongside them against the French. They have been famous through history as sailors and fishermen and were the greatest whalers in the world from the Middle Ages, when whales were thick in the Bay of Biscay. The last whale was caught at Biarritz in 1686. The Basque fishermen followed the whales to Scotland, Iceland and to Spitzbergen. Above all, they started to fish the banks off Newfoundland for cod until Louis XIV's disastrous wars led to the Treaty of Utrecht in 1713, which gave the Newfoundland fishing rights to the English. Then they turned to a little piracy to augment their incomes. Today the boats from St Jean-de-Luz catch mainly tunny and anchovy.

The Basques have always been farmers too, growing wheat and fruit and producing mountain cheese, lamb, the famous ham smoked around Bayonne, and poultry, and they also fish for trout and salmon in the mountain streams. Like all people of the Pyrenees, the Basques were smugglers for centuries. They regarded the Spanish Basques as their brothers, members of the same nation, and they saw no reason why the foreigners of France and Spain should have a right to tax them for trading with each other. They smuggled wool from Spain and Armagnac to Spain, then later cattle and sheep, using the old paths which still exist. In wars and times of trouble, they smuggled across men, refugee families and arms. During the Spanish Civil War Republicans fleeing from Franco's forces were led across from Spain, and in the Second World War the Basques took heroic risks helping Allied airmen who had evaded capture and escaped Allied prisoners of war. Some of my friends in the RAF went home that way. The worst problem was Franco's police. The Basques from France would pass over the escapees to the anti-Franco Basques in Spain, who would pass them through a network of Republican families to the British or American Embassies in Madrid. Spain was officially neutral but Franco's police would often beat up escaped Allied prisoners and return them to the Nazis or even torture them to get information about who had helped them.

In the 1950s I was taken to see an old Basque smuggler in his cottage near St Étienne-de-Baïgorry, very near the Spanish border. 'What do you smuggle now?' I asked.

'Finished – all over,' he said. 'No smuggling now. I am old.'

'If you were young, what would you smuggle?'

'It's finished. No smuggling.'

'But just let us pretend that it has started again,' I persisted. 'What would you smuggle?'

'Transistors,' he said immediately.

'Why transistors?'

He roared with laughter. 'People in Spain can't get transistors. They are easy to hide. You were a prisoner of war. You were searched often enough. You know where to hide transistors!'

They were also smuggling spare parts for American motor cars, which were contraband then. They brought back sheep.

France was still short of mutton, lamb and wool after the Nazi occupation.

I hired what they called locally a 'jeep'. It was an old Citroën with a raised chassis to give it ground clearance and big wide wheels and tyres, obviously converted by a local garage – or smuggler! I drove it on the old mule and cart tracks, bumping around like a car with broken suspension on the East African Safari, got lost, found myself in Spain. I retreated quickly. Franco was still in power.

Recently I was driving in a Rover saloon along an official tarmac road about four miles from the frontier and was stopped by the French police. I wonder what the Basques smuggle now? Still Armagnac, I hope – not drugs.

The cliché of the 'bounding Basques' comes not only from their exuberance but because they delight in dancing and singing, especially at their fêtes. Their folk dances are for fun, not as a tourist attraction, and they are joyous – either athletic, leaping dances, accompanied by piercing whoops, or else elaborate attractive dances, beautiful when performed in brilliant costumes. In 'Danse du Verre' the dancers circle round a glass of wine and step on it for a fraction of a second without breaking or spilling it.

The Basques are great games players (especially, of course, of their own game of *pelota* – *see* Bayonne, page 68). One of France's most famous tennis players, Jean Borotra, was a Basque who was known world-wide for his great athletic feats on court. The south-west as a whole is the centre of French rugby. The famous fish restaurant at Ciboure, near St Jean-de-Luz, the Arrantzaleak, has this notice: 'Rugby teams assured a great welcome', which is not true in every restaurant in France or Britain. At Larrivière, just across the Adour river from Grenade, 10km south-east of Mont de Marsan, is a church dedicated to Notre-Dame de Rugby!

As you go inland, the peaks grow higher into Hautes-Pyrénées, with Vignemale, 50km south of Lourdes on the Spanish border, reaching 3298 metres. You can see it best by driving to La Gavarnie and on to Col de Tantes, then walking the last stretch to the top (*le pic*) at 2322 metres. The panoramic views are superb. In fact this is an area of superb scenery, and Gavarnie is a great walking, climbing and skiing centre. Along this border with Spain is the Parc National des Pyrénées, set up in 1962 to protect nature. It runs for 100km between the Aspe valley and Pic de Néouvielle. Hunting, digging up flowers, fires, camping, even dogs are forbidden. But if you follow the rules you can fish in the rivers and 230 lakes. There are salmon here and a lot of trout. There are twenty-four mountain refuge huts in the park and the GR10 (*Grande Randonnée*) long-distance footpath goes through parts of it and skirts it, with other paths from it leading into wilder stretches. The park is the refuge of the last twenty or so brown bears left in France and a few hundred marmots, 'squirrels' which live underground and hibernate.

In the Ice Age, the Central Pyrenees were swept by great glaciers, leaving behind the awesome cirques cut out of the older mountains of granite. Cirque de la Gavarnie is particularly spectacular.

There are few valleys leading into the mountains and many roads, of course, are snow-blocked in winter. Some roads are not for the faint-hearted, even in summer.

When snows melt in spring, the sheep are brought up in flocks to graze. The fast-flowing rivers are mostly called *gaves*, though some are called *nives* or *nestes*. Some are harnessed now for hydroelectric power. Many of the important *gaves* run through the Béarn, west and south of Pau, the area which was joined by Napoleon with the Pays Basque, to form the department of Pyrénées-Atlantiques. Béarn was originally Basse-Navarre, the kingdom which became a hotbed of Protestanism. Its rivers include the Gaves de Pau, Aspe, Azun, Ossau and Baretou. Its mountain slopes produce renowned lamb and sheep's-milk cheese. Much of the lamb's cheese used for the making of Roquefort in the Auvergne comes from Béarn. Its plains are famous for chickens, ducks and geese. So are the plains of Gers, the department north of the Pyrenees and east of Les Landes, still known over most of the world outside Paris as Armagnac.

Auch in Gers was the capital of old Armagnac. The delightful town of Condom is the centre of Armagnac brandy. With travellers this is a rather neglected area. Its villages are pleasant and still truly agricultural and its little towns are busy, unpretentious, friendly and have atmosphere. There are many *bastides*, too. Bastides were fortified villages started in the thirteenth century during the Hundred Years War, by both English and French, to protect farmers from wandering bands of hungry soldiers on both sides, and especially from 'routiers', the troops of soldiers who would fight for anyone who would pay them and looted everything they could. The peasants were bribed to move into the bastides with land outside to which they went each day, and with immunity from call-up as soldiers. French and British armies not only needed their food but also safe places to sleep overnight when on the march. They had fortified churches and market squares with arcaded stores.

Armagnac is a region of scenic rolling hills, and tree-lined roads through vineyards, fields of wheat and sunflowers, and past tranquil, inviting lakes. It is an area to explore to find the spirit of south-west France in more senses than one.

Despite recent industrialization, mainly around Toulouse and Bordeaux, the Gascons remain close to the fields and especially to vineyards. The hearty, hard-drinking, heavy-eating, hard-fighting, independent Gascon who bows to nobody was not an invention of writers.

It is no accident that the heart of French rugby is in the south-west – Bordeaux, Toulouse and Les Landes, as well as the Pays Basque. The rugby players' commitment to half-slaughter the other side on the field then drink happily as friends after the game is still very Gascon. Alexandre Dumas had it right in *The Three Musketeers*, even if he was a northerner. But then D'Artagnan was based on a real live Gascon, and before he wrote the story, Dumas had read a highly romanticized 'life' of D'Artagnan (*see* Auch, page 61).

Dumas made D'Artagnan brave, gallant, hard-drinking and womanizing and few Gascons would quarrel with that. But he also returned to tend his Gascon estates between Army duties. That fits, too.

HOW TO GO

AIR
Heathrow–Bordeaux (Air France, British Airways).
Gatwick–Bordeaux (Euro Express – seasonal).
Heathrow–Biarritz (Air France – seasonal).
Heathrow–Toulouse (Air France).
Gatwick–Toulouse (Euro Express; Nouvelles Frontières – 071-629-7772).
Gatwick–Lourdes/Tarbes (Dan Air).
        Lourdes (Euro Express).
Gatwick–Pau (Air Littorel – 081-759-1818).

RAIL
TGV high speed trains Paris–Bordeaux.
French Motorail car-carrying trains:
Boulogne–Biarritz (13 hrs), Bordeaux (11 hrs), Toulouse (12 hrs) – all seasonal.
Paris–Biarritz (8 hrs), Bordeaux (6½–8 hrs), Tarbes (9½ hrs), Toulouse (12 hrs).
Lille–Biarritz (10–12 hrs) – seasonal.

ROAD
Motorways from just outside Boulogne/Calais/Dunkerque right through to Bordeaux and Toulouse via Paris. Or pick up A10 motorway at Orleans or Tours to Bordeaux, then A62 to Toulouse. A65 from Bordeaux to Bilbao in Spain via St Jean-de-Luz already built in stretches at each end, missing in the middle, where you use double-tracked N10.

HISTORY

When in 56BC the Romans under Crassus came to south-west France and called it Aquitania (Land of Water) because of its many rivers and coastline, Gaulish tribes already had large settlements around Bordeaux and Toulouse, and the Basques were already on the coast near Bayonne. They were on one of the main trade routes which linked Greece to England through southern France. Caesar Augustus spread Roman rule to the Loire and Massif Central and the Romans divided Aquitania into three provinces – Aquitania Prima, east of Limoges and Cahors, with Bourg as capital; Aquitania Secunda from Poitiers to Agen and Bordeaux, with Bordeaux as capital; Novempopulania, stretching south from Bazas to the Pyrenees. The Basques were more or less left to themselves. Bordeaux was the most important place because of its port and its position as meeting point of routes, and there over 400 years a powerful and prosperous Gallo-Roman culture grew up.

The poet and teacher Ausonius was a Bordeaux man, tutor to Gratian, the Roman emperor's son, a Roman consul, and theoretically at least, a Christian. He was a keen wine producer, and one of the best wines of St Émilion is still called Château-Ausone.

As the Roman Empire collapsed, the wine was almost all that remained of the Roman influence. Roman civilization was destroyed by the invasion of the Visigoths from Spain, who swept through the Pyrenean passes up to the Loire, taking Aquitaine. Then they met the Franks, who were sweeping south, and were defeated. The Franks reached the Pyrenees but Aquitaine was too remote for the rule to be effective, and in the sixth century an Iberian tribe called the Vascones, with their own language, came through the Pyrenees and took the flat lands to the river Adour. Over the years they spread their rule to the Garonne, and mingling with the population became known as Gascons, developed a new dialect called Gascon.

The Moors crossed the Pyrenees in the eighth century, sweeping through France as they had through Christian Spain, and threatening to turn Europe into a Mohammedan empire. Edward Martel defeated them at Poitiers to save Europe and

Christianity, and they fled south, destroying everything in their path.

Charlemagne, grandson of Edward Martel, King of the Franks and Emperor of the Romans, who spread Christianity across Europe at the point of the sword, ruled Aquitaine, crushing frequent revolts ruthlessly. Only the Basques succeeded against his all-conquering army. As he was marching from conquests in Spain to put down a revolt by the Saxons, the Basques waylaid his army in the pass at Roncevaux and destroyed all his rearguard by rolling trees and huge stones down on them from the mountainsides. Charlemagne made Aquitaine (based on Poitiers) and Gascony into separate Dukedoms. But on his death in AD 814 his empire was split between quarrelling sons, and invaded by the Norsemen who swept up almost every river and tributary of western France in their long boats each spring, looting, burning, killing and raping, to sail back north in the autumn with their loot and prisoners. In 848 they destroyed Bordeaux. They attacked Bayonne, Dax, Tarbes and Condom, too. But when the Norsemen suddenly settled in Normandy and became Christians, the Dukes of Gascony took over and the towns were rebuilt. In 1058 the duchies of Gascony and Aquitaine merged under the title of Aquitaine. Béarn was ruled by the Dukes of Foix. Both remained separate from France and French kings had no power over them.

Religion brought much of their prosperity. The great pilgrimages had begun around 950 to the tomb of St James at Compostela on the Spanish coast just south of the Pyrenees. Rich and poor from all over Europe made their way to Compostela. They spent money as they went and the rich gave great gifts to the Church to build churches, monasteries and hospitals, the houses which sheltered pilgrims. Five of these pilgrim routes went through Aquitaine, through what was then called Basse-Navarre, the part of Navarre on the north side of the Pyrenees. The gathering point to cross the mountains was St Jean-Pied-de-Port. Bands of fake pilgrims called *coquillards* used to attack and rob the true pilgrims.

It was on a pilgrimage to Compostela in 1137 that William X, Duke of Aquitaine, died. He ruled Gascony, Périgord, Limousin, Poitou, the Saintonge, part of Auvergne and the county of Toulouse. His heir was his fifteen-year-old daughter, Eleanor, and he had just arranged for her to marry Louis, heir to the French throne. The French were delighted to rush the marriage through. The lands she had just inherited were her dowry. The same year, he became King Louis VII and, with France and Aquitaine in his kingdom, the richest ruler in Europe. Alas, Louis was extremely pious, liked to dress in the woollen robe of a penitent and dine on plain fare. He had hoped to go into the Church until his elder brother was killed in an accident and he became heir. Eleanor was intelligent, well-educated and strong-willed. She was also beautiful and romantic. This was the age of troubadours and she had listened to their romantic songs and to the tales of chivalry and war from minstrels in her father's castle halls since she was a child. She was motherless and her father had let her sit beside him, listening and learning. She needed a strong husband. The vassal lords of Aquitaine were a quarrelling, warring lot and a girl of fifteen was unlikely to be able to control them.

She had the wrong husband. She was no penitent. She liked lovely clothes, music, wine, sunshine, excitement. She was soon bored with the grey skies of Paris and the cheerless court of Louis. She was what would now be called 'fun loving'.

Her two children were both girls. Louis the Pious showed no signs of giving her an heir. She complained that he was more like a monk than a husband.

When Louis started his disastrous crusade to the Holy Land, she insisted upon going with him. While he was busy out there in the sunshine of Palestine his fun-loving wife was enjoying herself with the odd knight. That, anyway, is what Louis later accused her of doing, and it is likely to be true.

In 1152 the Count of Anjou, called Geoffrey Plantagenet because he wore yellow broom (*planta genista*) in his hat, took his wife Matilda, granddaughter of William the Conqueror, and their eighteen-year-old son Henry to the court of Louis and Eleanor in Paris. Henry was already Duke of Normandy and had claims to the English throne after the death of Stephen. He was athletic, handsome, with flaming red hair, and full of life. Matilda's idea was to betroth him to the five-year-old Marie, elder daughter of Louis and Eleanor, so that one day Henry might rule England, Normandy, Aquitaine and France. But it was Eleanor, bored, beautiful and thirty, who cast her eye on this young man.

Whether the divorce from Louis was her idea, his or egged on by the French court who needed an heir for France is not known. Divorced they were, on the grounds that they were too close blood relations to have been married in the first place. She was to leave her children behind in Paris but Louis returned her dowry of the Duchy of Aquitaine, which shows how much he wanted to get rid of her.

She had to flee quickly to Aquitaine. She was a great prize and two landless younger sons of rulers tried to kidnap her to make her marry them. But within two months she was married to young Henry. Next year he was confirmed as heir to the English throne, and by 1154 he was Henry II of England, ruler from the Tweed to the Pyrenees, of England and of what was called the Angevin Empire. His capital was at Poitiers, then in Anjou. He was hardly an Englishman. He had been born at Le Mans, he had Norman ancestry, he died at Chinon and spent much of his life warring in France, including with his own sons.

There seems little doubt that Eleanor was really in love with Henry for some years, and she produced five sons. The eldest died in childhood. The second, Henry, born in 1155, was his father's favourite and at fifteen was crowned as associate and heir to Henry as the Young King. Richard was Eleanor's favourite. He was very handsome, with golden-red hair, clever, a poet, musician and brave soldier. At fifteen Eleanor had him made Duke of Aquitaine. Geoffrey, the next brother, was killed in a tournament in Paris. The youngest son was John, a weak lad known as John Lackland, because his father and mother had apportioned all their estates to the others before he grew up.

Henry II kept his hands on the power and the purse. While he was away in England, Eleanor ruled Aquitaine. They both, it seems, found life lonely when apart. Henry's girlfriends included the Fair Rosamond – Rosamond Clifford, who bore him two sons. The story that she was murdered by a jealous Eleanor was invented in the fourteenth century, and 'improved' through the centuries. Eleanor was rumoured to be busy herself with troubadours and especially a page. This is supposed to have been the reason why Henry imprisoned her in a tower. There is a more likely reason.

Young Henry was impatient to get his hands on the throne of England. A new king of France, Philippe-Auguste, who wanted to topple the Angevin Empire, encouraged him to revolt. Young Henry went to join him in Paris. Richard followed and Eleanor decided to join them. The story is that Eleanor, dressed as a man, was caught by Henry II's guards and after that she was interned by her husband.

Young Henry, supported by the French, and egged on by Eleanor, fought his father, but finally could not pay his troops and stole the treasures of the shrine of Rocamadour. He died in agony in Martel of a disease which even he believed was sent by God as a punishment for his sacrilege.

Richard Coeur de Lion continued to help the French king fight his father and then Henry's new favourite, John, turned against him, too. Henry, defeated in battle, simply gave up and died of exhaustion. But Philippe-Auguste now found a tougher opponent in Richard, who fought him successfully. Richard went on a crusade and was captured and imprisoned in Germany on his way back. When he did return he had to go to England to put down discontent stirred by his brother John. Luckily Eleanor looked after his Angevin Empire so successfully that, despite John's intrigues and feuding lords in Aquitaine, Richard's far-flung lands remained intact.

After he was killed through carelessness in a minor siege in 1199, John took over and was no match for the guiles of France's Philippe-Auguste. Philippe had no physical courage but he was a clever and cunning fighter and diplomat and John lost all of the Angevin Empire in Europe within twenty-five years except the cut down Aquitaine from the Garonne to the Pyrenees. Eleanor was still in charge of Aquitaine, even when she had officially retired to the abbey of Fontevrault. Eleanor, who was now seventy-eight years of age, even protected John for the sake of her beloved Aquitaine, although he had double-crossed Richard when he was at the crusades, and tried to seize Richard's lands. At eighty she held the town Mirabeau for John until his army arrived. She died at Fontevrault in 1204.

The Gascon lords quarrelled among themselves under English rule but the Gascons as a whole were in favour of it. They did not feel like an occupied people, especially under Richard. They regarded him as a local boy. The English gave them autonomy and brought them great prosperity from trade with Britain. You could meet Gascons on the streets of London just as English wandered the streets of Bordeaux. In fact it was the English who wondered sometimes if the togetherness was worth while. Aquitaine was expensive to England and its lords were often troublesome, seeking to undermine each other's influence or steal each other's lands. One Count of Toulouse in particular was a troublemaker, although he was married to Richard's sister Joanna.

The French kings were not the only ones to covet Aquitaine. In 1205 Alfonso VIII of Castile in Spain claimed Gascony as part of the dowry of his wife Eleanor, daughter of Eleanor of Aquitaine. He made an alliance with Philippe-Auguste, gained the support of local lords such as the Viscount of Béarn, a great troublemaker to the English, and even of the Bishop of Bayonne, and invaded, expecting a walkover. But the people of Bayonne closed their gates and defended themselves. The successful resistance in the north was led by the Archbishop of Bordeaux. The Spaniards retired hurt. Aquitaine maintained a surprisingly successful fight against French and Spanish take-overs through the Middle Ages.

Henry III of England, a misguided monarch who followed John, got himself into great trouble trying to take back the Poitou which John had lost and he unsettled Gascony so much that the notoriously fickle Gascon lords saw another chance to feather their nests, attacking each other and disturbing the peace in Aquitaine. Henry decided to send a strong man, the Earl of Leicester – none other than Simon de Montfort, third son of the Simon de Montfort who had led the vicious 'crusade' for the Pope against the Albigensian rebel Christians in south France and used it to push his own interests. This younger Simon de Montfort had the most useful family connections in France, Aquitaine and England and had gone to the English court as his best chance of gaining power and fortune. Simon had a tough job. The lords of Aquitaine, he complained in a letter to King Henry III, 'rob the earth, burn and pillage, riding by night in the manner of thieves'. Once again the worst was Gaston de Béarn, the Viscount of Béarn, who would change sides in a flash if it were to his advantage. Simon discouraged him by imprisoning his neighbour, the Viscount of Soule, for not answering a summons to court and a truce was called. And he settled a family vendetta in Bordeaux which was virtually a civil war.

Simon's methods were very harsh. He used the toughest penalty in a wine-growing country – he confiscated men's vineyards or cut down their vines. Complaints against him by Gascons poured into London, led by Gérard de Malemort, Archbishop of Bordeaux. Henry recalled Simon de Montfort, sent for Gascon leaders and held an inquiry which was conducted like a shouting match on both sides. The English barons saw to it that Simon won the case but Henry III promptly reversed the decision, no doubt to avoid revolt in Aquitaine. However when Simon returned to Aquitaine, he started reprisals against his enemies and the Gascons replied with enthusiasm. Henry settled the matter by paying off Simon de Montfort and making his own son Edward Duke of Aquitaine. The lad was thirteen years of age, and the new king of Castile, Alfonso X, saw his chance to claim Aquitaine and encouraged Gascon barons to join him. Gaston de Béarn, of course, did so.

Henry's settlement of this problem had a strange side-result. He went to Gascony and sent back to London a request for an army and money to defend it. In return for providing this, he agreed that two elected knights from each shire in England should go to Westminster to agree the grant to the King. It was the first step to formation of the Parliament which de Montfort and the barons later forced on Henry after defeating and capturing him at the Battle of Lewes.

He settled Aquitaine's problems by typical medieval diplomacy. He married off the fifteen-year-old heir to the English throne, Edward, to Alfonso of Castile's half-sister, Eleanor. To subdue Gaston de Béarn, he bribed de Montfort to come back to Aquitaine and do the job!

At the beginning of the Hundred Years War between France and England, fought over the hereditary right to the French crown (1352–1453), Edward III of England made his son Edward (the Black Prince), Prince of Aquitaine after his remarkably brilliant command of a wing of the army at Crécy at the age of sixteen.

A dashing, brave and intelligent soldier with a flair for show, he was just the type to appeal to the Gascons, especially after his great victory at Poitiers when his Anglo-Gascon army captured the French King Jean II and many important French nobles. The Gascons shared in the money from their ransoms. Among those he captured was du Guesclin, the great Breton soldier and French national hero who fought for French kings.

After Joan of Arc rallied French morale, the French gradually won Aquitaine. The people of Aquitaine felt no particular enthusiasm for Joan and none for France, but the war was ruining them. The Black Death which had swept Europe and the losses of men in the war had left vineyards in a sorry state, some ruined, some without men to work them. Trade with England was very greatly reduced. The population of English Gascony fell from 600,000 around 1300 to about 150,000 by 1414, but Bordeaux stayed remarkably loyal to England to the end. It had fewer population problems than the rest of Aquitaine, for peasant families had fled there from the bands of roving 'routiers', the freelance soldiers and thugs who went around in gangs during the Hundred Years War looting, stealing, raping, burning down houses, and killing families.

As the French forces won victories elsewhere, many Gascon barons decided that backing the French was a safer bet than staying on the English side. Bordeaux was finally taken by an army under the brilliant soldier Dunois, 'the bastard of Orléans', who had been Joan of Arc's beloved companion in arms and had continued her work of throwing out the English after her death. Bayonne fell to Dunois shortly after Bordeaux.

The Bordelais were soon accusing French officials of breaking their surrender agreement and made it plain to the English that they would like them back. The old English General Talbot, once a great soldier and hero but now aged over seventy, arrived with a small fleet and army and retook Bordeaux with the help of the citizens. Alas, Talbot was lured to Castillon to fight a French force, was fooled by a false report into believing that the French were fleeing, rushed out to chase them and fell into a trap. Most of his troops were destroyed by the clever use of artillery by Jean Bureau, who had been Bordeaux's master of artillery under the English. Talbot was killed, but a good Bordeaux wine is still named after him. The French besieged and took Cadillac (*see* page 141) castle, then attacked Bordeaux, which fought bravely, even taking on a French fleet from La Rochelle with its own little ships.

When inevitably surrender came, the English were allowed to leave, the Gascon leaders were banished from the French kingdom, Aquitaine was lost to England.

Charles VII of France, 'the little Dauphin' into whom Joan of Arc had had to instil the courage to become king, fined Bordeaux heavily and took away all the privileges that the English had given it, such as self-rule and freedom from tax on wine. Charles built castles to keep the citizens from revolt and made Bordeaux pay for them and for the cost of the occupying French soldiers. Bordeaux became so impoverished that the people were seething with revolt and Charles was forced to reduce the fine and grant very limited self-government. When Louis XI became king in 1461 he gave back self-government, cut the tax on wine drastically, exempted the city from other taxes, and granted the city two important fairs each year. No one, not even officials accompanying the king, would be lodged at the city's expense.

As a result, the wine trade with England was renewed, forming the basis of the prosperity of north Aquitaine.

The Albret family, kings of Navarre, became the powerful family of the Gascon Pyrenees, controlling Béarn, Foix and Bigorre, though in 1512 they lost the lands of their kingdom of Navarre south of the Pyrenees to Ferdinand of Aragon, the King of Spain. In 1527 Henri d'Albret married Marguerite d'Angoulême, sister of the French King Francois I, and when their daughter Jeanne succeeded to their titles she became a Protestant, which changed the history not only of the south-west but of France (*see* Pau, page 85). When the Religious Wars broke out, she and her son Henri de Navarre became leaders of the Protestant cause. Henri went to La Rochelle to join the Protestant army and fought as a commander at the Battle of Jarnac. He became leader of the Protestants, but during a lull in the wars married Marguerite de Valois, sister of Charles IX of France.

All the leading Protestants were invited to their wedding in Paris on St Bartholomew's Night and massacred by the men of Catholic Duc de Guise. Henri took over his armies again, won battles and gained a favourable peace. The death of the Duke of Anjou made him heir to the throne. He returned to Aquitaine to collect more troops and money and won battle after battle against the extreme Catholic League who were making the Catholic cause unpopular. After the death of Charles he was technically barred, as a Protestant, from taking the throne and the Catholics opposed him. 'Paris is worth a Mass,' said Henri, and became a Catholic. Some say that he did it to get the crown, others that he did it to unite France and put a stop to the Religious Wars. He was soon offered the keys of Paris and was crowned Henri IV. He was the most popular of the French kings, though not with the barons, for he curtailed the power of local governors and nobles, collected taxes to make France solvent, and built roads which encouraged commerce but discouraged local despots.

It is said that he never returned to Pau. But by his Edict of Nantes, making the Protestant faith legal, he brought a temporary peace to the south-west. And in his life style he behaved very much like a Gascon. He loved good food, wine and women and never shrank from a fight.

Pau became the Protestant centre. After Henri was murdered by a monk inspired by the Jesuits, the Edict of Nantes was repealed, the persecution of Protestants began again and the south-west suffered barbaric oppression once more as Louis XIV and Richelieu set out to destroy the Protestant faith. Aquitaine was forced into further control from Paris.

Even the bourgeoisie of Bordeaux and the Gironde department backed the French Revolution. They thought it was time for a change from a corrupt royal rule which stifled trade and left the people desperately poor and, rather naïvely, they thought that the Revolution was the change they sought. At first, the Girondins, as they were called, were such a powerful party that they led the National Assembly and the country. But these doctors, lawyers, merchants and teachers were not trained to run a country and were soon overpowered and then literally killed off by the blood-thirsty Jacobins led by Robespierre (*see* Bordeaux, page 75).

Napoleon's attempt to add Spain to his Empire drew Aquitaine into his wars, and as Wellington's army defeated Soult's French army and chased them through the Pyrenees, the fighting came to the Pyrenees and Aquitaine in 1813. When Wellington chased Soult out of the south-west he left behind a small force to besiege Bayonne, which fell. It was the last French town to do so before the return of Napoleon for his Hundred Days of Glory and defeat.

Gironde continued to prosper until the 1850s by exporting wine to the rest of France and especially Britain. Then the dreaded phylloxera disease hit the vines and it took until near the end of the century to strip the vineyards, clean the soil, replant vines grafted on to clean stock from California – much of which had come originally from Bordeaux – and to mature the vines until they produced great wine again.

Meanwhile Napoleon III had married a lovely Spanish girl, Eugénie, daughter of the Countess of Montijo. She had spent happy childhood holidays in a fishing village called Biarritz on the coast near Bayonne, and she persuaded Napoleon to take her there. They built a holiday home there, Villa Eugénie, and, of course, the village suddenly became fashionable with princes, the rich and famous, and those pretending to be rich or famous. Queen Victoria's visit ensured British support. Napoleon III lost his empire and fled to Chislehurst in Kent, where he built another villa which later became the clubhouse of the golf-course. But Biarritz made the Basque country a fashionable holiday area until the Second World War. Now it is more popular than fashionable.

In the 1860s the Pyrenean spas became fashionable too, especially after the Route Thermale was built from Eaux Bonnes to Bagnères-de-Bigorre. Skiing started to become popular from 1920. During the Second World War Bordeaux was inevitably a centre of the Resistance, with its ties with Britain, the independent spirit of its people, its port and, of course, its nearness to the Pyrenean smuggling routes. Earlier, in 1940, the French government had moved to Bordeaux away from the Nazi armies sweeping across the north, and it was there that the French premier Paul Reynaud pleaded with the generals and other politicians to keep France fighting, from North Africa if necessary. At Bordeaux France received Churchill's offer of an Anglo-

French Union, with twin citizenship for French and Britons. Alas, General Weygand and Marshal Pétain had their way. France capitulated. And it was from Merignac airfield at Bordeaux that General de Gaulle boarded a small plane and flew to England to continue the fight under the banner of his Free French.

Bordeaux became a Nazi submarine base, U-boats sinking much Allied shipping. Merignac airfield was used for four-engined Focke-Wulf bombers which directed submarines on to Allied convoys around Ireland, but RAF raids took their toll on these.

The post-war decline in agriculture led inevitably to some industrialization in Gascony, difficult for the people, for they had never been deeply involved in industry. The harnessing of power from the mountain rivers for electricity came later than in the Alps because of the hot, dry summers and lack of glaciers to provide summer water. But now the problem is solved by using mountain lake water to regulate the flow through the year. Huge dams have been built at very high levels, like Barrage de Cap-de-Long near Lac d'Orédon. The discovery of very big oil- and natural-gas deposits at Lacq just west of Pau, and of oil at Parentis in Les Landes have turned the south-west into a producer of a third of France's gas consumption. But, like North Sea oil, gas deposits are beginning to run out, so the industries which followed the gas bonanza (aluminium, sulphur, fertilizers, chemicals) will have to find a new power source by the year 2000) – probably nuclear power. Then what will happen to the network of brightly coloured pipes and cylinders which look so out of place in the valley? Lacq is run by the big state-controlled company Elf-Aquitaine.

The name Aquitaine is sneaking back. When Paris divided France into 'régions' for economic development and planning they called one of them 'Aquitaine' with Bordeaux as capital, but its boundaries are artificial, though not so completely artificial as those of 'Midi-Pyrénées', of which Toulouse is a rather bemused capital. The 'régional' set-up was the cause of great political and local wrangling. It finally came into being between 1982 and 1986, when the first régional elections were held.

So the name of Aquitaine lives officially again. But the

région is not the Aquitaine of which Frenchmen have talked and dreamed for centuries – nor will it be for a few years yet.

ARTS

Bordeaux's great man of letters was not actually born in Bordeaux. Michel Eyquem de Montaigne, the man who invented the word and literary form which we call the essay, was born at Château de Montaigne at Montcaret in Périgord in 1533. His great-grandfather, Ramon Eyquem, was a Bordeaux wine merchant who bought the château to buy himself into the aristocracy.

Michel had an eccentric upbringing. He was made to speak nothing but Latin at home until he was six. Then he was sent to the College of Guyenne at Bordeaux to be taught by the Scottish humanist George Buchanan. He studied law at Toulouse University and practised at the Bordeaux bar, which he hated. He gave it up at thirty-five when his father died and left him the family estate. He wrote and published his *Essais* and other works.

He was persuaded against his will to be Mayor of Bordeaux during the terrible times of the Religious Wars. A Catholic and loyal to Charles IX, he was a personal friend of Henri of Navarre, the Protestant leader, and tried to bring the extreme Catholic Leaguers and the Protestants together. His philosophy contradicted modern theories of competition and striving to succeed: to live an orderly and tranquil life was the true aim, not to win battles, and gain wealth, land or property. Constantly advocating tolerance in a highly intolerant age, he pointed out that no two men had the same opinions on the same thing, which did not endear him to the Catholic Church or the political powers of the time. He had a fine sense of humour. He had strong opinions on smells. He disliked the smell of Paris but loved the smell of good food.

One of Montaigne's closest friends who had an influence on him was Étienne de la Boëtie (born 1530 in Sarlat). He was a counsellor in Bordeaux Parliament at twenty-four, wrote poetry and powerful essays, and translated classics from Greek to

French. But he did not publish his works. He became better known after his death through Montaigne's *Essay on Friendship* about him. Montaigne published a number of his works. The one which made the most impact was subversive stuff for those days – 'Voluntary Servitude'. It argued that the root of a tyrant's power was not his own strength or ability but the sycophancy of those who supported him to gain position or profit. He wrote that it was unbelievable that anyone could give up personal freedom for position and profit. Those who did not rebel against tyranny were as guilty as the tyrants.

Another Bordeaux writer and reluctant politician was Charles Secondat who became Baron Montesquieu. He was born at the wine Château of La Brède in the Graves area in 1689 (*see* page 141). He was talked into becoming President of Bordeaux Parliament but much preferred to be back in his library reading. He claimed that there was no depression in life which could not be cured by an hour's reading. He was a great Anglophile, sold much of the wine from his two estates in Graves and one in Entre-Deux-Mers to the English, and was a friend and travelling companion of the Earl of Chesterfield, politician, traveller and essayist. Montesquieu's great works included *Esprit des Lois* published in 1748, suggesting widespread changes in French law. It had some influence on the French Revolutionaries forty years later. Another important work was *Grandeur et Décadence des Romains* – an inspiration possibly for Gibbon's *Decline and Fall of the Roman Empire*. He was known in his lifetime for a novel told in letters called *Les Lettres Persanes* (1721), about a humorously licentious Persian harem intrigue. In it two characters visited France, giving him a chance to satirize Parisian society. His Utopian race of cave-dwellers dated their troubles from the day they elected a King once more. The Gascon disdain for Paris and the Royal court shows through.

The third 'M' of Bordeaux was born there in 1885 into a pious, severe Catholic family. François Mauriac, regarded by many as the leading novelist of the Catholic faith, moved to Paris when he was twenty but set many of his brooding novels in the woods of Les Landes. He wrote of temptation, sin and redemption – of damnation and divine grace, personified in his character Thérèse Desqueyroux, about whom three of his best books

were written. She was driven mad by the claustrophobic forest
and the narrow life she led. Mauriac's family had a strangely
Norman-looking gabled summer-house at St Symphorien, on the
D3 west of Bazas and on the very edge of Les Landes forest. Here
François spent happy holidays as a boy and the family still own it.
He wrote about it in his novel *Le Mystère Frontenac*.

Once, St Symphorien was in the wild boggy moors of Les
Landes, so treacherous that the shepherds in sheepskin coats took
to stilts to tend their flocks. As the sheep ate the coarse, poor
grass, these tough men knitted the wool they had spun in winter.
Then the forests were planted, leaving *étangs* (lagoons) between
the trees, and that is how it was when Mauriac wrote his books. In
1949 came a terrible forest fire when more than 150,000 hectares
were destroyed. Now it has become a holiday area with holiday
and retirement bungalows in the forest clearings.

Later Mauriac himself had a holiday home, a mansion called
Malagar near Verdelais, among vineyards with views across the
Garonne to Langon and the vine-clad hills of Château d'Yquem.
Less than a kilometre from the grounds of the house is the
cemetery where the painter Toulouse-Lautrec was buried in
1901 (*see* Verdelais, page 246). He had come to his mother's
château of Malromé 3km away to try to recover his health, but
he died there.

FOOD

The Gascons have always eaten heartily and the people of the
Pyrenees just as heartily but with more spices. Half-raw ducks'
breasts in raspberry vinegar, mousses like Grandma used to
make for babies, décor on a plate in the form of fingers of meat
with slivers of carrot and kiwi fruit – these were never for the
Gascons nor Basques. Their traditional dishes – *garbure*, *confits*
of goose and duck, *cassoulet*, *poulet en pot*, *salmis* of partridge
and pigeon – are filling, fattening, luscious and rewarding. Yet
here in the little spa of Eugénie-les-Bains in Les Landes the
great Michel Guérard launched his *cuisine minceur* – his gastronomic diet for slimmers (*see* page 159). But Guérard is a master,
and his *cuisine gourmande* for those not in the slimming mood

would seduce a penitent sworn to bread and water to break his vows.

Very few restaurants outside Bordeaux flirted with yesterday's fashion for nouvelle cuisine. Bordeaux likes to think of itself as being in the top three gastronomic centres of France with Lyon and Paris, even if Michelin does only give stars to six of its restaurants, and so it was inevitable that some restaurants provide for the well-heeled young bourgeoisie who until recently followed the Gault-Millau guide like a gourmet's bible. It seemed rather perverse to offer nouvelle portions within a short drive of splendid fresh vegetables, superb Bazas beef, lamb of the Pauillac marshes rivalling the salt-marsh lamb of Normandy, milk-fed lamb, all the superb ducks, geese and turkeys of Les Landes. But I am glad to say that, as Marc de Champérard, the gourmet-guide writer, said in his 1990 edition, 'Nouvelle cuisine is the cooking of yesterday.' Modern (or 'young') regional cooking ('*La Jeune Cuisine du Terroir*') is in, and that means we shall again be offered the local dishes of France, even if the sauces and the portions are a little lighter than when I was young.

The return to old regional cooking has quite frightened some young chefs brought up on nouvelle. One asked me anxiously if I knew any good old recipes of his area.

I heard no such anxiety in Aquitaine. Very few Gascons ever abandoned their own regional dishes made with fresh local ingredients. Fish is inevitably splendid around here. Fishing boats land their catches at Bordeaux and St Jean-de-Luz in the Basque country. The Gironde estuary is along the Médoc wine road from Bordeaux. Arcachon's oyster beds are just down the coast. Freshwater fish come from the Dordogne and Garonne rivers, and the rivers further south which flow down from the Pyrenees are rich in trout and still produce salmon. Adour salmon poached in red wine is an old delicacy of Bayonne. The Adour produces *piballes* (young eels) too. These appear in late winter and early March, are fried, and are very much nicer than you would think.

On the Bordeaux waterfront they still clean and open oysters outside little restaurants to lure you inside. There the oysters may be served very cold with hot spicy little sausages

called *crépinettes*, hunks of bread and dry white Bordeaux wine. You swallow an oyster, take a bite from the sausage, a bite of bread and a large draught of wine, than start again. In very posh places, the *crépinettes* will be truffled.

Mussels are cooked in red wine and tomatoes or in mouclade (white wine and cream). Little red mullet (*petit rougets*) are baked with chervil (*cerfeuil*). *Bar aux cèpes* (sea bass in cèpe sauce) is delightful but the cèpes are often replaced with lesser mushrooms in cheaper restaurants. *Cèpes* are found in autumn in woods, mainly around Margaux. Some are canned or dried to use later but they are at their very best fresh, stewed with parsley and garlic in butter in Bordeaux area, in olive oil in other places. Sometimes grape juice is added.

Lamproies (lampreys), migratory eels caught in the estuaries and rivers, are sliced and cooked with leeks, red wine, garlic and, if possible, blood of the eels – *à la bordelaise*. Leeks used to grow wild in the vineyards and were called 'wine workers' asparagus', but now they are cultivated because pesticides killed off the wild ones.

Dishes described as *bordelais* or *à la bordelaise* have no consistent ingredients. *Sauce bordelaise* is made of shallots, red or white

wine (usually red), butter, tarragon, parsley and should include
bone marrow. Fish and shellfish *à la bordelaise* are usually cooked
in wine with vegetables or herbs. *Homard à la bordelaise* is boiled
lobster flamed with Armagnac brandy, and served with white
wine and egg sauce. *Morue à la bordelaise* is salt cod cooked in
white wine with tomatoes, garlic and red peppers. A beautiful
dish of red mullet is called *rougets à la girondine*. The fish are
cooked in butter with shallots, then a sauce is made of garlic,
onions, shallots and mushrooms, preferably *cèpes*, all finely
chopped and cooked until golden in butter and oil. Flour is
stirred in, white wine and Armagnac are added, with seasoning
and a bouquet garni of herbs, and it is all simmered for ten
minutes; then the fish are removed and some fish stock or water
is added to the sauce, which is then strained and poured over the
mullet.

In the Pyrenees, salmon steaks and trout are braised with
mushrooms, tomatoes and shallots in dry white Jurançon wine,
with cream stirred into the liquid (*saumon au Jurançon*). Another
great dish is trout stuffed with duck. *Chipirons* is the Basque
name for squid (ink fish). It is often stuffed with tomatoes and
stewed in its own ink.

In harder times, like sieges, *entrecôte bordelaise* was the cynical
name for a rather unappetizing dish – rats grown fat in wine
warehouses, soaked in wine and grilled. Now gourmets insist
that it is not the *real* dish unless the beef comes from Bazas. To
most of us it is any *entrecôte* (rib steak) grilled and served in wine
and shallot sauce with tarragon and preferably sliced beef marrow. It is now sometimes called *marchand de vin*, which can mean
any of a variety of red-wine sauces. *Entrecôte maître de chai* is
grilled over vine twigs (*sarments*).

Lamb of the Pauillac salt marshes is often eaten very young
and breaded. To my mind it has little taste and is better when
older. This lamb appears from January to about mid-May. The
Basques roast shoulder of lamb off the bone stuffed with a lot of
garlic, shallots, parsley and breadcrumbs soaked in white wine,
and serve it surrounded by slices of red and green peppers
cooked in the fat of the joint (*épaule de mouton basquaise*). *Épaule
landaise* is rolled shoulder stuffed with veal, pork, Armagnac and
herbs. Traditional braised veal, called *carbonnade gasconne*, is

slices of veal baked with a layer of sausage meat, garlic and shallots over it. *Chou rouge landais* is shredded red cabbage in apple, green pepper, onions, garlic and sugar, baked with a large garlicky sausage and red wine.

Tourin bordelaise is an onion and garlic soup thickened with egg yolks. In other places they add tomatoes. In Béarn it is called *ouliat*, in the Pyrenees *toulin*. The great traditional soup-stew is still served during the *vendange* and is called simply *soupe de vendanges* (grape-pickers' soup). It used to be made in old laundry boilers or something similar. Beef must be plentiful in it. Slits are made in the beef in which are put spices, garlic, salt, pepper, bay and fresh grape seeds. With it in the pot should go a leg of veal. Then the pot is stuffed with leeks, garlic, turnips, cabbage, celery, rosemary, mixed herbs, salt, lots of pepper, fresh grapes and plenty of cloves. It is covered in water and simmered for hours. The liquid is served as soup, the meat and vegetables separately.

Ttoro is a Basque fish soup-stew of white fish and eel, plus mussels, langoustines and fish heads with carrots, onions, garlic, tomatoes, sweet peppers, chilli, leeks, herbs, water and lots of ground pepper. It is served poured over bread rubbed with garlic.

The superb soup-stew of the south-west, especially Béarn, is *garbure*. It is made in an earthenware pot called a *toupin*, bulbous at the base, narrow at the top. It is a vegetable stew including cabbage, soaked white beans, broad beans, garlic, herbs and usually chestnut with pieces of meat – ham, pork, turkey or what you will. But it should include *confit* of duck or goose or both. As you empty the bowl you pour in a glass of red wine and drink the liquid. That is called *faire chabrot* or *faire goudale*. White beans are always used. Other vegetables are those in season. The best I have tasted was at the Arcé at St Étienne-de-Baïgorry (*see* page 217).

The geese and duck of Les Landes and Béarn are fattened for *foie gras* as in Périgord and Lot, and the legs, thighs and wings are preserved in their own fat in earthenware jars to make *confit*. You can buy *confit* in bottles or cans and it makes some wonderful dishes. It is delightful just fried in some of the fat with the rest used to fry sliced potatoes and garlic. It is used to

enrich stews and casseroles, and is essential for the true Toulouse version of *cassoulet*.

Goose or duck fat is used for cooking over most of the
south-west and gives a totally different flavour from butter or oil
– a very rich flavour indeed. The fat is sold in tubs or cans and
personally I buy it to bring home whenever I find it.

The French love of ducks' breasts – *magret de canard* – has
increased the duck population of France, including Les Landes,
by almost alarming numbers, although the turnover must be
very high indeed. One old French chef who was cynical of
modern cooking fashions said to me 'The French love *magret* so
much these days that they would rather eat it raw than wait for it
to be cooked properly.'

Henri IV's *poule au pot* that he said every family should have
once a week was made with a large boiling fowl stuffed with
bread soaked in chicken's blood or milk, giblets, onion and
garlic, and simmered with carrots, leeks, turnips, cabbage or
something similar (originally they used *blette* – Swiss chard,
leaves of white beet). Henri was simply implying that every
family should have one really good meal a week. They didn't in
those days. Now it is a luxury dish stuffed with ham and liver
and cooked in wine.

Cassoulet is named after the earthenware dish in which it is
cooked, and everyone who makes it has his own recipe. With
some it is almost a religion. It must have soaked white beans,
garlic, pork rind, herbs and meat. The three major versions are
from Castelnaudry, Carcassonne (both in Aude) and Toulouse.
All claim to have the original recipe. All contain various parts of
pork, cured, smoked or fresh, and sausage. Carcassonne adds
lamb or mutton, and the rich add partridge. Toulouse has a
complicated version, with lamb, the famous Toulouse sausage
and *confit* of goose or duck with goose fat, sprinkled with breadcrumbs on top and dotted with goose fat. When the crumbs
form a crust, that is stirred in and more breadcrumbs added. In
the old days when *cassoulet* would simmer for days, the stirring
was done at least six times. Now chefs usually stir once, twice for
holidays, three times for weddings. But some only simmer it for
a mere three to six hours. In Montauban they add tomatoes.
This is regarded as sacrilege in Toulouse.

Toulouse sausage is a long, fat, soft sausage of hand-chopped pork. There is splendid charcuterie in the south-west, especially from Béarn, which is pig country as well as sheep and poultry. The famous Bayonne ham comes mostly from Orthez in Béarn, but is cured by having Bayonne salt rubbed in. Most is eaten raw, though it is used to add flavour to stews, and in egg dishes. *Jambon à la bayonnaise* is soaked to get rid of the salt, skinned and braised in Madeira wine, which is then used for the sauce. The Basque sausage *tripotchpa* is a sort of *boudin blanc*, veal innards with blood and strong spices boiled in a herby bouillon.

Eggs and peppers play a big part in Basque meals. One dish, *oeufs frits à la bayonnaise*, is getting smaller these days. It is as many eggs fried in oil as you can eat piled on a piece of bread fried in oil, with alternate slices of fried Bayonne ham. You are far more likely to eat *piperade*, a delicious simple dish, described variously as an omelette or scrambled eggs with green and red peppers and tomatoes. Local chefs are keen to point out that it is really peppers and tomatoes, with onion and sometimes a small red chilli cooked in oil with beaten eggs stirred in at the end. It is served with Bayonne ham.

Pommes basquaise are baked potatoes stuffed with peppers, ham, tomatoes and garlic.

Game from Les Landes and the Pyrenees is fairly prolific in season, especially partridge (*perdreau*) and *palombe* (wild pigeon, usually more tender than our wood pigeon, especially in Béarn where corn is grown). *Palombes à la béarnaise* are marinated, braised in white wine and Armagnac, and served with puréed artichokes. Pigeon is also made into a *salmis* – roasted until half-cooked then finished in red wine with small onions, diced ham and mushrooms.

Desserts are often made with a superb pastry of layers of very fine leaves, like the filo pastry of Greece, strudel of Austria and superb leaf pastry of Turkey and North Africa. *La croustade* is made of this pastry with layers of apple or of plums and sugar. Do try if you can *gâteau qui a des ailes* (winged cake!) for which the pastry leaves are perfumed with orange flower-water and Armagnac, folded twice, topped with knobs of butter and baked. Traditionally *lou pastis* (or *pastis gascon*) from Les Landes and the Basque country was fruit in a pastry baked with goose fat. Now butter is usually used. *Pastis landais* is pastry with prunes. *Gâteau à la poêle* from Béarn is a thick savoury pancake. *Gâteau basque* is a thick tart filled with custard or cherries or plums.

Touron is a sweet of ground almonds, pistachio nuts and crystallized fruit – a sort of almond nougat. Fruit preserved for months in Armagnac is served with cream or put into cakes; the liquid is often drunk as a sort of liqueur. In fancy bottles sold in confiseries or pâtisseries this fruit steeped in Armagnac is very expensive.

It is a pity that so much of the sheep's cheese from Béarn is sent to the caves of Roquefort in Rouergue to make Roquefort cheese. But you can find other blue cheeses in local markets of the south-west, made from cow's or sheep's milk. *Bethmale*, made on farms, is a lovely tangy cow's milk cheese, but most actually comes from Arriège just outside our area. One is also called *Cierp de Luchon*.

Ardi-Gasna in Basque means simply 'local cheese', I am told. It is a nutty-flavoured sheep's cheese from mountain farms, used mostly for cooking. The best-known Basque cheese is *Iraty*, made in mountain farms from a mixture of cow's and sheep's milk and it varies according to the amount of each used, but is always strong. *Ossau-Iraty* is also made in Béarn. It is made from sheep's milk, matured in a humid atmosphere for three months and is creamy-white with an earthy taste. Its full name is *Ossau-Iraty-Brébis-Pyrénées*! *Amous* sheep's cheese from Landes has a shorter name and a stronger flavour.

WINE

Modern expertise in growing grapes, and particularly in making wine, has revolutionized the industry and there is now a bewildering choice of good, drinkable wines. Great claims are made for the wines of California, Australia, New Zealand, the Rioja region of Spain and even of Chile. Some are extravagant, many are justified, particularly for the white wines of Australia and New Zealand, and some red wines of California and Rioja. But I have noticed one thing. The claims nearly always include some phrase like, 'We have wines to compete with Bordeaux now.'

Bordeaux and Burgundy are still the standard by which the world measures wines. There are no other wine areas where *all* the wines are good, many are very good and some unsurpassed. If I were advertising Bordeaux wines, I should simply say: 'If it's Bordeaux, it's good.' The University of Bordeaux has done wonderful research work on wine-making, from preventing rot to control of temperature at which wine is fermented. The traditional wooden vats (*cuves*) for fermentation have mainly been replaced by stainless-steel ones lined with enamel, glass or concrete, which make it much easier to control the temperature of fermentation. Fermentation takes about five to ten days and takes place at 28 to 30°C (82 to 86°F) instead of the old method of allowing temperature to rise to 34°C (93°F).

Another change is that chaptalization (adding sugar to the must to help fermentation) was illegal in Bordeaux until 1962, but is now used except in years of the best grapes when it is unnecessary.

Machine-picking took a long time to reach Bordeaux. Now it

is fairly general except for the Premier Cru wines. It would spoil the atmosphere of the vineyards.

Red Bordeaux wine is matured in oak casks of about 225 litres and for the best wines new casks are used every year. But wines below Premier Cru (First Growth) classification use new casks every third year. It is interesting that in nearby Bergerac, where some traditional growers boasted of the age of their casks, modern wine-makers have adopted the Bordeaux method and improved their wines almost sensationally, ridding them of the overdose of tannin which could never be eliminated even by ten years' maturity. In Bordeaux, the length of time in cask before bottling varies according to the type and quality of wine. Most wines are bottled earlier than previously. The average time in cask for First Growths is now reduced from three to two years.

Methods of making dry white wines have changed greatly in recent years. Just as Australia and California have learned a great deal from Bordeaux about making red wine, many French wine-makers have begun to learn from Australian modern methods of making delicious white wine. I have heard leading French wine producers admit in private that the Australian Alan Crozer is probably the best white-wine-maker in the world. Stainless steel, horizontal presses and low-temperature ferment-ation have changed enormously the flavour and quality of white wine, making it fruity, fresh and clean, often with a splendid perfume. The return to popularity of the Sémillon grape as part of the blend for dry white wine has added greatly to the spicy flavour. Only special wines, like the very good Graves, spend more than a few months in cask. Most wines are bottled within six months to keep fruit and freshness.

Sémillon is the main grape used in the sweet wines of Bordeaux, such as Sauternes. For them it is allowed to stay on the vine until it has *pourriture noble* (the noble rot), a fungus called *Botrytis cinerea* which attacks overripe grapes, dehydrating them and concentrating the sugar. Fermentation goes on for weeks. The best wines mature in cask for more than two years.

Classification of Médoc wines started in 1851 when the Second Empire of Napoleon III was deciding which wines should represent Bordeaux at London's Great Exhibition. A commission of Napoleon's courtiers were given the job of tasting; their results were published in 1855 and has been the official order of merit ever since. Only one wine, Château Mouton Rothschild, managed to get its position changed. It joined the Premier Grand Cru wines in 1973 after years of lobbying by Baron Philippe de Rothschild, who died in 1988. Only the red wines of Médoc and the white wines of the Sauternes were included, plus Haut-Brion from Graves.

After the Second World War, Graves and St Émilion got their own classifications. In 1985 St Émilion classification was revised amid much fury and gnashing of teeth. The 1855 Médoc Classification is very out of date, although few would argue with the Premier Cru list of Lafite-Rothschild, Latour and Mouton Rothschild from Pauillac, Château Margaux from Margaux, and Haut-Brion from Pessac in the Graves area. Some vineyards have amalgamated, divided and deteriorated, then have been revived. These include especially Boyd-Cantenac, Beychevelle,

Old wine press

and Château Duhart-Milon-Rothschild, once unworthy of its 4ème Cru classification, then taken over by the Rothschilds who run Lafite and now one of the very best of Pauillac wines, well worthy of promotion. Château Lagune, a 3ème Cru Haut Médoc wine went down badly, then became a sort of experimental *chai* for modern techniques in stainless steel and mechanical racking, and was bought by the Champagne house of Ayala, who have turned it into a wine of great elegance, becoming very rich with maturity. It has a lovely bouquet. It is well worthy of promotion to 2ème Cru. Alas, the 1973 and 1975 I bought at bargain prices have now all gone – drunk by my family.

Opinions vary on Château Lynch-Bages, which is softer and fruitier than most Pauillac, with a definite taste of blackcurrants which experts so often find in wines. I think it is worth much more than its 5ème Cru classification. Médoc reds have 5ème Cru classifications plus Cru Bourgeois de Médoc. EEC regulations allow only the words Cru Bourgeois to appear on the label, but in the Médoc they divide Bourgeois wines into three categories. Cru Bourgeois must have at least seven hectares, the wine must be made on the property (not at a co-operative) and be of good quality. Cru Grand Bourgeois must also be matured in cask. Cru Grand Bourgeois Exceptionnel are very good quality wines grown in the Haut Médoc and must be château-bottled. These are well worth seeking, but as you will no longer be able to tell them by the label, here is a list: from St Estèphe commune – Andron-Blanquet, Beausite, Capbern, Le Crock, Haut-Marbuzet, Marbuzet, Meyney, Phélan-Ségur. From Ludon – Agassac. From Moulis – Chasse-Spleen, Dutruch-Grand-Poujeaux, Poujeaux (really exceptional – has beaten Grand Premier Cru wines in blind tastings). From St Laurent – Cannone Ste-Gemme. From Cissac – Château Cissac. From Avensan – Citran. From Listrac – Fourcas-Dupré, Fourcas-Hosten. From St Julien – Du Glana.

The Appellation d'Origine Contrôlée system (AOC, sometimes shortened to AC) was enacted in 1935. It lays downs the area limits of a name (such as St Émilion), grape varieties which can be planted, density per hectare of vines and how they shall be pruned, maximum yield for each hectare, minimum degrees of alcohol, and amount of chaptalization allowed (sugar added to must in years when insufficient ripeness brings too little alcohol). Grape varieties allowed are:

Red

Cabernet Sauvignon Most important grape for Médoc and Graves wines. Produces deep-coloured wines with the famous 'blackcurrant' bouquet, and which improve with age. Does best on gravelly soil.

Cabernet Franc A good foil to Cabernet Sauvignon, especially in Graves, Médoc and St Émilion, where it is often called Bouchet.

Merlot Blends well with the Cabernets in Médoc, and the dominant grape in St Émilion and Pomerol, where it gives the wines that plummy, velvet taste which makes them so easy to drink.

Malbec Called Pressac in St Émilion, it was used extensively in Fronsac, Pomerol and Côtes de Bourg in the past and in Médoc as a counter to the tannin in Cabernets. Used much less now because of growing problems, except in Côtes de Blaye and Bourg. Low alcohol strength and high acidity.

Petit Verdot Seen little now except in Médoc because it ripens fully only in good years, giving wine colour and tannin.

White

Sémillon For long the major grape for Bordeaux white wine, it was replaced in some areas by Sauvignon Blanc but is making a big comeback. It needs to age, to bring out its lovely rich, honeyed bouquet, and it has paid some growers to switch to Sauvignon to give a quicker return and also a drier wine, now in fashion. But the full flavour of Sémillon is being appreciated more and more and it blends very well with Sauvignon. For good sweet wines it is essential, for it is susceptible to *pourriture noble* (the noble rot) and gives the magnificent honeyed flavour to great Sauternes.

Sauvignon Blanc Very fruity, this is the grape used in the Loire for Sancerre and Pouilly-Fumé, and now in many wine areas of France where it can produce rather acidic wine when it has not ripened enough. But in Bordeaux it produces a finer wine, high in sugar and alcohol. It is now used on its own in some areas of Bordeaux, especially Entre-Deux-Mers, sold as Bordeaux Blanc Sauvignon. Margaux's white wine Pavillon Blanc is made entirely of Sauvignon.

Muscadelle Another grape which is slowly regaining popularity. Its musky bouquet is so heady and its sweetness so rich that it is usually used in small doses with Sémillon and Sauvignon. Some is used in larger doses to make sweet wines for early drinking in the Premières Côtes de Bordeaux around Loupiac and Sainte-Croix-du-Mont.

The proportions of each grape used depends on the soil and the aims of the wine-maker. Château Margaux, I believe, contains 75 per cent Cabernet Sauvignon, 20 per cent Merlot and 5 per cent Cabernet Franc and Petit Verdot, while Château Kirwan (named after its founder from Galway who lost his head in the Revolution) which is a 3ème Cru wine from the Margaux commune, uses 40 per cent Cabernet Sauvignon, 30 per cent Merlot, 20 per cent Cabernet Franc and 10 per cent Petit Verdot.

In St Émilion, one of the two most highly classified wines, Château Ausone, uses 50 per cent each of Merlot and Cabernet Franc, and the other top wine Cheval Blanc (which is red) uses 65 per cent Cabernet Franc to 35 per cent Merlot. One of the oldest Cru, Château Berliquet, owned by the Vicomte et Vicomtesse Patrick de Lesqueu and now climbing back to the top where it was in the eighteenth century, favours 75 per cent Merlot, the rest shared by the two Cabernets.

Wine-makers say that the character of a wine comes from the grape, its soul from the soil. And in Médoc they say that if you can see the river and feel the gravel under your feet, you can make good wine.

I have not suggested routes through the vineyard communes because what you can see or want to see depends so obviously on the time you have, whether you want to stop often to taste wine, or whether you are interested in the few old genuine châteaux among these 'châteaux' vineyards. Some are very attractive or historic, like Beychevelle, Margaux, Langoa-Barton, Pez, La Brède and Malle. I have written of some of these in the Places section. Nor have I room in a travel guide to give an extensive list of châteaux or of those which give tastings to the traveller unconnected with the wine trade. I have given a general account of each wine area.

For an extensive list of vineyards, their classification, which grapes they use, and a truly professional opinion of their wines, do read David Peppercorn's pocket guide to *The Wines of Bordeaux* (Mitchell Beazley). He is one of the most respected merchants of Bordeaux wine in the world and describes some 800 châteaux. The vintages are up to 1985.

Not many of the grand vineyards have time to receive amateur visitors and their wines are certainly too precious to give away. Apart from the cost of growing, picking, throwing out grapes not up to standard and making the wine, think of the capital tied up for anything from ten to twenty years. In 1986, when I was last at Château Latour, a million bottles were maturing there at a value of more than £20 a bottle! But there are some Grand Cru wines to be tasted and many very good Bourgeois Cru wines. For information on vineyards all over France which give free tastings without a lot of fuss and organization, see my book *Eperon's French Wine Tour* (Pan, £6.95).

For suggested wine tours or other information on the Bordeaux vineyards, pay a visit to the Maison du Vin at l cours du XXX Juillet, 33000 Bordeaux (tel. 56.48.18.62). Here, stained-glass windows, a superb tapestry and paintings are all dedicated to the noble drink. You can get very useful booklets and maps on the wine and the vineyards, including a booklet on Médoc called *Découverte Médoc* with a list of around 230 vineyards, most of which you can visit and some where you can taste wine. And there is a bar at the Maison du Vin at which you can taste wines representing each district.

VINEYARDS

MÉDOC

The best route to the Médoc châteaux is along D2. Take N215 north-west from Bordeaux, and D2 is on the right approximately 4km past the turn-off for the A10 motorway to Paris. The Médoc wine area is on the Gironde river side of the peninsula north-west from Bordeaux to the Pointe de Grave. The vineyards are along the river on a gravel and sand strip between 5 and 10km wide. Most are just away from the river to avoid the rich silt which vines don't like.

Médoc is divided into two appellations – 'Médoc' is north of a line from St-Seurin-de-Cadourne to Vertheuil; 'Haut-Médoc' stretches from this line south to the outskirts of the city of Bordeaux.

Haut-Médoc is the truly great wine area with the famous communes of Margaux, Moulis and Listrac, St Julien, Pauillac and St Estèphe.

Among the châteaux on D2 or near to it are La Lagune near Ludon, Giscours (one of the oldest and largest in Margaux) at Labarde, and Cantemerle (famous old property producing an underestimated light, elegant wine) at Macau. Around the Cantenac plateau is a string of good châteaux: Château Palmer (named after a British general who fought with Wellington; its reputation has deservedly soared recently); Boyd-Cantenac and Pouget (under the same management, and producing very similar well-made wines) and Château Prieuré-Lichine (a former priory, later European home of Alexis Lichine, true wine expert and great maker, who was born Russian, became French, finally American).

At Château Margaux you can visit the *chai* (above-ground

wine store), see the vinification plant, and admire from without the beautifully proportioned house. Here, too, in Margaux commune are Lascombes (the original Lichine property, sold in 1971 to Bass-Charrington, the British brewers), Château Malescot-St-Exupéry (a charming château in Margaux village, once owned by the St-Exupéry family to which the French airman-poet Antoine de St-Exupéry belonged), and Rausan-Ségla, one of the oldest and most famous Cru in Margaux, bought in 1960 by the Liverpool firm John Holt, now part of Lonrho.

In St Julien commune alongside the river is Château de Beychevelle, most beautiful and historic château in the Médoc. Try to visit it (for description and visiting times *see* below). It makes a fine St Julien wine – elegant, lovely, fresh ripe-fruit flavour when drunk young, even better and more harmonious when kept, matching a Pauillac.

Some lovely wines are made here in St Julien in some beautiful châteaux. Châteaux Langoa-Barton, almost rivalling Beychevelle for beauty, and Léoville-Barton have both belonged to the Barton family since the 1820s. The original Barton, Hugh, was an Irish wine merchant.

The Anglo-Irish connection with Haut-Médoc crops up in one vineyard after another. But not at Château Lagrange. The Japanese distillers and wine merchants Suntory bought this 3ème Cru vineyard on the St Julien plateau behind Gruaud-Larose in 1983 and have been increasing its size since. But a very experienced Frenchman, Marcel Ducasse, runs it. There is another Lagrange in Pomerol. Lynch-Bages in Pauillac was named for the son of John Lynch who fled here from Galway in 1690 after the Battle of the Boyne. His son Tom wisely married an heiress who inherited Domaine de Bages at the gates of Pauillac. His son became Mayor of Bordeaux and Count Lynch under Napoleon. They sold out in 1842. For three generations it has been run by the Cazes family. Grandad Cazes drank the wine liberally and lived to be ninety-five. His son André became the energetic Mayor of Pauillac. Grandson Jean-Michel now lives in the big château and runs the vineyard (*see* Visits and Tastings, page 44). Château Lafite Rothschild, Château Mouton-Rothschild and Château Latour are in Pauillac. The argument in recent years between the branches of the Rothschild family, who were cousins, is a legend of the Haut-Médoc and the whole wine world.

Château Mouton was bought by Baron Nathaniel Rothschild in 1853 but in 1855 it was surprisingly classified only as a 2ème Cru. His great-grandson Baron Philippe took over in 1926 and immediately worked flat out to improve his wine, publicize it world-wide and get it promoted to Grand 1er Cru – something which had not happened to any other wine. Meanwhile James Rothschild, brother of Nathaniel, had bought Château Lafite in 1868. It was a Grand 1er Cru wine, famous already when Madame de Pompadour and Madame du Barry served it. By appointment to the Royal mistresses, it seems. Oddly, it was the Rothschilds of Lafite who were against the promotion to 1er Cru of Mouton. After Mouton made the top there was an odd contest to see which cousin could sell his wines for the highest price. In 1973 the bubble burst for wine prices and the battle ceased.

Baron Philippe died in 1988. Until the end he remained one of the great characters of wine. In later days he sat in bed each morning with a bottle of wine doing business round the world by phone. His secretary brought in his mail. His dog sat on his bed. No one was allowed into the room until he strode out to tour his vineyards just before lunch. He owned two other vineyards in Pauillac – Mouton d'Armailhac, renamed Mouton-Baronne-Philippe, and Clerc-Milon. Also he bought Château Clarke in Listrac, a huge estate originally planted by Cistercian monks in the twelfth century, and producing now a light wine fit for a light luncheon or snack. He and his wife built up a wonderful Mouton Wine Museum, a superb collection of old drinking vessels, goblets, tapestries and paintings, and hundreds of works of art concerning wine, including the delightful wine labels he commissioned from Braque, Henry Moore, Dali, Masson, Villon and other well-known artists. Beneath is a blackened cellar of 100,000 bottles of vintage wine from all over Bordeaux, including nearly every vintage of Mouton Rothschild since 1859.

The third Grand Premier Cru wine here, Château Latour, was owned from 1963 until very recently by the Pearson Investment Group of London. The monumentally great wines will last so long that the 1970 wine is only just about ready and lovers of Latour as they grow older fear that they will not live long enough to taste the best recent vintages. I shall simply not be rich enough.

There are far too many good Pauillac Châteaux to mention. The strangest château is in nearby St Estèphe; Château Cos-d'Estournel, on a hill overlooking Lafite, has a façade like a pagoda with turrets and wooden carved doors from the palace of the Sultan of Zanzibar. In fact this is the *chai*, not the château.

St Estèphe produces a lot of wine (about 650,000 cases) of which only a fifth comes from its four Grand Cru Châteaux. The wines are not so subtle as Pauillac but very quaffable and satisfying – a big mouthful with a long-lasting taste. My favourite is Château Calon-Ségur, dating from the twelfth century and belonging in the eighteenth century to Marquis de Ségur who owned Lafite and Latour but said that his heart was in Calon, hence the heart-shaped device on the label. The wine is soft, fruity, easy to drink and not too pricey.

Château MacCarthy has not prospered as well as other 'Irish' vineyards. It is down to six hectares but does produce a very drinkable Grand Bourgeois wine. Château Montrose has no Scottish ancestry. It means Mont Rose – the rose-coloured hill. But it produces a 2ème Grand Cru wine. I think Château de Pez is underrated. Classified only as a Cru Bourgeois Supérieur, it is an attractive wine with rich fruit, and smells of spice.

St Laurent-de-Médoc on D1 coming back towards Bordeaux has two 5ème Cru – Château-Belgrave (a tip for the future) and Camensac (run by Spaniards from Rioja).

Listrac and Moulis further down the road have no Grand Cru wines but some good Bourgeois growths, powerful and fruity. The Grand Listrac Co-operative wines are good value.

Médoc wines from the north of Médoc tend to use more Merlot than Haut-Médoc wines because soils are heavier.

Château Loudenne, by the river just over the border, is a charming eighteenth-century rose-pink château owned by W & A Gilbey, the British gin company, since 1875 and once famous for the Gilbey family's spectacular parties. Its wines are better than most Bourgeois AOC Médocs – light in colour with lovely perfume and finesse – and improve noticeably with age.

The white is crisp and tasty – young or old. The château has an interesting wine museum (*see* Visits and Tastings, below).

At Blaignan near Lesparre, when D2E meets D1, in a fine old manor house called Château La Gorce, friendly Henri Fabre makes a full-blooded wine which 'seduces when young, delights when older'. He says that my readers can taste his wines morning or afternoon so long as they 'wear a large smile'. They will after being seduced by the full-blooded wine (tel. 56.09.01.22).

VISITS AND TASTINGS

MOUTON-ROTHSCHILD (56.59.22.22). Visits to cellars and museum by appointment only – Shut Saturday, Sunday, August

MARGAUX (56.88.70.28). Two weeks notice to château Margaux, 33460 Margaux, France. Groups preferred. Shut Saturday, Sunday, August, during picking. Visits to cellars, vineyards, not inside château.

BEYCHEVELLE, ST JULIEN (56.59.23.00). Early June–end September. Shut Saturday, Sunday. Tastings.

LOUDENNE, ST YZANS-DE-MÉDOC (56.09.05.03). Phone preferably. April–October, Monday–Friday. English spoken.

HAUT-MARBUZET (56.59.30.54). At Marbuzet on D2 just before it joins D204. Superb Cru Bourgeois Exceptionnel. Drunk young or old.

CHÂTEAU DE PEZ, ST ESTÈPHE (56.59.30.07). Fine old turreted château. Wine should be classified as Grand Cru. Shut Saturday afternoon, Sunday.

CHÂTEAU HANTEILLAN, CISSAC-MÉDOC (56.59.35.37). On D204 between Lesparre and Pauillac, marked on yellow Michelin map. Run by the elegant Catherine Blasco, former designer, engineer, agronomist and sheep-farmer. Wine should be classified 4ème Cru.

LYNCH-BAGES, AT GATES OF PAUILLAC (56.59.19.19). See text. Phoning appreciated, not necessary. English spoken.

BELGRAVE (56.59.40.20). On D101 between St Laurent-de-Médoc and St Julien. Good value. Improving.

FOURCAS-HOSTEN, LISTRAC (56.58.01.15).
World-renowned wine.
PRIEURÉ-LICHINE, CANTENAC (56.88.36.28). 4km SE
of Margaux on D2. Alexis Lichine's English-speaking
hostess will teach you a lot about Médoc wines. For
tastings, ask beforehand. Superb collection of old
firebacks.
GISCOURS, LABARDE (56.88.34.02). Next to Cantenac
on D2. Phone, ask for PR. English spoken. Both wine
and Napoleon III château splendidly restored recently.
Full-bodied yet delicate wine.
LA LAGUNE (56.30.44.07). Ludon-Médoc, just off D2,
10km S of Margaux. See text. Phone if possible. No
English spoken, but nearest important Médoc château
to Bordeaux.
MAISON DU VIN, place La Trémoille, Margaux. Sells 27
different, excellent Margaux wines. No tastings.

Further Information
SYNDICAT VINICOLE DE MÉDOC ET DU HAUT-MÉDOC,
33250 Pauillac (56.59.02.92).
SYNDICAT DES CRUS BOURGEOIS DE MÉDOC, 24 cours
de Verdun, Bordeaux (56.44.90.84).

GRAVES

The Graves wine area sweeps around the city of Bordeaux then
down the left bank all the way upstream to beyond Langon, with
three riverside gaps for Cérons, Barsac and Sauternes. When I
was young, most Britons and Americans thought of Graves as a
white wine, very slightly sweet. Apart from the 1er Grand Cru
wine of Château Haut-Brion, they thought of red Graves as
something drunk by locals. This was strange because the wine
the English called 'claret' and imported since the Middle Ages
was the light *clairet* produced in Graves.

Exactly the same amount of red and white is produced and
on the whole the French regard the red as superior, though the
white is the best in Bordeaux. The red grapes are grown on

gravelly soil (quartz pebbles of different colours) which gave the wine its name; the white on sandy and clay soils.

Yield per acre and grape types are strictly controlled. Grapes for both are the same as for Médoc wines – Cabernet Sauvignon, Cabernet Franc, Merlot, Malbec and Petit Verdot for red, Sémillon, Sauvignon and Muscadelle for white. Red wines must have 10% alcohol and white wines 11%, sweet white wines 12%. Most are stronger.

Red Graves is not so delicate as Haut-Médoc but has more body. 'Médoc is a delicate tasty woman,' said a French négociant to me. 'Graves is an earthy powerful man.' Their bouquet improves greatly with age; many good vintages can be kept for thirty years, but are usually drunk after five. Whites are ready after two years, many are kept for five years and some last twenty years. Locals are proud that 'the city of Bordeaux is in Graves'.

Fifteen Graves Châteaux have been classified since the Second World War. Those producing classified red and white wines are Haut-Brion, Carbonnieux, Domaine de Chevalier, Malartic-Lagravière, Olivier, La Tour-Martillac and Bouscaut. Reds classified are Pape-Clément, La Mission-Haut-Brion, La Tour-Haut-Brion, Haut-Bailly, Fieuzal and Smith-Haut-Lafitte. Whites classified are Laville-Haut-Brion and Couhins.

The best growths are along the N650 road to Arcachon, starting with Mission-Haut-Brion, Tour-Haut-Brion, the white Laville-Haut-Brion, then the great Haut-Brion itself and next to it Pape-Clément.

Haut-Brion was long called Pontac, after a wealthy Bordeaux tradesman and landowner Jean de Pontac who bought it in 1533 and must have thrived on drinking it, for he died in 1589, aged 101, still an active, powerful businessman and politician. By then, his wine was so famous that many Graves producers were calling their wine 'Pontac'. Generations of his family ran the vineyards and often the Bordeaux Parliament as well. The name Haut-Brion gradually became known. Samuel Pepys wrote in 1663 that at lunch in the 'Royall Oake Taverne' he drank a French wine that he had not met before 'Ho Bryen which hath a good and most peculiar taste'. 'Peculiar' meant singular or unusual in those days! Then François de Pontac started to sell his wines personally in London and set up a fashionable tavern called 'The Pontac's Head' to push the sales. The wine got honourable mentions from John Evelyn, Daniel Defoe, Dryden and Swift.

Haut-Brion passed through marriages to the Fumel family, who introduced bottles instead of casks for exporting and found that bottle-age improved the wine. Thomas Jefferson, the American Ambassador to France, ordered his Haut-Brion in bottles so that it could not be adulterated! Comte Joseph de Fumel, elected first Mayor of Bordeaux after the Revolution, was a Girondin (*see* Bordeaux, page 75), and was guillotined under Robespierre's Terror. So were the owners of Châteaux Lafite, Latour and Margaux.

Haut-Brion was bought in 1935 by the American financier Clarence Dillon, and his manager, Jean Delmas, was the first great Bordeaux producer to install stainless steel in place of wooden vats. Dillon's granddaughter, the Duchess of Mouchy, now runs it with her husband.

I had a sad experience at Haut-Brion. In the 1960s I was invited to a dinner at which the Mayor of Bordeaux was guest of honour – a superb dinner, served by flunkies with powdered wigs and splendid costume, with magnificent wines. These included two of the very last bottles from the cellars of Haut-Brion 1924, decanted into superb Louis XIV decanters. Alas, one of the flunkies was ham fisted. He jammed the top into the decanter so hard that in trying to extract it, he broke it off. The nectar was firmly corked, the beautiful decanter ruined. We drank a later vintage, not really *chambré*.

Recently the Dillon company bought from the Woltner family Mission-Haut-Brion, La Tour-Haut-Brion and Laville-Haut-Brion, whose tiny production of classic spicy white kept in the cask for a year is mostly sent to the US. Tour-Haut-Brion is made at La Mission-Haut-Brion. It matures quickly, is treated as a second wine to La Mission and is good value.

I love La Mission. Made in glass-lined vats, it is deep coloured, rich, full flavoured and lasts well. I still look longingly at my magnum of '72 – empty, alas, but the emptying is a happy memory.

Further down N650 behind trees is Château Pape-Clément, a vineyard from medieval times. In the thirteenth century it was owned by the Archbishop of Bordeaux, Bertrand de Goth. He became Pope Clément V in 1305 and was the Pope who moved the Papacy from Rome to Avignon. The red wine has a lovely bouquet and can be drunk young.

There are good vineyards around Léognan, including Domaine de Chevalier, producing fine red and white in very small quantities; Carbonnieux, one of the oldest vineyards, which makes an honest rustic red and a super white with 65 per cent Sauvignon, 30 per cent Sémillon, lovely and fruity when young, spicy and flowery after two years as the Sémillon takes over. Château Haut-Bailly is an excellent red with a nice bouquet, light colour, little tannin; a fine old manor and farm. Château La Louvière in Léognan is a historic monument. The very perfumed red with a delicious flavour is good value. The outstanding white is delicate and fruity.

VISITS AND TASTINGS

PAPE-CLÉMENT (56.07.04.11). 216 ave du Dr Nacel-Pénard, Pessac, Bordeaux. Tastings.
HAUT-BAILLY (56.21.75.11). 12km S of Bordeaux by D651. Tastings.

The village of Podensac is in Cérons (*see* Sauternes area, below) but produces red Graves and sweeter white wines. At the following you can taste and buy good value Graves wines:

CHÂTEAU DE MAUVES (56.27.17.05). 25 rue François Mauriac, Podensac (N113 SE Bordeaux on Garonne river). Good value to take home – ruby colour, fine perfume, mellow.
MAISON DES VINS DE GRAVES (56.27.09.25). 2 rue François Mauriac, Podensac. If tasting, try to phone. Represents 44 communes in Graves and sells many wines.

SAUTERNES, BARSAC, CÉRONS

Sauternes and Barsac are from a very small area near Langon, producing strong, sweet wines from grapes picked at the maximum concentration of sugar. There are several pickings of grapes for the greatest Sauternes. Each time only berries completely coated with '*pourriture noble*' (the noble rot) are picked. This mould which develops on the overripe grapes causes sugar to concentrate and leads to formation of glycerine. When gathered the berries are shrivelled, withered, nearly purple in colour. The juice coming from the presses is thick and rich in sugar. Fermentation stops automatically when the alcoholic content reaches 14–17°, leaving enough sugar to give natural sweetness. Australian and Californian wines called 'Sauternes' or 'Sauterne' are from a different world and not to be compared.

Both Sauternes and Barsac have a fine straw colour, with yellow reflections. Their bouquet alone is inimitable. Sauternes is usually more luscious. Barsac is lighter with a lemon taste.

The greatest Sauternes of course, is Château d'Yquem, from just north of Sauternes village – one of the original 1855 Premier Grand Cru wines. Back in 1787 Thomas Jefferson used to go to the château to buy Sauternes from the owner, Comte de Lur-Saluces. Today Comte Alexandre de Lur-Saluces, his great-great-great grand nephew, owns and manages it. It is made with 80 per cent Sémillon, 20 per cent Sauvignon and 100 per cent care and attention, and no one but a fool would drink it until it was at least ten years old. A great Mayor of Bordeaux told me to drink it as elevenses for good health and temper. I wish I could afford to. The Count himself says that his wine can be drunk with any dish in the meal or all through the meal. It is absolutely superb with *foie gras*. By the year 2000, the 1981 should be in splendid shape for drinking. The vineyard of 90 hectares makes 7,500 cases of wine in years when there is no spring freeze or summer or autumn heavy rain or hail. Mists of autumn are essential. In certain years Yquem makes a dry white wine called 'Y', said to be rich, full bodied with a honey smell. Alas, I have never tasted it.

There are five communes of Sauternes-Barsac – Barsac, Fargues, Preignac, Bommes and Sauternes. Signs from N113 marked 'Circuit du Sauternais' take you on a delightful drive through wiggly country lanes past many châteaux, and if you buy some of the lesser-known wines you may have some bargains. There are also eleven Premier Cru wines – Coutet and Climens in Barsac, La Tour-Blanche (once regarded as one of the finest wines in France), Lafaurie-Peyraguey, Clos-Haut Peyraguey, Rayne-Vigneau, Rabaud-Promis and Sigalas-Robaud in Bommes, Suduiraut in Preignac, Reiussec in Fargues and Guiraud in Sauternes.

Château Suduiraut adjoins Château d'Yquem. Its lovely

seventeenth-century château, where Louis XIV stayed, looks run-down, but the park laid out by Le Nôtre, who made the Versailles gardens, is well kept. The wine is nearly back to its historic greatness. So is Château Guiraud since it had a shot in the arm in 1981 from an Anglo-Canadian Hamilton Narby. He also makes a good secondary Sauternes called Le Dauphin de Lalague, a dry white Bordeaux Sec and a red Bordeaux Supérieur.

Château de Malle, in the family of the Comtesse de Bournazel for 500 years, straddles Graves and Sauternes and produces both wines well. The Sauternes is fruitier than most with a gorgeous bouquet and can be drunk chilled through a meal. The red Graves is fruity and aromatic, and there is a dry white Sauvignon. The château is magnificent (*see* Visits and Tastings below.)

The future of Sauternes is not bright. Production costs, with several hand-pickings of grapes and no Sauternes wine produced in years when the weather is wrong, mean high prices. Now fewer people will pay them and some producers have been forced to cut corners to survive.

Cérons, north of Barsac, produces good alcoholic fruity and sweet white wines without quite the finesse or gorgeous flavour and bouquet of Sauternes, but cheaper and very drinkable. It also produces reds very similar to Graves.

VISITS AND TASTINGS
Château de Malle (56.63.28.67). From N113
Preignac right turn across VC4. Malle marked on yellow
Michelin near A62. Open 15.00–17.00 hrs Easter–15
October. Visits to wine *chai* by phoning Secrétaire.

PREMIÈRES CÔTES DE BORDEAUX – LOUPIAC, CADILLAC, STE-CROIX-DU-MONT, ST MACAIRE

These are the wines on the right bank of the Garonne, opposite Graves, Sauternes and Barsac, running from Bordeaux to just past St Macaire, which is opposite Langon.

Coming from Bordeaux, the Premières Côtes north of Cambes produces red wines known for their softness, though they can be harsh when young, which is the way the French drink them. Buy a stronger wine with the commune name in it (e.g. Premières Côtes de Bordeaux Quinsac), keep it five to six years, and you have a lovely ruby-coloured generous wine, easy to drink and excellent value.

The white wines from south of Cambes are semi-sweet and sweet, rich and perfumed – excellent value.

Cadillac is a charming village (*see* page 141) and the old castle of the belligerent Protestant Ducs d'Epernon is very interesting inside and is partly owned by the wine producers, who give tastings to visitors. The wine is a surprisingly good sweet or semi-sweet white made from the classic grapes (Sémillon, Sauvignon, Muscadelle) and the best white of the Premières Côtes. It has an AOC. Drink it young and very cold. It is quite cheap. Château Cadillac vineyards are owned by a very good St Émilion producer, Robert Giraud. Try also Château Fayau.

The sweet white of Loupiac, too, has its own appellation. Minimum alcohol content is fairly high, 12.5%. Grapes are picked overripe when affected by the noble rot, producing a golden, luscious, fruity wine with a honey bouquet which will keep up to twenty years. Try drinking it young, very cold, with fruit desserts. Drier wine from younger grapes is sold as 'Bordeaux'.

The same is true of Ste Croix-du-Mont sweet white wines, made in the same way. In Loupiac, the best-known wine is Château de Ricaud, in Ste Croix it is Château Loubens. St Macaire makes nice white wine with a pleasant bouquet.

VISITS AND TASTINGS

CHÂTEAU CADILLAC (56.27.31.08). One-hour guided
visits. Shut Monday.

DOMAINE DE CHASSE-PIERRE CADILLAC (56.21.12.72).
Sweet white and red wine. English spoken.

CHÂTEAU VERTHEUIL (56.63.25.71).
Ste Croix-du-Mont. English spoken.

CHÂTEAU RONDILLON (56.27.03.11). Clos Jean,
Loupiac. English spoken.

ST ÉMILION, POMEROL, FRONSAC

In the late 1940s and 1950s, we used to sit on the terrace of St Émilion's Hotel Plaisance by the Old Bell Tower, looking over the crowded rooftops of the steep little medieval city to the vineyards beyond, sinking a bottle of Premier Grand Cru St Émilion and dreaming. When we were old, we would tell ourselves, this was where we should like to die in peace and quiet, after finishing a bottle of rich, deep red Cheval Blanc.

Now that I am over seventy and almost old, my dreams have changed, like St Émilion. Trees and shrubs block the view from the terrace. The Plaisance is posher and charges higher prices for its wine for Parisians and Americans. From spring to autumn streets are thick with visitors on wine pilgrimages as well as religious pilgrimages to see the cave home and chapel of the hermit saint himself (*see* St Émilion, page 216). At the cave of the producers' union in the tiny place du Clocher beside the Plaisance, you can still taste good wine, and buy a bottle, a case or two, or, as I do, *en vrac* in a plastic barrel to take home, bottle myself and keep for two or three years. That way I get a good St Émilion at half the home market price or less.

I eat now at the little Logis de la Cadène in the small market square (place Marché au Bois, tel. 57.24.71.40) where the Mouliérac family serve good-value traditional regional meals and their very own Grand Cru classé wine, Château la Clotte. It's a delightful wine – 85 per cent Merlot, 15 per cent Cabernet Franc, giving it delicacy, smoothness and a lovely bouquet. Too easy to drink!

St Émilion's Jurade which controls the quality of wine and classifies châteaux was first set up by King John I of England in 1199, and was restarted in 1948. Wines are classified as Premier Grand Cru, Grand Cru Classé, Grand Cru and AOC St Émilion, in descending order. Simple AOC St Émilions can vary greatly in quality and Grand Cru wines are often worth the extra cost. They should be rich, deep coloured, with concentrated fruit and very little tannin. Most of the 1000 producing vineyards are very small. In outlying villages a similar wine is produced and they are allowed to add St Émilion to the village name. The best are Montagne, Lussac, Puisseguin and St Georges.

The Merlot grape is the key to St Émilion. In some wines it is 85 per cent of the juice, around 50 per cent in most wines.

The two top châteaux are Château Ausone, named after the Roman poet Ausonius, and Cheval-Blanc. They are at opposite ends of St Émilion, and on quite different soils.

A good vineyard to visit and to buy wine to take home is Château Canon-la-Gaffelière (*see* Visits and Tastings, page 55). A Grand Cru Classé wine, it matures quickly and is easy to drink – not great, but good and dependable. Comte de Neipperg is the owner.

At the back of the old port of Libourne (*see* page 185) which once rivalled Bordeaux for exporting wine, is Pomerol. Its wine is very underestimated. The area is small, growers are many, and much wine is sold to private clients. The Merlot grape is predominant but clay soil gives a different wine from St Émilion. Pomerols are richer, and slightly more tannic, though this becomes less obvious after four to seven years. The near-legendary Pomerol is Château Pétrus, a connoisseur's wine which matures superbly. It is hard to find. It became extremely fashionable in the 1960s among such people as the Onassises, the Kennedys and the Duke and Duchess of Windsor, and then among all who would be fashionable. Alexis Lichine blamed Henri Soulé, who ran Le Pavillon restaurant in New York, for its popularity. It is 95 per cent Merlot, 5 per cent Cabernet Franc. Another excellent wine is Château Latour-à-Pomerol. Lalande-de-Pomerol to the north produces a wine nearer to St Émilion on sandy soil.

Fronsac red wines, which early last century cost more than St Émilion, come from downstream from Libourne on the Dordogne. The wine is rich in colour with a lot of body and improves in the bottle. It should be kept at least four years. Do try it – it goes well with meat or cheese and most wines are excellent value. It usually contains about 50 per cent Merlot grapes. Canon-Fronsac wines come from a small area in the middle of Fronsac and often are the best. Château Canon-de-Brem has fruit and a lovely flavour.

Jacques Borie at Château La Rivière (*see* Visits and Tastings, below) is standard bearer of Fronsac wines. In blind tastings, his fruity wines have upset the form-book many times. A very grand château with huge cellars. Vines have been grown here for 1300 years. A tower built for Charlemagne still exists.

At Verac in north Fronsac Sir Henry Peat and family produced a Bordeaux Supérieur at the former hunting lodge of the Dukes of Chambord – Château l'Eperon!

VISITS AND TASTINGS

St Émilion

UNION DES PRODUCTEURS DE ST ÉMILION (57.24.70.71) place Clocher. Shut Sunday. 380 producers form this union, which makes AOC and Grand Cru wine – also much praised Château Berliquet. Good place to taste and buy.

CHÂTEAU PAVIE (57.24.72.02). On St Émilion to Laurent-des-Combes road. Must phone and you cannot buy it here, but a great wine, worth seeking.

CHÂTEAU CANON (57.24.70.79). Just outside walls of St Émilion, marked on yellow Michelin map as Domaine de St Martin. Lovely smell, silky, long-lasting flavour.

CHÂTEAU CANON-LA-GAFFELIÈRE (57.24.71.33). Off D172 into city from D670. English spoken.

Further Information

ASSOCIATION DES PROPRIÉTAIRES DE GRANDS CRUS CLASSÉS DE ST ÉMILION (57.24.71.41). Les Templiers, rue Guadet, 33330 St Émilion. Can arrange châteaux visits.

SYNDICAT D'INITIATIVE (57.24.72.03) place des Crémaux.

Fronsac

CHÂTEAU LA RIVIÈRE LA RIVIÈRE (57.24.98.01) St Michel-de-Fronsac, NW from Libourne for 6km just past St Michel. Rich in colour and fruit, full-bodied, long-lasting taste. Very welcoming to visitors. English spoken.

ENTRE-DEUX-MERS, GRAVES-DE-VAYRES, STE-FOY-BORDEAUX

Entre-Deux-Mers should be called Entre-Deux-Fleuves (Between Two Rivers) for it is a huge area between the rivers Dordogne and Garonne, but Gascons are not given to understatement. It is the largest source of good dry white wine in Bordeaux and the area under vines has increased enormously, with large vineyards, mechanical picking and modern cool fermentation. The wine is drier than when I was young – following fashion, no doubt. A much underrated red wine is produced, but it can only be called Bordeaux or Bordeaux Supérieur.

Many of the vineyards have several secondary labels for their wines. The most impressive château is Château Bonnet, an elegant eighteenth-century château with a huge vineyard in Grézillac, due south of St Émilion. Owned by a well-known Graves producer, André Lurton, it is very well run and equipped, and produces lovely fruity wine with a delicious smell. The red wines are nice, too. Other very good wines are Château Launay and Château de Toutigeac.

Graves-de-Vayres is on the left bank of the Dordogne just SW of Libourne bordering Entre-Deux-Mers. Its white wines, sweet and dry, have body. So have the whites of Ste-Foy-Bordeaux, which is on the Dordogne at the eastern end of Entre-Deux-Mers.

VISITS AND TASTINGS
CHÂTEAU BONNET (57.84.52.07). Grézillac.
Must telephone.
CHÂTEAU BARON D'ESPIE (57.24.24.08). Branne.
Open Monday–Friday.
CHÂTEAU LAUNAY (56.61.31.51). Soussac.

CÔTES DE BLAYE, CÔTES DE BOURG

Wines of Blaye and Bourg on the right bank of the Gironde opposite Médoc came back into popularity a few years ago when Haut-Médoc prices shot up. The wines are still regarded by some as poor relations to Haut-Médoc, Graves and St Émilion, but have improved enormously and are well-worth knowing. In the fifteenth to sixteenth centuries they were considered to be the best wines of Bordeaux, and merchants would sell only if the buyer was prepared to take some of the 'plonk' from Médoc with them! Into the 1960s, oxen were still used for ploughing and carting. The *pieds-noirs* refugee growers from Algeria introduced tractors.

Premières Côtes de Blaye wines are soft, fruity, have a most attractive bouquet, are lighter than Côtes de Bourg and usually drunk young. Côtes de Bourg's gentle slopes led to its landscape being called 'La Suissse Girondine' – surely by an advertising man! On the hillsides are grown the classic Bordeaux red grapes to make a full-bodied red wine, deep in colour, with finesse. The French underestimate it because they usually drink it too young. Kept four to six years or more it is a real rival to many wines across the river in Médoc and Haut-Médoc. Try Château Brûlesécaille and try to keep it ten years!

Dry white wines of Blaye are best drunk young, and are good value. A little Côtes de Blaye sweet white is produced. There are some fine old châteaux in both areas.

VISITS AND TASTINGS

CHÂTEAU DE BOUILH (57.43.01.45). On D115 just N of St André-de-Cubzac, marked on yellow Michelin map. Home of Comte de Feuilhade de Chauvin (*see* Cubzac-les-Ponts, page 153). Visits with tastings 1 May–1 October. Thursday, Saturday, Sunday afternoons.

CHÂTEAU BRÛLESÉCAILLE (57.68.40.31). Tauriac, Bourg, on D669 going E from Bourg, turn left at La Lustre turning. English spoken.

CHÂTEAU BARBÉ (57.64.32.43). Take D937 for 4km E of Blaye. Open Monday–Friday. Carreau family have lived in this attractive eighteenth-century house for eight generations.

CHÂTEAU SOCIONDO (57.64.33.61). Ave Ferrand, Berson, at meeting of D937 and N137. Lovely award-winning Blaye red, rather like St Émilion.

Further Information
BLAYE WINES TOURIST OFFICE (57.42.12.09).
11 cours Vauban, Blaye.

JURANÇON

One of the great old wines of south-west France, Jurançon, from the Pyrénées-Atlantiques, is becoming scarcer as wine-makers pick the grapes early to catch the modern market for dry white wines. They make more money and don't take so much risk with the weather. The vineyards spread over about twenty-five villages from Jurançon village, 8km south of Pau, along the left bank of the Gave de Pau river.

Jurançon is made from three local grapes, Petit Manseng, Gros Manseng and Courbu, allowed to grow high, supported by trellises. The wine is about the same weight as Sauternes but quite different – gold in colour, a rich bouquet, honeyed, with a touch of nutmeg, and a luscious taste. It can be drunk young, is much better when kept at least five years, makes a pleasant aperitif, goes well with rich pâtés and *foie gras* and as well with fruit. It is delicious with strawberries. It is much underestimated. Prestige d'Automne is a beautiful wine.

Nine out of ten bottles are now dry white wine, called simply Jurançon Sec. It is pale, slightly spicy, fruity but slightly tart. Makes a good aperitif and is all right with fish or chicken.

TASTINGS
CAVE DES PRODUCTEURS (59.21.57.03). 53 ave Henri
IV, Gan, on N134. Phone if possible. 300 growers
belong to this Co-op.

MADIRAN

Madiran red wine is underestimated, too – probably because the French, in particular, often drink it too young. It comes from the left bank of the Adour in Pyrénées-Atlantiques, north-east of Pau and north-west of Tarbes, and is made from about half Tannat grapes (robust and tannic) with Fer (which give it a dark colour), Cabernet Sauvignon and Cabernet Franc. It rivals

Cahors in deep colour and long-living and is very rough when young. It has to spend twenty months in wood before bottling, and the tannin can persist, so it is best to keep it at least five years, preferably ten. Then it can be rich, full and fruity. It goes perfectly with local cured ham, red meat and game and is the best wine to drink with *cassoulet*.

OTHER WINES OF THE SOUTH-WEST

Irouléguy – from a small wine area between St Jean-Pied-de-Port and St Étienne-de-Baigorry. Very little white is produced. Biggest production is of rosé, always popular in a tourist area. This one is orangey-rosé coloured, full flavoured and drunk young. The red is quite the best, with a lovely ruby colour, lots of fruit and spicy, but lighter than Madiran.

Béarn – has an Appellation Contrôlée. Most is produced by Co-ops and drunk at one to two years old – red, rosé and white; fruity, light, easy to drink.

Pacherenc du Vic Bihl (AOC) – dry or slightly sweet white produced from vines trained on 2 metre posts and wires (pachets-en-rang, hence the name). Good aperitif. Small production.

Côtes de St Mont (VDQS) – from Gers and Eastern Landes. Reds have 70 per cent Tannat grape, are fruity, and like a rougher version of Madiran. Whites are pale straw colour, dry but not acidic.

Tursan (VDQS) – from Landes, around Aire-sur-l'Adour and Geaune. The white is made from its own special grape, Baroque (90 per cent), has flavour, no bouquet and is drunk very young. Refreshing. The red is quite tannic and solid.

Condomois (Vin de Pays) – from around Condom. Light white with acidity, drunk young. The red is light, easily quaffed and drunk locally.

Côtes-de-Gascogne (Vin de Pays) – red, dry white, rosé from Gers. Becoming popular in Britain.

Côtes-de-Bruhlois (Vin de Pays) – red and dry white from Gers and Lot-et-Garonne. Whites are refreshing when young. Reds have a bright ruby colour, are fruity and good with meat.

The Basque liqueur called *Izarra* is a copy of Chartreuse but made from Armagnac instead of Cognac. The Chartreuse monks were banished to the Pyrenees in 1403 under anti-clerical laws and did not return to the Dauphiné until 1932. Izarra is made with much the same mountain herbs and comes in green (very strong) and yellow (sweeter) like Chartreuse. It tastes similar.

Auch

[MAP 4, page 254]

The ancient city of Auch, once capital of Gascony, strides the Gers river. From boulevard Sadi, which runs along the left bank, you can walk up a vast monumental stone staircase of about 230 steps to the tree-shaded place Salinis and the Cathedral of Ste Marie. At the first platform as you take a breather you see a statue of a dashing seventeenth-century soldier, renowned in his day, made legendary last century by Alexandre Dumas. D'Artagnan was probably the only one of Dumas' Musketeers who really lived, though the famous Three have been claimed as local seigneurs in Gascony. D'Artagnan was born Charles de Batz around 1615 at the Château de Castelmore, near La Teñarèze. He wanted to join the Royal Guards of Louis XIV but realized that he would get nowhere without a more important family name, so he took the name d'Artagnan from his mother's family. It worked. He was favoured by the all powerful Cardinal Mazarin, then by Louis XIV himself, who gave him special missions to perform. When Nicolas Fouquet, Louis' finance minister, was indiscreet enough to build himself the most magnificent château in France, Vaux-le-Vicomte, and to invite the King to one of the most lavish parties in history, it was d'Artagnan who was sent to arrest him for having his hand in the Royal purse. And when the Gascon soldier the Duc de Lauzun was bold enough to have an affair with the Duchesse de Montpensier, royal cousin and known as 'La Grande Mademoiselle', d'Artagnan again was sent to take him to prison. He was a brave, tough soldier and was made captain-lieutenant of the élite First Company of Royal Musketeers, the King's official guard. He was also, it seems, a hard-drinking, womanizing roisterer in the tradition of Gascon soldiers. He died bravely at the Siege of Maestricht in 1673. Around 1700 a hack writer called Gatien de Courtilz wrote a wildly imaginative fake of his memoirs which was long forgotten when Alexandre Dumas picked up a copy and used it as the basis of his *Three Musketeers*.

At the top of the steps is the fourteenth-century Tour d'Armagnac, rising 40 metres, in biscuit-coloured stone and looking particularly sinister after you discover that for a long time it was a prison. There are long views on fine days from place Salinis, even to the Pyrenees. In the square and in the narrow roads around the cathedral are fine old houses, including some medieval half-timbered ones.

The imposing light-golden stone cathedral of Ste Marie was built between 1489 and 1568, its Renaissance façade masking its Gothic origins. The two square bell towers were not finished until 1678. You will see the impressive façade from place de la République round the corner from place Salinis. Inside, though cluttered, the cathedral is made more impressive by the eighteen stained-glass windows behind the choir. The colouring is superbly vivid and rich, the 360 figures full of life and character. The Crucifixion is powerful, the Nativity realistically tender. They are the work of a Gascon artist, Arnaut de Moles, born around 1465, who is believed to have worked in Toulouse.

Unfortunately the other great work of art in the cathedral, the choir stalls, carved by local woodcarvers from 1515 to 1531, can only be seen with a guide, and it is difficult to study detail. But the whole is magnificent – 113 oak stalls decorated with more than 1500 figures from the Bible and from mythology and legend. On the underside of the choir stools are erotic scenes which must have caused giggles from choir boys during boring sermons.

Above the main entrance to the cathedral is a porch containing a famed organ, built in 1694 and still used for recitals during the June classical music festival. It was built by Jean de Joyeuse of the same local family as Admiral Villaret de Joyeuse, defeated by Admiral Howe in 1794 off Ushant in the Battle of the Glorious First of June.

Next to the cathedral, behind a great gateway, is the old Archbishop's Palace, now the Prefecture. On a corner of place de la République is the Tourist Office in the delightful fifteenth-century Maison Fedel. Place République is a pleasant place to sit outside a café, but the centre of activity in old Auch is place de la Libération. Here is the town hall built by Antoine d'Étigny, Intendant in the eighteenth century and the man who regenerated the town physically and culturally. Fittingly, the theatre is inside. The fountain is modern. The old Hôtel de France, splendidly ornate and part of the scene, has two Michelin stars.

In place Louis Blanc, a steep walk from the cathedral, is an old Jacobin convent made into a museum with exhibits varying from a room of puppets, prints, paintings and books about d'Artagnan to Gallo-Roman archaeological discoveries and South American colonial art (shut Monday).

Little lanes and staircases on both sides of the cathedral hide medieval and Renaissance houses. From rue de la Convention, south of place Salinis, are three very steep and narrow staircases called les Pousterles, running to the lower town. These are the postern steps of the ancient fortified town, leading to the town gates. One of these, porte d'Arton, still stands.

The lower town by the river is quite lively in tourist season, for Auch is at the junction of many busy roads. It is on the route from Toulouse to the Atlantic, to Tarbes and Lourdes, from Agen to the same places on the N21, and Toulouse to Bayonne. Auch is renowned for Armagnac and pâtés. From mid-July to mid-September local gourmet products can be tasted and bought at Maison de Gascogne in the eighteenth-century covered market in place David opposite the post office (tel. 62.05.12.08).

TOURIST INFORMATION Tourist Office, place
Cathédrale (62.05.22.89)
MARKETS Wednesday morning, Thursday, Saturday
FESTIVALS June – classical music festival

HOTELS

France et Restaurant André Daguin, place Libération (62.05.00.44). Luxury hotel with three restaurants, cooking by André Daguin and son Arnaud, décor and smooth running by Jocelyne Daguin. Great old Gascon meals of beef from Bazas, local goose, chicken and duck. Superb *garbure* (vegetable soup-stew with preserved goose, pork). Inventive dishes, too, using local ingredients. ROOMS G. *Restaurant Daguin*, MEALS G (Shut January, Sunday evening, Monday); *La Neuvième Bistro* MEALS D (Open all year); *Côte Jardin*, MEALS E (Shut mid-October–30 April). Hotel open all year.
Relais de Gascogne, 5 avenue Marne (62.05.26.81). Cheap and useful. ROOMS B–E. MEALS B–F. Shut 22 December–12 January.

RESTAURANTS

See Hotel France.
Claude Lafitte, 38 rue Dersoles (62.05.04.18). Excellent traditional regional cooking. Find out how the Gascons eat! Seventeenth-century house. Charcuterie attached. MEALS C–G. Shut Sunday evening, Monday.

Bayonne

[MAP 5, page 255]

It is easy to underestimate Bayonne if you come in on the N10 from Dax and leave on the road to Biarritz and Spain. You see it as a busy port, crowded with traffic, exporting unromantic products such as sulphur, making cement and aircraft parts. You must park and explore to begin to discover this elegant but lively city with arcaded streets, rich in history and charm.

The river Adour has inevitably controlled the life, history and prosperity of the city which regards itself as capital of the Pays Basque. It grew to the south of the Ardour river striding the smaller river Nive which flows into the Adour near its main bridge, Pont St Esprit. The most interesting area is still there, though the modern industrial town has spread along the north bank way beyond the nineteenth-century northern suburbs.

The Romans used Bayonne as a port but in the eleventh century the Adour changed course and the town became an obscure market centre until Eleanor of Aquitaine, who owned these lands, married Henry II of England in 1152. Bayonne lived under the English for the next 300 years and gained prosperity and power. It became a great trading port, doing a lot of business with England.

As with Bordeaux, the English gave Bayonne freedom from important taxes and its own elected parliament. It ranked with Bordeaux as an English administrative base. It traded with Castile and Navarre in leather and oil as well as with Bordeaux and England, and controlled the commerce of the Adour as Bordeaux did of the Dordogne, Gironde and Garonne. Even the smallest tributaries were trade routes.

Most of the people of Bayonne were very pro-English. When Alfonso VIII of Castille tried to grab Aquitaine with the help of the French King Philippe-Auguste, the Bishop of Bayonne backed the Spanish, but the people closed the town gates and resisted the Spanish army.

Bayonne did have trouble from the Basques. Although it likes to be called capital of the Basques, it was not really a Basque city. As the Bayonnais had the sole right to trade on the sea and to tax goods supplied to the surrounding area, the Basques not unnaturally objected. The Mayor of Bayonne was Pé de Puyanne, a successful sailor who had been given the job by Edward III of England after he led the Bayonne ships fighting with the English in battles which broke the French sea power. De Puyanne immediately oppressed the Basques outside the city. In particular he put a tax on cider, their staple drink. Any Basque caught smuggling to avoid the tax was to have his right hand cut off. The Basques refused to pay, so in 1343 he and his sailors attacked some Basque merchants celebrating the feast of St

Batholomew at Château de Moitz, killed most of them and took five prisoners. These were tied to the arches of the bridge to drown as the tide rose. Immediately two hundred Basques, led by a famous Pyrenean hunter Jean Amachon, attacked the garrison of the bridge-protecting tower. A bloody battle was fought on the tower's staircase. The Basques won. The Black Prince ruled that the Bayonne people were to blame, fined them and banished Pé de Puyanne to Bordeaux. He was murdered two years later when visiting his own vineyard.

Meanwhile Bayonne was having trouble with the river Adour. Normally it flowed into the sea at Cap Breton but in 1310 a huge storm blocked the channel with sand so the river diverted itself ten miles north to Port d'Albret. The new channel was wide and shallow, so ships had to unload at the river mouth instead of coming into Bayonne. The city's trade and prosperity slumped.

The English were driven from Bayonne in 1451 by Dunois, the Bastard of Orléans, friend and companion in arms to Joan of Arc. He did more than anyone after Joan's death to drive the English from France. The Bayonnais resisted strongly but they were a hard-headed people and they must have realized that the English cause was virtually lost in France. To help them make up their minds to surrender, a strange cloud formation made a white cross in the sky. This was cleverly interpreted by the French as a sign from God that the city should pull down its English flags carrying the red cross of St George and replace them with the white of the French fleur-de-lis. This was called the Miracle of Bayonne, celebrated now by a plaque in the cathedral.

The French promptly fined the city a huge sum for not giving in immediately and took away all its privileges, including freedom from export taxes and right of self-government. French taxes were high. The people resented having to use French instead of Gascon as their official language. Like Bordeaux, Bayonne was soon sighing for the good old days of English rule. It had lost its English market, too, and the channel to the sea was allowed to silt up. It was one hundred years before work began to clear the Adour channel again and there were several failures until a storm helped to clear the sand. The river flowed again to Anglet bringing back export trade and ship-building. The lake at Hossegor, loved by holiday-makers, is all that is left of the old river outlet.

In the eighteenth century Bayonne was made a free port. Trade flourished with many countries, its fishing fleet sailed to the Newfoundland banks, its privateers preyed on Atlantic shipping and brought back great wealth. Its iron foundries produced weapons, including the new 'bayonet' named after the city. But the Revolution and the Napoleonic wars destroyed its prosperity. The British blockaded it. The port was at a standstill. In 1813, when Wellington's forces from Spain crossed the Pyrenees, the French under Soult were in strong positions around Bayonne. Wellington's forces drove them from everywhere except Bayonne city. Wellington left a holding force to besiege it and pressed on. Bayonne did not surrender to the British until after Paris fell. It was the last French city to fall – ironic, considering it had been English for 300 years.

Now the port is prosperous again. A great breakwater extending a kilometre into the Atlantic has stopped the sanding up of the channel and big ships can dock. Natural gas and its by-products come from the foothills of the Pyrenees. So do fertilizers. And Bayonne still produces its famous home-made chocolates. In the sixteenth century Spain had a monopoly of chocolate-making from the cocoa of its American colonies. But the Spanish kings drove out the Jews and they brought the secret of chocolate-making to Bayonne. You will have no problem in finding shops that sell chocolates and *tourons* (almond meringues).

The old part of the city south of the Adour is small enough to be explored on foot. Follow the busy rue Thiers from place De Gaulle and you come to Château Vieux. The English built it, the French rebuilt it as soon as they took over, then it was strengthened by Vauban, the great military architect in 1674–9, when he fortified Bayonne for Louis XIV. Now it is used by the Foreign Legion. Vauban built the citadel on the north side of the Adour in the district called St Esprit where most of the factories are built. He also strengthened Château Neuf, built eastwards across the river Nive in 1489 and built the southern ring of battlements around the city. He made Bayonne so strong that it withstood fourteen sieges. Now the battlements are attractive gardens.

In Château Vieux the French hero du Guesclin was imprisoned by the English until his ransom was paid. He cost France a lot of money in ransoms but repaid the cost in his nuisance value to the English, who must have wished finally that they had just kept him in prison.

A short walk along rue des Gouverneurs takes you to Ste Marie's cathedral, the most important Gothic building in this part of France. Built on the site of a Roman temple, it was started in the thirteenth century; the work was then held up by fires but it was restarted and finished in the sixteenth century. On the north door is a thirteenth-century knocker, a 'ring of sanctuary'. A fugitive could claim sanctuary from his pursuers when he touched it. The north tower was added and both towers crowned with steeples in the 1880s by Boeswillwald, a pupil of Viollet-le-Duc. The effect is ornately elegant. Inside it is tall with wide aisles and side chapels with some good stained glass. The loveliest window, from 1531, lights the chapel of St Jérome.

The cloisters, much restored, are very beautiful, with slim pillars and lovely tracery design. The pathway is partly paved with seventeenth- to eighteenth-century tombstones.

The streets around the cathedral are rich in fine old buildings. The delightful old five-storey arcaded houses in rue du Pont have shops and cafés on the ground floor, busy midday with shoppers and chocolate drinkers. From place Pasteur by the cathedral walk along rue Monnaie into rue Orbe past fine old houses to carrefour des Cinq-Cantons, where five old streets meet, then take rue Pont de Castets and you reach the delightful quays of the river Nive.

The Nive has several nice little bridges and pleasant walks on its right bank. Just over Pont de Castets, in a delightful Basque seventeenth-century house on quai Corsaire, is Musée Basque – a truly interesting museum of Basque life and culture. Even if you are not normally a museum explorer, do see this one and take time over it. You might, with the help of a museum guide, be able to unravel some of the mysteries of the Basque people from their early tombstones or even understand the game of *pelota*. You are sure to see this fast, athletic game being

Ste Marie Cathedral, Bayonne

played in the Basque country in good weather by young men in white shirts and trousers, with a colourful sash. Their team may well include a young priest with his black skirts hitched up. It is played against a wall (*fronton*) with a little hard ball, by teams of two or three. There are various forms, but usually the ball is hit with the right hand covered in a *gomme* (glove) with a wicker scoop attached. In one version players use a small stringed racket and rubber ball. Young boys practising or playing an unorganized game against the school or church wall use bare hands, hitting the hard ball with their palms or knuckles. That is called '*à main nu*'. You can see the connection with *jeu de paume*, the old French game, and with British rugby fives. *Pelota* is played indoors when the Atlantic winds blow.

The museum has a reconstruction of a Basque bedroom and living room. Another interesting display in the museum is of *makhilas*, the sticks used for walking the mountains and for fighting. There are also models of the great Basque fishing boats (*see* St Jean-de-Luz, page 219). Museum shut Sunday.

Quite close by in rue Jacques Lafitte is Musée Léon Bonnat, one of the great art galleries of south-west France. Much of the first floor is given to works by Léon Bonnat, born in Bayonne in 1833. A very successful portraitist of the rich and important, he was also a great teacher. His pupils included men who became great artists, including Braque, Dufy and Toulouse-Lautrec. Many of his works here are copies made in his youth of masters of painting such as Leonardo da Vinci, Titian and Vélazquez. An excellent portrait of Bonnat was painted by one of his admirers – Degas. Bonnat's portraits made him rich and most works in the museum came from his large collection. They range over four centuries and include excellent pictures like Van Dyck's *Martyrdom of St George*, Girodet's portrait of Napoleon, fine works by Ingres, including a *Female Bather*, Constable's *Hampstead Heath*, a Goya Self Portrait, and works of Murillo and Rembrandt. In one room oil sketches are picked out dramatically by spotlight. They are by Rubens, some made for tapestries such as *The Triumph of the Eucharist* now in a Madrid convent, many others for scenes from Ovid's *Metamorphoses* commissioned by Philip IV of Spain (museum closed Tuesday; open daily mid-June to mid-September; open afternoons rest of year, plus mornings at the weekend).

Much of Bayonne's history is tied up with neighbouring Spain. Here in 1565 Charles IX of France, with his mother Catherine de' Medici, met his sister Elizabeth, married to Philip II of Spain, to plan the elimination of Protestantism – a crusade which led later to Philip's disastrous attempt to invade England with the Armada. In 1808 Carlos IV of Spain, for fear of Napoleon, surrendered the Spanish crown to Napoleon's brother Joseph Bonaparte in nearby Château de Marrac.

Although Bayonne ham is not produced in Bayonne but at Orthez in Béarn, Izarra is. This liqueur – yellow or green – is pleasantly like Chartreuse. The distillery is on quai Amiral-Bergeret on the Adour river (visits: tel. 59.55.09.45).

TOURIST INFORMATION place Liberté (59.59.31.31)
MARKETS Tuesday, Thursday, Saturday
FESTIVALS Easter Wednesday, Thursday, Saturday –
Ham and Charcuterie Fair;
end July – International Folklore

HOTELS

Agora, avenue Jean-Rostand (59.63.30.90). Modern (Mercure group). Garden with nice riverside terrace. ROOMS E. MEALS B–E. Open all year.
Loustau, place République (59.55.16.74). Convenient position beside Adour river bridge. Front rooms noisy. Good cooking. ROOMS D–E. MEALS B–D. Shut mid-December–mid-January; Saturday afternoon, Sunday in winter.

RESTAURANTS

Cheval Blanc, 68 rue Bourgneuf (59.59.01.33). Greatly under-estimated outside Bayonne. Excellent cooking of lovely local

ingredients, especially fish and Pyrenean lamb. MEALS C–G.
Shut 8–end January; Monday in winter.
Miura, 29 rue Cordeliers (59.59.49.89). Simple, charming.
Excellent value for good cooking. MEALS B–D. Shut 1–15 July;
20–30 December; Sunday evening; Wednesday.

Bordeaux

[MAP 2, page 252]

Bordeaux is a truly great city – elegant, friendly, prosperous and
rich in history and in great museums. It owes its importance to
its protected position on the wide river Garonne, its wealth to its
history and its elegance to its wealth. Even the new industrial
Bordeaux, with its two new river bridges, its motorways and
flyovers and its modern apartment blocks, is more admirable
than most in Europe.

Its great half-moon sweep of wide water made it certain to
become a great seaport, and the Romans made it a great trading
centre and Imperial city. But it was the English who really built it
up, making it the capital of their lands of Aquitaine and the
major port for their supplies and trade. They gave its people the
freedom to elect their own mayor and run their own affairs and
they gave them a near monopoly of wine exports. The wine
which they exported, and wool which they imported were
exempted from customs duties. The merchants of Bordeaux
made certain that the wines were from their own area and not
poled down the river on *gabarres* from Dordogne and Lot. They
drove the rival wine port of Liborne out of business.

Bordeaux was the English capital of Aquitaine for 300 years,
and in the Hundred Years War the Black Prince had his court
there. His younger brother Richard of Bordeaux, who became
Richard II of England at the age of nine, was born there.

The Bordelais, especially the bourgeois merchants, did not want to become French, and fought the French armies with great tenacity. They had done very well under the English, had never been part of France and did not *feel* French. When the English were defeated at Castillon in 1453, the French at last got their hands on Bordeaux and treated it like an occupied country. All its freedoms, privileges and above all the freedom from tax on wine were taken away. Though many of the anglophile Bordelais had gone to England, the rest revolted and Paris was forced to reduce taxes to the same level as they were under the English and later to give Bordeaux its own *parlement*. As late as 1585 the elders of Bordeaux were complaining that 'we live in a conquered territory'. Henri IV, a Gascon, was the only king Bordeaux really accepted. To this day, there is little love between Bordeaux and Paris, although the French Government moved temporarily from Paris to Bordeaux in 1870 when the Prussians took Paris, and in 1914 when the German advance threatened to reach Paris and the Channel ports, and very briefly in 1940 as France collapsed.

All that is left of Roman Bordeaux are a few arches of an amphitheatre, Palais Gallieni in rue Dr Albert Barraud. It was not a palace. Little is left from the 300 years of English rule. In the eighteenth century, the medieval city within the crumbling medieval walls was knocked down. Hardly surprising that the walls were crumbling. The gates of the city had been shut at 8 p.m. in winter and 10 p.m. in summer for security reasons. The independent Bordelais simply knocked illegal holes in them or dug tunnels underneath. Foreigners, Jews and Protestants were not allowed to build or live within the walls. So some of the finest houses had been built outside them – mansions belonging to shipowners and merchants who, from there, could watch the sailing and returning of ships. Bordeaux had grown rich. Its money came not only from exporting wine, but from slaving from the coast of Africa to the French colonies in America and the Caribbean, and from importing spices from the Indies, silks and cottons from the Orient, and wood from Africa. The suburb outside the walls become the in place to live. Louis XIV's chief minister Colbert had appointed regional governors (Intendants) to run the French regions to break the power of the aristocrats and force them to pay taxes. An Intendent of Bordeaux who *was* an aristocrat, Aubert, Marquis de Tourny, decided to knock down the walls and crumbling medieval houses and build a noble city of stone. He did for Bordeaux what Haussmann did for Paris, but more elegantly. The town was virtually turned around to face the river.

The masterpiece is the Grand Théâtre, neo-classical, with huge statues of the nine muses and three Graces above its superb Corinthian colonnade. It was designed in 1773 by Victor Louis, a Bordelais who was the greatest pre-revolutionary architect in France, and it is still one of the most beautiful theatres in the world. The double staircase leading from the colonnaded foyer and lit by a glass dome was imitated for the staircase in l'Opéra in Paris. The auditorium, a perfect semicircle, is lit by an enormous crystal chandelier. The ceiling was repainted in 1918 as Robin had painted it originally.

In the heyday of eighteenth-century Bordeaux the theatre was very much the centre of high life. Arthur Young, the English agricultural expert who travelled through France just before the Revolution, reported in 1787 that performances in the theatre took place every night, including Sundays; that leading actors and actresses came from Paris to perform; that a famous dancer, Dauberval, and his wife from London were paid the fortune of 28,000 livres a year as ballet master and lead dancer; and that rich merchants paid girl singers and dancers salaries 'which ought to purport no good to their credit'.

The theatre today is the centre of Bordeaux's 'Mai Musical' festival.

When the French Government fled to Bordeaux in 1870, the Grand Théâtre was used as the National Assembly. It was built on the site of a Gallo-Roman temple which Louis XV had knocked down, and quite recently excavations for a car-park revealed Gallo-Roman remains.

Down-river from the theatre is the tree-lined place des Quinconces, laid out in 1818 on the site of Château Trompette built in 1455. It is one of the biggest squares in Europe, with some good parking space nearby, in a city notorious for lack of parking. Here stands a memorial to the Girondins, liberal martyrs of the Revolution, erected in 1895. Oddly it was dismantled in 1943 and its fifty-two tonnes of bronze sold as scrap. They were found later in an Angers scrapyard and the monument was painstakingly reconstructed in 1982. Its 50 metre column is topped by a statue of Liberty. Two remarkable bronze fountains of chariots pulled by sea-horses symbolize the Republic and Concord.

The Bordelais workers and bourgeoisie rather naïvely joined the Revolution, believing that it was time for reform, and that the Revolution was truly to bring in a world of '*Liberté, Egalité et Fraternité*'. They formed with other liberally minded people in Gironde a party called Girondins, which came to power in the National Assembly in the early days of the Revolution. They were mostly middle-class liberal merchants, doctors, lawyers and writers and were quite untrained to make any order out of the chaos in France. They made many mistakes. The powerful Jacobins, under Robespierre, had twenty-nine of them arrested as traitors to France and the Revolution, and a trial was held under puppet judges. But the reasonable arguments of the Girondins in court began to sway the ordinary people on the public benches so successfully that Robespierre cut short the trial and declared them guilty. They went to the guillotine singing the Marseillaise. One said prophetically to the Jacobins: 'I die on the day that the people lost their reason. You will die on the day that they find it again'. That was in 1792. The people of Bordeaux set up the memorial to them a hundred years later.

Within a triangle from near place Quinconces, at place Tourny, along allées de Tourny to the Grand Théâtre, then along cours Intendance to place Gambetta, and back along cours Clemenceau to place Tourny again are most of the beautiful terraced houses with iron balconies of the rich eighteenth century merchants, overlooking boulevards lined with plane trees. In cours Intendance, place Gambetta and rue Ste Cathérine are luxury shops, including *haute couture*. It is still fashionable to sit at lunchtime in Gambetta taking an aperitif. At No. 57, Casa de Goya, the Spanish painter Goya died in 1828. It is now a Spanish cultural centre (open afternoons except Saturday and Sunday; also Wednesday morning).

Tourny's statue stands inevitably in the perfectly circular place Tourny, but this has been ill-treated since he planned it.

The Grand Théâtre, Bordeaux

Some of its low buildings with attractive roofs have been
knocked down to make way for roads, others de-roofed to add
more storeys. Place des Grands Hommes, another symmetrical
circle, has suffered less and is still attractive. Its centre is filled
with the covered food market, and around it are attractive little

shops. The market, alas, though interesting inside, is of concrete, though the stalls around it have colourful awnings and give out a blend of perfumes from pork butchers to flowers.

Place Gambetta, too, is little altered, though crowded. Here they set up the guillotine in the Revolution.

From the corner of place de la Comédie opposite the theatre you can pick up rue Ste Cathérine which runs through Old Bordeaux to Porte d'Aquitaine in place de la Victoire. A very busy shopping street, it can become packed with people and traffic, especially on Saturday. Here, during the civil war of the Fronde, a full-scale battle took place between the Royal forces using canon and artillery and Fronde supporters from Bordeaux armed with muskets, and at the end of the battle 450 people lay dead in the street.

In a side street, rue de Cahernan, in 1206 a stranger battle took place. Bordeaux was under siege from the King of Castile and its citizens near to starving. Even wine was running out. They sent a message to the Spanish King. Neither side, they said, would give in and there would be much death and suffering on both sides before it was settled. Why not avoid horrors by settling the argument now by single combat between a champion from each side? The King of Castile agreed. He, too, was short of food and he thought that he had a trump card – a seven feet tall, tough Goliath of a man called Fernand. Bordeaux chose as its David a skilled soldier called Chevalier de Lalande.

The huge giant flayed at the Bordelais with a wicked two-edged sword. But Lalande was as nippy as a Bordelais scrum-half. Lalande ducked under his guard and pierced him through the heart, then cut off his head with an axe.

The Spanish King surprisingly stuck to the rules and withdrew his troops. Fernand's head (Cap Fernand) was carried along rue Ste Cathérine amid dancing.

To the right of rue Ste Cathérine coming from the theatre, a road leads to the cathedral of St André, almost as big as Notre-Dame in Paris. Begun in the eleventh century, some Romanesque features survive but it is mostly thirteenth to fourteenth century, though it has been altered over the centuries since. Alas, the controversial 'restorer' Abadie got at it in the last century, as he did the cathedrals at Angoulême and Périgueux.

At Périgueux he added a lot of towers fit for an Eastern mosque. At Bordeaux he destroyed the cloisters. Though rather hemmed in by the town walls, the church has rich decorations and one lovely doorway, the thirteenth-century Porte Royale with superb sculptures.

When the nineteenth-century architect Viollet-le-Duc was restoring Notre-Dame on the banks of the Seine in Paris, he had moulds made of Porte Royale's statues of the apostles to reproduce them on the restored Paris cathedral. The flamboyant François I, the man who met Henry VIII of England in the most ostentatious picnic ever, held at the Field of the Cloth of Gold near Calais, was married at St André. He organized the occasion with his usual sense of showmanship and drama. He and his bride entered the city from opposite ends. Both were mounted on capering horses and followed by richly dressed noblemen and their ladies, musicians, drummers and soldiers. They met in the city centre and continued together to church.

Standing separately at the east end of the cathedral is its belfry, Tour Péy-Berland, built between 1440 and 1446 and named after the archbishop who had it built. Alas, the top came down in a storm and now it is capped by an incongruous and huge nineteenth-century statue of Notre-Dame. It stands alone because this part of Bordeaux used to be marshy and they needed to build it on solid ground.

The town hall beyond the cathedral was built by one of the immensely powerful and rich Rohan family when he was made Archbishop of Bordeaux in the eighteenth century. The Rohan motto was: 'I cannot be King. I disdain to be a Prince. I am a Rohan.' This one controlled eleven abbeys, forty-four monasteries, thirty nunneries, 390 parishes, Bordeaux University and a host of colleges, schools and hospitals. He wanted a palace, fit for a Rohan, with a superb garden, a courtyard big enough for huge feasts, suites for his 'nieces' who lived with him and even a laboratory for scientific studies.

It took a long time to build – too long, he insisted. And he was right, for he was moved to Cambrai to be Archbishop there before it was finished and it was Champion de Cice, his successor, who moved in. Within five years the Revolution had come, the Republic was proclaimed from the palace steps and tribunals were held in its halls while the superb bedrooms became offices. Napoleon held court there as one of his Imperial Palaces. It became the town hall last century and still is, but its galleries round the gardens are museums, including Musée des Beaux Arts (*see* page 81). The main town hall can be visited at 2.30 p.m. on Wednesday (guided visit – apply at Tourist Office).

The second great church is the Basilique St Michel, near the waterfront south of St Pierre bridge. This fine church, built over a hundred years from 1396, was badly damaged in 1940 and its medieval stained-glass windows destroyed. The church was restored, the windows replaced by modern works of Max Ingrand. Although the brightly coloured abstracts may appear out of place to some, the biblical scenes in superb colours of scarlet, green, gold and yellow, with people who look alive, are masterpieces. Two artists greatly underestimated even in France are Max Ingrand and great modern master of tapestry Jean Lurçat. The fifteenth-century tower with a spire 100 metres high stands apart from the church, for this land was very marshy and peaty. When the medieval cemetery was dug up, the bodies were found to be mummified. There was nowhere to re-inter them. So they are in the tower, once a macabre sight but now closed to visitors.

There is still a flea market swarming round St Michel in the squares of Chanteloup and Meynard from Monday to Friday in the morning. On Saturday it becomes a food and clothes market (Marché Royal).

The twelfth-century Ste Croix church southwards was once part of a rich abbey. It was 'restored' last century by Paul Abadie, who could not resist adding a tower to make it more 'balanced', a Byzantine dome and an incongruous statue of St George. Some pillars in the church still have iron rings where the mentally ill were chained during Mass because it was believed that the revered St Monmolin could cure them.

West from St Michel is the very impressive clock tower Grosse Cloche, once the city hall. The belfry stands over a gateway, its turrets topped with witches caps. Mostly from the fifteenth century, it is loved by the Bordelais, for the bell used to be tolled to mark the official beginning of the *vendange*, the picking of the grapes. The bell had to be replaced several times and each time the new one was given expensive christening gowns in fine cotton and silver, while the town held a feast. After the Bordelais revolted in 1548, the French King took away the city's privileges and its bells. They had to use sundials to tell the time until 1556, when the bells were restored with much feasting. The Bordelais love an excuse for a feast. With their wine, that is hardly surprising.

North-west from St Michel along the Garonne river is the eighteenth-century Porte des Salinières, still called Porte de Bourgogne by some locals. Opposite is a crescent of handsome Louis XV buildings. The porte is opposite Pont de Pierre, 501 metres long with 17 arches, built in 1810–21.

Porte Cailhau upstream was originally the entrance to the Palais de l'Ombrière, palace of the Black Prince and the Dukes of Aquitaine. Charles VIII built a triumphal arch in 1495 to celebrate his victory at Fornova. It was much restored last Century, but is still most impressive.

Quai de la Douane along the river leads to the elegant classical place de la Bourse. It was designed and built from 1733 by Jacques Gabriel and then his son Jacques Ange Gabriel, architect of place de la Concorde and École Militaire in Paris. It is an attractive square, open on one side to the river, with angled corners to avoid formality and surrounds a garden and fountain of the three Graces, with tall houses of the wine merchants along the quay. Its most impressive building is the great Hôtel de la Bourse, the old Exchange now housing the Chamber of Commerce. An enormous building, beautifully restored after damage in 1940, it has great carved pediments outside, and inside a great hall with an ornate wrought-iron grille and impressive main staircase. The old Custom House (*Douane*) is now a museum of the history of custom officers, imaginatively told (shut Monday).

From the place you can see the contrast between this old Bordeaux and the modern industrial zone across the river which has given Bordeaux most of its post-war prosperity. The zone stretches 20km north along the right bank of the river. The man responsible for that is Jacques Chaban-Delmas, Mayor of Bordeaux, President of France's National Assembly and Prime

Minister from 1969–72, a liberally-minded Gaullist who announced what he called 'the New Society'.

Chaban persuaded Paris to build or help to build the motorways, flyovers, ring roads and the Pont d'Aquitaine suspension bridge, 1767 metres long, 55 metres above the water, joining the A10 Paris motorway with the west ring road connecting Mérignac international airport and joining in the south the A61 Toulouse motorway. Just west of the bridge the road crosses a huge lake alongside a great new international exhibition park and congress centre – one of the most important in Europe. Dozens of great fairs are held there, including, of course, the biennial Vinexpo international wine and spirit fair.

Chaban persuaded the merchants of Bordeaux to break out of their caution and used his influence in Paris to persuade companies who had state contracts to set up new plants. Thomson CSF electronics moved to Bordeaux, in 1971 Ford opened their first plant in France there, and chemical works, oil refineries, aircraft factories, ship-building works have arrived in Bordeaux. A big new deep-water port for tankers and container-ships was built at Le Verdon on the end of the Médoc peninsula and opened in 1976.

A new university was built in the south-west suburbs of Pessac-Talence as well as a super modern sports stadium with a one-span roof. Small wonder that other French cities talked of blatant favouritism. But all Aquitaine benefited and shook itself free of the sort of economic decline which turned regions like the Dordogne and Auvergne into lands of abandoned villages and crumbling towns, saved only by tourism and the people from Paris and abroad buying second homes there.

Bordeaux has become an active cultural centre as in the eighteenth century, with two renowned orchestras, four theatres, a superb May music festival and very good museums.

Musée d'Art Contemporain (Entrepôt Lainé, rue Foy) has four exhibitions of modern art each year, each with a theme and much work in plastic, often created especially for the vast spaces of the hall (shut Monday). It is also used for films, lectures and conferences on art.

Musée Beaux Arts in cours d'Albret next to the town hall

started in 1801 with fourteen masterpieces saved from riots in Versailles and Paris, including works of Rubens, Titian and Van Dyck. In 1829 over 300 paintings were acquired from the collection of the Marquis de Lacaze (mostly seventeenth-century Dutch) and after that the museum grew enthusiastically. Two works of Rubens include a very strange *Martyrdom of St Just* showing the saint holding his decapitated head and conversing with two friends. Of the Dutch paintings, a landscape and a picture called *Oak Struck by Lightning* (1638) are by the realistic landscape painter Jan van Goyen, who would bring a feeling of fresh air and peacefulness into his work.

The nineteenth-century French paintings are especially interesting and include good landscapes by Corot and Boudin and an excellent painting *Greece Expiring on the Ruins of Missolonghi* (1826) by Eugène Delacroix, great Romantic artist who combined vivid colour and energy with violent or exotic subjects. There are many works by the local painter and lithographer Odilon Redon (1840–1916), whose charcoal sketches included symbolic images inspired by Edgar Alan Poe's writings and who turned later to vividly coloured paintings and pastels. Another local is Albert Marquet (1875–1947) who worked with Matisse but remained more conservative (museum closed Tuesday).

Musée d'Aquitaine, in cours d'Albret (closed Tuesday, Sunday) dates back to 1781 and has very interesting archaeological finds including *Venus of Laussel* made 20,000 years ago and a bronze statue of Hercules from the second century AD, found in a drain beneath a house. The modern exhibits illustrate Bordeaux's agriculture, commerce and maritime life.

Musée des Arts Décoratifs, in a lovely mansion (36 rue Bouffard) is delightful, with elegantly panelled drawing rooms and collections of interesting furniture, enamels, glassware, jewellery and wrought iron, much from the great eighteenth century period and the Grand Théâtre. The collection of Pots-Jacqueline is fascinating. These are rustic figurative jugs from Lille, not unlike Toby Jugs but with more variety (shut Tuesday).

Centre Jean Moulin in place Jean Moulin houses a collection of items from the Resistance, Deportation of French to German forced-labour camps and of the Free French Forces, named after a great Resistance leader (open afternoons except Saturday, Sunday).

Several boats will take you on trips round the docks and on the Garonne, Dordogne and Gironde rivers. Ask at Aquitaine Tourisme Fluvial, 12 place de la Bourse (tel. 56.90.91.28). The *Aliénor* has a restaurant on board and gives trips with lunch to Château Cadillac (*see* page 141). Apply Grands Bateaux d'Aquitaine across from quai de Queyries (tel. 56.86.50.65).

For Bordeaux wine and vineyards see pages 33 and 51. Information on wines and visits from Conseil Interprofessional de Vin de Bordeaux, 1 cours du 30 Juillet.

TOURIST INFORMATION BORDEAUX 12 cours du 30 Juillet (56.44.28.41)
AQUITAINE REGION 24 allées de Tourny (56.44.48.02)
GIRONDE DÉPARTEMENT 21 cours de l'Intendance (56.52.61.40)
MARKETS Les Capucins, place Capucins; Grand Marche, cours Victor Hugo; Grands Hommes, allées de Tourny; Chartrons, place des Chartrons; Lerme, place de Lerme – all mornings except Sunday. Open Air – places Meynard et Chanteloup, mixed on Monday, flea market Tuesday – Friday; food and clothes Saturday. St Pierre, place St Pierre – organic produce Thursday.
FESTIVALS May – fortnight Music Festival based on Grand Théâtre (must book ahead – 56.48.58.54). May – horseshow; June (biennial) – Vinexpo International Wine Fair

HOTELS

Bordeaux has dozens of hotels and good restaurants of all types. It vies with Paris and Lyon as a gourmet centre.

Grand, 2 place Comédie (56.90.92.37). Opposite the theatre. Modern rooms behind eighteenth-century façade. Good value. Restaurant open weekdays for lunch only. ROOMS E–G. MEALS B–D. Open all year.

Terminus (Mapotel), gare St Jean (56.92.71.58). Traditional railway hotel; comfortable; big rooms. Restaurant.

Relais St Jean, former station buffet serves excellently cooked classical and regional dishes. ROOMS E–G. MEALS C–E. Open all year.

Gambetta, 66 rue de la Porte-Dijeaux (56.51.21.83). Another central modernized old hotel. No restaurant. ROOMS D–E. Open all year.

Saint-James, (at Bouliac 4km SE, D113 towards Langon) 3 place Camille Hostein (56.20.52.19). Modern and regional cooking, varied, at times brilliant, especially when simple. 'The best peasant terrine in the world,' says Champérard. Modern building in lovely position. Very expensive. ROOMS G (book). MEALS G. Open all year.

RESTAURANTS

Chapon Fin, 5 rue Montesquieu (56.79.10.10). In an original fin-de-siècle setting, Francis García (a Catalan) serves delicately cooked classical dishes of south-west France and Spain. MEALS G. Shut Sunday, Monday; end July–mid-August; 13–19 February.

Pavillon des Boulevards, 120 rue Croix de Seguey (56.81.51.02). Refined classic bourgeois cooking. Excellent! MEALS G. Shut Saturday lunch, Sunday; 25 March–2 April; 7–20 August.

Vieux Bordeaux, 27 rue Buhan (56.52.94.36). Very good classic cooking, slightly angled towards modern. Excellent value. MEALS C–F. Shut Saturday lunch, Sunday; August; one week in February.

Les Provinces, 41 rue Saint-Rémi (56.81.74.30). Classic and regional dishes of the south-west and Auvergne at bargain prices. MEALS A–E. Open all year.

Pau

[MAP 5, page 255]

Pau is a singular town, lovable despite the inevitable modern
buildings of mediocre design which followed the discovery of
natural gas in 1951 at nearby Lacq. It is cosy in winter, an oasis
of warmth in a world of snow. In summer the sun lights up its
south face, and its splendid position on a high ridge above the
river Gave du Pau gives it superb panoramic views which stretch
to rising rows of permanently snow-capped mountain peaks
which seem to be peering over each other's shoulders.

Like so many attractive towns in France it was born of a
lord's love of hunting. In the eleventh century the Count of Foix
built a château on this remote ridge to use as a hunting lodge. A
village grew around the castle, which was fortified with a huge
brick keep in the fourteenth century and walls of stone from the
hillside by the most colourful of the Counts of Foix, Gaston
Phoebus, who even wrote a book on hunting. It became the main
residence of the lords of Béarn and the principal town of the
west Pyrenees.

In 1527, Henri d'Albret, lord of Béarn, titular King of
Navarre, married Marguerite d'Angoulême, sister of François I
of France, and she made the castle into a home, its medieval
fortress softened by Renaissance decoration. Marguerite of Navarre, as people now called her, was a brilliant woman, author
and poet, who encouraged agriculture, arts and learning. *Corps
féminin, coeur d'homme, tête d'ange,'* they said of her – a woman's
body, a man's heart, an angel's head. She wrote a remarkable
collection of seventy-two amorous tales called *Heptaméron*, told
by men and women supposedly cut off by floods in a Pyrenean
abbey and based on the real amorous adventures of her court
contemporaries. Rabelais dedicated one of his volumes to her
memory. She was influenced by Plato and her court was the
birthplace of the Platonism which became so popular in France
with the idea of woman as the centre of spiritual love. She
protected Clément Marot when he was accused by the Sorbonne

of heresy for translating the psalms into French. Yet despite all the learning and culture, her court was the centre of fêtes, balls and music. It remained so until her daughter, Jeanne d'Albret, who had succeeded her, became a Calvinistic Protestant, when such pleasures ceased.

When Jeanne was expecting a child, she was driven almost non-stop for nineteen days by coach from Picardy so that it should be born in the castle at Pau. The baby was a boy and before his father showed him to the people he followed the tradition of moistening his lips with garlic and wine from the Jurançon vineyard of Clos de Gaye. Perhaps that is why the son Henri of Navarre, the Protestant leader and soldier who gained the crown of France as Henri IV by professing to become a Catholic, loved food, wine and women all his life. There is hardly a wine area of France which does not boast that 'Le Vert Galant' said that their wine was one of the best in France.

After Henri had become King of France and Navarre, Béarn became part of France and in 1620 his son, King Louis XIII, ceremonially entered Pau. He threw out the Protestants. After that the little town started to grow as monasteries and the university were founded.

One of the joys of Pau is the truly splendid boulevard des Pyrénées, a great platform built on the very edge of the river valley, from the château to the beautiful Parc Beaumont. It was built to the orders of Napoleon, and you have only to spend a while here looking southward towards the Spanish border to know that Pau is a town of the mountains.

The defeat of Napoleon's Armies under General Sault in 1813 started the British influence in Pau. After the fall of Toulouse and Bayonne, a British regiment was stationed in Pau. Some of the officers were so loathe to leave the intoxicating air and mild winter climate that after they were posted home they returned in autumn and winter with their families. They built a Protestant church in rue des Cordeliers. When his French regiment was stationed there in 1828, Alfred de Vigny, who was to become a great novelist, married an English girl, Lydia Bunbury, though like a good Frenchman of his day, he had a beloved mistress, the actress Marie Dorval.

One of those motley British colonies in Europe grew up,

especially after a respected Scottish doctor Alexander Taylor set up a winter 'cure' clinic in 1842. The colony included not only people seeking relief from illness or the effects of excess food and alcohol, but retired officers who could live on their frail pensions better there than in Cheltenham or Bath, refugees from creditors, and husbands and wives who had changed partners and were ostracized at home.

One of the first things the English did was to establish a fox-hunt, dressed properly in hunting pink, of course. It still meets in Pau. Then came a steeplechase course at Pont-Long, still there and one of the most difficult in Europe after Aintree. In 1856 they laid out a golf course, the third outside Scotland after Blackheath and Calcutta. By 1860 the British colony made up 3000 of Pau's 21,000 inhabitants, apart from British winter visitors. But in 1889 Queen Victoria chose to stay in Biarritz instead of Pau. Fashion followed her. The Pau colony declined, although many sportsmen stayed, including the naturalist Sir Victor Brooke. So his son, born at Bagnères-de-Bigorre in 1883, spent his childhood in Pau. He became Field Marshall Sir Alan Brooke, Chief of the Imperial General Staff 1941–6, chief strategic advisor to Winston Churchill and later Viscount Alanbrooke.

The British left behind a tradition of sport which makes Pau still a centre for sporting holidays. It is also a training centre for French Army parachutists.

The château is now a national monument containing a museum of the life and history of Béarn. The massive brick keep named after him remains from Gaston Phoebus's strong fort. Tour de Montauzer, much rebuilt in the sixteenth century, is still there. Its name derived from 'monte-oiseau' because its ladders could be pulled up in the air in case of siege.

Gaston Phoebus, Count of Foix and Viscount of Béarn, was tempestuous and notorious. A great soldier and cunning politician, he spent much time amassing wealth by gangster methods. He attacked his neighbours who paid him protection money to keep the peace. He received 400,000 florins to leave Languedoc in peace, 200,000 florins to restore towns he had attacked, 500,000 florins in ransom for Jean I, Duke of Armagnac, after he had captured him. Then in 1376 he made peace with Jean II of Armagnac, whose daughter Beatrice married his son. But he was convinced that his son was trying to poison him to gain his land and titles, and killed him. He died on a bear hunt, without heir, so the Albrets family got his lands and titles instead. The château was their home until Henri of Navarre became king and lost interest in it. It was neglected for 200 years until the nineteenth century when King Louis Philippe and then Napoleon III over-restored and partly reconstructed it.

The result of these changes is that when you stand in the pleasant triangular courtyard you see a strange mixture of buildings around you, different in style and in the stone and brick of which they are made. Renaissance ornament from the time of Marguerite still stands out.

Inside the château, the vaulted kitchen, with a model of Pau from around 1830, and the dining-room, with a massive table to seat a hundred guests, are interesting. The Gobelin tapestries here are copies of the famous Flemish *Chasse de Maximilien* works. The tapestries with a red background on the second floor are Gobelins, too. Here, there is a museum devoted to Henri IV, with the turtle shell which was supposed to have been his cradle and his backgammon board inlaid with ivory and mother-of-pearl. But his bedroom is a nineteenth-century reconstruction and most of the furniture nineteenth-century reproduction.

The Algerian national hero, the Emir Abd-El-Kader, who fought the French for Algerian and Moroccan freedom from 1832–47, was imprisoned in this part of the château when the French finally defeated him. Musée Béarnais on the third floor contains local natural-history collections and costume, furniture, household utensils and musical instruments of Béarn.

West of the château is a big wooded park, Parc National, and boulevard des Pyrenees, lined with imposing buildings, which runs from the château to the very pleasant Parc Beaumont with woods, a lake, open-air theatre and the casino. About 450 metres from the château the boulevard meets place Royale. Opposite is a funicular down to the river and the railway station.

Behind the château eastwards are the streets of old Pau which are worth exploring. In rue Tran just off place de la Libération is a museum in the house where Jean-Baptiste Bernadotte was born in 1763, now devoted to his remarkable life (museum shut Monday). Son of a Pau lawyer, he joined the French Army as a private soldier, rose to officer and became an ardent Revolutionary. He rose to command a division, and caught the eye of Napoleon in Italy. He became a Marshal of France in 1804 and for his conduct at Austerlitz was made Prince of Pontecorvo! His successes continued, but Napoleon never liked rival heroes. He was made commander of French troops in Germany and Denmark but after another success at Wagram returned to Paris. He had become friendly while in Denmark with the ailing King of Sweden, Charles XIII, who in 1810 made him heir to the Swedish throne. He changed his name to Charles John and, just as the Protestant Henri IV became a Catholic to gain the crown of France, he became a Protestant to gain the crown of Sweden. He was soon running the country for the sick king and when Napoleon made demands which he knew to be against Sweden's interests he went to war with his old chief, taking an important part in the victory over Napoleon at the Battle of Leipzig in 1813.

He became King Charles XIV of Sweden in 1818 and was regarded as a wise and good king until he died in 1844. He remained married to a draper's daughter Desirée Clary even when King. The present Swedish royal family are descended from them. So was Count Folke Bernadotte, the mediator and peacemaker of two World Wars, who was appointed by United Nations to mediate in the Palestine-Jewish troubles and was assassinated by Jewish terrorists in 1948.

The centre of Pau, place Clemenceau, is not very exciting. Rue Foch from the north-east corner takes you to Musée des Beaux-Arts, with one of the most interesting collections in south-west France (shut Tuesday).

The Spanish paintings are particularly good, including works by El Greco (*St Francis*), and Juan de Juanes. A strange painting attributed to a Neapolitan called Gaspare Travessi is the *Drunkenness of Noah*. Perhaps that is where G. K. Chesterton got the idea for the line in his poem 'Wine and Water' in which Noah says: 'I don't care where the water goes if it doesn't get into the wine.'

There are three works of Rubens and two British paintings by George Romney and David Wilkie. The most famous is

Degas' *The Cotton Exchange, New Orleans*, said to be the only painting of Degas bought by a public gallery in his lifetime. The oddest painting is *Pneumatic Greeting* by Alfred Courmes showing the very pneumatic Michelin-type man giving an 'Ave Maria' to a sexy girl in black suspenders. One room is devoted to nineteenth-century paintings of women.

Pau has many good restaurants and the wine town of Jurançon is just across the river (*see* Vineyards, page 58) – most convenient.

TOURIST INFORMATION place Royale (59.27.27.08)
MARKETS Daily; also Monday – poultry, cattle and chestnuts in season
FESTIVALS Spring – show jumping; June – motor race Grand Prix de Pau; July – Theatre Festival.

HOTELS

Continental and Conti Restaurant, 2 rue Maréchal-Foch (59.27.69.31). Classic grand hotel, modernized, elegant, well soundproofed. Very good restaurant. Regional products with variety of dishes for most tastes. ROOMS E–F. MEALS C–E. Open all year.
Commerce, 9 rue Maréchal-Joffre (59.27.34.39). Renovated, comfortable, quiet rooms in town centre. Very good-value meals. ROOMS D–E. MEALS B–D. Restaurant shut Sunday except evening 1 May–30 September.

RESTAURANTS

Pierre, 16 rue Louis Barthou (59.27.76.86). Best in Pau. Old local dishes like Henri IV's own *poule au pot* (chicken in the pot) which he said every French family should have on Sunday, *cassoulet, garbure*, local salmon, with some more sophisticated dishes. Raymond Casau is a true master. Lively, popular, happy restaurant; but not cheap. MEALS F–G. Shut Saturday lunch, Sunday; mid- –end February.
Pyrénées, place Royale (59.27.07.75). Unassuming, informal. Good cheap menu. MEALS C–E. Shut Sunday; 1–22 August.

Toulouse

[MAP 4, page 254]

These days Toulouse is a city for the young and fit. They make Concorde and the European Airbus here; it is France's space centre. People seem to be trying to keep up with Concorde, and drivers seem to be practising for stock-car racing. Dozens of restaurants stay open until 2 a.m., many night clubs open until 6 a.m. and traffic of cars and people goes on most of the night. Yet behind all the frenzy and traffic jams is a charming old city of red brick, warm and cosy, beautiful in sunshine.

The fourth largest city in France, Toulouse lies in open country where the Garonne river swings west. The Romans built here because there was a ford. They called it Tolosa. The Visigoth King Alaric made it his capital in the fifth century but it came under the Franks after Alaric was beaten by the Frankish King Clovis. It was virtually ruled by the Counts Raymond from the ninth to the thirteenth centuries because it was so far from Paris.

Toulouse became powerful and important. One Count, Raymond IV, led a crusade against the Moors who had occupied much of Spain. He married a princess of Aragon and had close links with that province, and then he got possession of Provence. So Toulouse ruled much of what is now southern France. Another Count, Raymond V, beat off attacks by the Plantagenet English Kings Henry II and Richard Coeur de Lion.

When Simon de Montfort was running his vicious 'crusade' of murder and devastation on behalf of the Pope against the heretical Albigensian sect, he accused the Count of Toulouse of complicity in the murder of a Papal legate, entered Toulouse and began a regime of murder and terror. De Montfort wanted to be made Count of Toulouse, but while he was away, the Count retook the town. Montfort returned in 1218 to besiege it and was blessedly killed by a stone from a giant sling. No one in France regretted his passing except the freebooters he employed as soldiers.

The Pope made Count Raymond VI pay penance, part of which was to maintain for ten years four masters in theology, two in canon law, six masters of arts and two directors of grammar. The University of Toulouse was thus born.

Soon after, Raymond VII was forced by Louis VIII of France to give his daughter and heir in marriage to Alphonse de Poitiers, brother of the future King Louis IX. When Raymond died, Toulouse came under the French crown and was made capital of a newly defined province called Languedoc, which stretched from the Pyrenees to the Rhône and which had a separate culture from the rest of France. Languedoc came from the language 'Langue d'Oc'. The Romans had no word for 'yes'. They used *hoc ille* meaning 'this that' or, translated very freely, 'that's it'. In Northern France this developed into *oïl*, then *oui*. In the south it became '*oc*' – thus 'the oc tongue' – langue d'oc. Not until 1539 was northern French made the official language, and then the ancient language of Oc (also called Occitan or Provençal) was still used until the early nineteenth century when, under Napoleon, the language was made illegal in schools. It was not legal again until 1951, since when efforts have been made to revive it, but among intellectuals, poets and writers, rather than vineyard and factory workers.

A huge fire in the fourteenth century destroyed much of Toulouse, but happily it was rebuilt in the pinky-red bricks made from local clay. Then in the sixteenth century a new crop was planted in nearby fields – a woad plant from which an indigo dye was made. The local merchants made so much money from it that they were able to build fine and beautiful houses. The dye trade only lasted about a hundred years but many of the houses are still there, proudly boasting towers to show the power and importance of their original owners. Many more fine old houses were knocked down last century in an orgy of vandalism in the name of progress. Toulouse did not progress. It remained a provincial town of around 100,000 people, long since stripped of its power and importance as a southern capital by Napoleon. It was called 'the anti-Paris'. It had only 180,000 people in 1939. Now with its suburbs it has 500,000 people and is a great industrial city with huge suburbs of ugly concrete apartment blocks, factories, warehouses and supermarkets, surrounding the lovely old red-brick city. It is said that the true Toulousians live in the old city, and in the suburbs the newcomers – the scientific whiz-kids of the aircraft, electronic and aerospace factories, the factory workers, resourceful Pieds Noirs businessmen who came to live here after Morocco, Algeria and Tunisia gained independence, the ambitious young who in France tend to regard jobs in provincial cities as a stepping stone to Paris.

Toulouse's scientific gold-rush and industrial expansion did not start immediately after the war, as it did in Grenoble, Nantes, Lille and other big French cities. Toulouse was left wing, anti-Gaullist and living rather lazily in the southern sun. The city fathers would not accept Paris-dictated plans for the future. Paris noticeably kept Toulouse short of funds compared with Bordeaux, Grenoble and other more co-operative cities. Then the Gaullists won an election by a very narrow margin and Toulouse had a Gaullist mayor. Immediately things began to happen. Money poured in from Paris. The Gaullists were not going to lose their new-found majority if they could help it. Young brains with modern minds came from all over France and beyond. There are now more than 300 research laboratories in Toulouse and more than 5000 researchers. Concorde, the first faster-than-sound airliner, was born here and in Bristol.

The entry of Spain into the EEC has given Toulouse new markets, too. While Franco lived, there was no love lost between Spain and Toulouse, where many thousands of Spanish refugees from Civil War days lived. These Spanish immigrants gave Toulouse a Latin atmosphere and attitude which did not fit in with de Gaulle's and Pompidou's dream of a 'new technological France'. Today many of the cafés and nightspots have a strong Latin atmosphere, with Spanish music, and Spanish and South American musicians and singers.

It is a very cosmopolitan city now. As many people speak English as anywhere in France except the Channel ports.

The inner boulevards to the east bank of the Garonne contain nearly all of the most interesting sights of the city. The N20 road from Montauban and Agen and N88 from Albi lead towards the basilica of St Sernin, a very large, perfect Romanesque church little altered since it was built between 1080 and

1350, though restoration begun by the architect Viollet-le-Duc in 1855 continued until about twenty years ago. It is in red brick, splendidly ornate, with an enormous twelfth-century octagonal tower of five storeys, each narrower than the one below and the top crowned with a balustrade surrounding a narrow spire.

It was for a long time a major place of pilgrimage, which is why it is so enormous – 115 metres long, 64 metres across the transept and 21 metres high. The wide aisles were designed for processions. The huge, tall twelve-bay nave has galleried double side aisles. The great high altar of 1096 has been restored. Though built in 1670, the choir stalls are Renaissance. The tomb of St Saturninus is in the apse and there are seven interesting marble reliefs in the ambulatory. Romanesque wall paintings were discovered during restoration. It is a splendid church, well worth seeing.

Down rue du Taur, the fourteenth-century church with an odd bell tower, Notre-Dame du Taur, was actually named for St Saturnin's bull, which is even odder. St Saturnin (called Serrin now) tried to convert Toulouse to Christianity in AD 250. The price of failure was to be tied to a bull, which dragged him to his death – hardly, you would think, a Holy Bull. Along the rue du Taur are beautiful old mansions with courtyards behind their big old coach gates. They are mostly converted into flats.

Toulouse has very many churches as well as beautiful old houses, but it is far from being a dead 'museum' city. The centre of its activity and art is still the Place du Capitole at the end of rue du Taur. This great square is truly dominated by the town hall, called the Capitole from the seventeenth century when Toulouse (with Languedoc) was ruled by its own consuls (or *capitouls*) and was trying to show its independence from Paris and north France. At the same time Protestantism was becoming popular and Richelieu had a double reason to destroy États du Languedoc. He had the Governor, Duc de Montmerency, executed in the Capitole courtyard in 1632 as a warning. There were happier scenes and great festivity on 12 April 1814 when peace was declared. Wellington, who had brought his troops from Spain over the Pyrenees and scattered the Napoleonic army of Marshal Soult from its powerful positions in and around Toulouse, was received with honours and rejoicing.

Toulousians were not averse to the defeat of Napoleon, who had taken away the city's power, by the English, historic trading partners of Toulouse, and allies of their old trading partners, the Spanish.

The Capitole is very impressive rather than beautiful. The inside courtyard is from 1606, the long façade from the early eighteenth century. Upstairs rooms are grandly decorated. In the pretty gardens behind is the restored keep (Tour du Donjon) containing the Tourist Office.

Place Capitole is surrounded by cafés where housewives chatter in daytime and students put the world to rights through the evening until the early hours. The square is the true meeting place of Toulouse and centre for festivities. Brasseries and snack bars are full until after midnight. Even boutiques are still open. At the south end of the square is l'Opéra, the theatre for opera, music, ballet and plays.

Westward from the theatre along rue Gambetta, then left along rue Lakanal is a treasure of a church, Église des Jacobins, which a hundred years ago was used as stables and barracks by the French Army.

Originally it was the church of a monastery started in 1216 and finished at the end of the fourteenth century. It was founded by St Dominic when he was campaigning against the Albigensians, the first house of his Frères Pécheurs. A year later his followers arrived in Paris and settled by the Porte de St Jacques. They were called 'Jacobins'. Confiscated by the State after the Revolution, the church was commandeered by the Army in 1820 to be used as stables for 500 horses and barracks for their riders, grooms and vets. Damage and neglect brought it to ruin. A concerted campaign by church and city forced the Army out in 1863 but money was not provided to start restoration until the end of the nineteenth century, and the work was not finished until the mid-1970s. A glance inside from the south door will show you that the time and money were well spent. Its octagonal tower is superb Gothic, the pride of Toulouse, though the church is a little austere. Its cloisters, faithfully reconstructed after Army destruction, are elegant and big.

Inside, the vast double nave is truly breathtaking. The seven pillars in line which divide it are thick but so tall that they look slender. They support the roof with the help of slim brick arches fanning from the top to meet the arches from the outer walls to form vaulting. It is unique and very effective, especially with the sense of space given by the uncluttered floor paved with large stone slabs in grey and pink. The tall and narrow Gothic windows go almost all round the walls. The windows by Max Ingrand, flanking the west half of the nave are masterly. He has combined cool colours to the north with sunny reds and yellows to the south, aimed to bring colour to the stone floor. I believe that Max Ingrand is one of the most underestimated artists of the twentieth century. Even Michelin does not bother to name him as artist of these great works and the usually knowledgeable *Phaidon Cultural Guide to France* does not even mention the windows. The two high rose windows on the west wall have their original fourteenth-century glass.

Just past rue Lakanal on rue Gambetta is Hôtel de Bernuy, a mansion from 1530 and one of the many in Toulouse worth seeing. It has an octagonal stairway tower, the tallest in Toulouse, a superb vaulted Gothic arch and an arcade with a Renaissance influence in its fine courtyard. It is now a Lycée.

Other handsome mansions include Hôtel Béringuier-Maynier (once called Vieux Raisin) in rue du Languedoc opposite place des Carmes, with an Italian Renaissance style worthy of the Loire. It has a fine spiral staircase in its courtyard. Rue de la Dalbade, between place du Parlement and the church of Notre-Dame de la Dalbarde, now a pleasant side street, was once a residential street for rich merchants and members of the ruling parliament, and has some superb old houses. The man who had Hôtel de Clary built must have been very rich, for he used stone instead of brick for the front and that cost a fortune to bring here to the south in 1615. The house is true Renaissance, with rich carving in stone and wood. Step through the gateway into the courtyard and the rest of the mansion around you is of brick and is very handsome.

An even richer man had Hôtel d'Assézat built on the corner of rue Languedoc and rue Croix-Baragnon leading to the cathedral of St Étienne. It was built in 1555 by a merchant, named Assézar, who became a ruling *Capitoul* after making a fortune in the wool and dye trade. It is hidden behind a wall, but go through the gateway and you are faced with a grand palace built in red brick around a central courtyard, and a strange tower with more than a hint of the East rising from one corner. It was designed by Toulouse's own Renaissance architect Nicolas Bachelier and is regarded as the most beautiful building in the city. It is almost classical with adornment of Doric, Ionic and Corinthian pilasters. One side of the courtyard has attractive arcades with a wooden panelled ceiling but another side was never finished. The merchant Assézar became a Protestant, was banished and ruined. Now his house has a medical history museum on the second floor and is headquarters of six societies of learning and culture. One, the Académie des Jeux Floraux, is the oldest literary society in Europe. It was founded in 1323 by local poets who wrote in langue d'Oc and wanted to keep their language alive after the French took Toulouse. They called it La Compagnie du Gai Savoir (happy learning), but in the seventeenth century Louis XIV changed the title to the Floral Games. The games are annual poetry contests in the langue d'Oc and have been held since the society was formed. They are usually in May and winners are given flowers made of gold and silver.

St Étienne's cathedral is strange. Combining features from the eleventh to seventeenth centuries, it has none of the architectural harmony which the French love. It seems to be put together at random. Yet it has quaint higgledy-piggledy charm. The eighteenth-century rectangular tower is proud and imposing. The nave was built in instalments over centuries, none quite finished, each in a different style. The first single nave was built around 1100, the vaults added in the seventeenth century. Gothic additions came over the centuries so that now there is a broad nave with no aisles added to a wider section with side aisles. The severity is relieved by sixteenth- to seventeenth-century rather worn tapestries and by stained glass of various periods.

Rue du Metz, cut through the old town from the cathedral square to Pont Neuf in the nineteenth century, is the big shopping street.

There are pleasant walks along the quays of the Garonne river, especially from north of Pont Neuf at place Daurade north-west to Pont St Pierre. On the Garonne's left bank beside

Pont St Michel is a pedestrian area from the river to cours
Dillon. Place Président Wilson, east from place du Capitole, is a
pleasant square for sitting at an outside table eating or drinking,
facing a public garden dedicated to a seventeenth-century langue d'Oc poet.

Toulouse has several good museums, but the Musée des
Augustins is outstanding – one of the most imaginative in
France. It is housed in the remains of a fourteenth-century
monastery. The buildings were intact just after the Revolution
but during the conversion to a museum they were badly damaged. Then last century the refectory was knocked down and
replaced by a 'warehouse' designed by Viollet-le-Duc, who had
rebuilt Carcassonne so brilliantly, restored Notre-Dame in Paris
and Laon and Amiens cathedrals, and should have known better
than to do this to Toulouse. The beautiful old cloister remains.

I did not see the museum before 1970, but it is said to have
been sorry and neglected. New conversions, exposure of
medieval walls and reorganization have made it splendid. It has
a fine collection from most periods of great painters of many
schools, a most impressive and quite moving collection of
religious paintings displayed in the old monastery church, and
an inspired collection from Toulouse's own school of the seventeenth century which developed entirely separately from Paris,
more influenced by the Italians, especially Caravaggio.

In the former chapterhouse and the cloisters is displayed a
now-famous collection of fourteenth- to sixteenth-century
sculptures rescued mostly from cloisters and churches demolished after the Revolution. They include a large group of works
by the architect Nicolas Bachelier who designed Hôtel Assézat.

Religious paintings include a fine Murillo, the very dramatic
Rubens *Christ Between the Two Thieves*, once in a church in
Antwerp, and Van Dyck's *Miracle of the Mule*. Two powerful
paintings of the seventeenth century are by the Parisian painter
Simon Vouet who turned to religious and allegorical works after
years in Rome. The same was true of Nicolas Tournier (1590–
1638), greatest of the seventeenth-century Toulouse school, who
had been known for his scenes of eating, drinking and music
playing. Toulousians are furious that he is not better known,
and Michelin, too, claims that he should be. He was Caravaggio

with refinements. His people are more elegant, their faces more refined. He has three paintings in the church. In the Viollet-le-Duc building is his *Battle of the Roches Rouges*.

Some of the Toulouse seventeenth-century artists are still unknown. One whose name is known but not his background is Amboise Frédeau, who has two works in the church. Jean Chalette, who worked also in Italy and Aix-en-Provence, has a painting here called *Virgin and Child Blessing Prisoners*, painted to brighten a prison. Another Toulouse contemporary shows Italian influence in several works commissioned to decorate the Capitole.

In the nineteenth century section are paintings by Jean François Detroy, a Toulouse man who worked mostly in Paris. He painted everyday life scenes, very different from François de Troy, the portrait painter, who was a contemporary.

Toulouse-Lautrec, Delacroix, Courbet, Corot and Baron Gérard are all represented, too (museum shut Tuesday, Sunday morning).

Another museum housed in a Viollet-le-Duc building is Musée St Raymond on place St Sernin by the church, containing Romanesque carvings from former churches and the finest collection of Roman busts outside Italy (shut Tuesday except in July, August).

Musée Paul Dupuy, rue de la Pleau, shows arts and crafts from Middle Ages to today (shut Tuesday, Sunday morning).

TOURIST INFORMATION Donjon du Capitole, square
Charles de Gaulle (61.23.32.00); Haute-Garonne
Tourisme, 63 boul. Carnaut (61.23.52.52); Regional
Tourisme, 12 rue Salambo (61.47.11.12)
MARKETS Daily except Monday
FESTIVALS 24 August – Garlic Fair; mid-October –
Garlic Fair and Automobile Show; November –
Antiques Fair

HOTELS

Grand Hôtel de l'Opéra, 1 place Capitole (61.21.86.66). *See also Restaurant Les Jardins de l'Opéra*. Reasonable room prices for such luxury. Also apartments. Good position for exploring.
Brasserie (Grand Café de l'Opéra) as well as restaurant (*see below*). ROOMS F–G. Brasserie MEALS F.
Concorde, 16 boul. Bonrepos, facing gare Matabiau (61.62.48.60). Hotel *de grand-standing* as the French say. Big rooms. Optimistic address for Concorde! ROOMS G. MEALS C–D. Restaurant shut Saturday, Sunday; August.
Orsay, 8 boul. Bonrepos (61.62.71.61). No restaurant. Less ambitious than Concorde but comfortable. ROOMS D–F. Open all year.

RESTAURANTS

Les Jardins de l'Opéra, 1 place Capitole (61.23.07.76). Young chef with appropriate name of Dominique Toulousy is reaching the top. He serves regional food, beautifully cooked, slightly modernized, while his wife Maryse, smiling, oversees the service and the cellar which is well-stocked with south-west wines. Expensive. MEALS E-G. Shut Sunday; 12–26 August; 2–7 January.
Vanel, 22 rue Maurice Fontvielle (61.21.51.82). The master of Toulouse chefs, Lucien Vanel, now has a young partner; dishes are lighter and less ambitious. Good choice of cheapish wines. MEALS G. Shut Monday lunch, Sunday; August.
Darroze, 19 rue Castellaine (61.62.64.70). Pierre Darroze's daughter-in-law Viviane has taken over at the cooker but all remains the same – regional, excellent cooking. Real river Adour salmon in season. Superb *piperades*. Expensive. Magnificent collection of Armagnac brandies. MEALS F–G. Shut Saturday lunch, Sunday; mid-July–8 August.
Chez Emile, Francis Ferrier, 13 place Georges (61.21.05.56). Very good fish on the ground floor, regional dishes on first floor. Delicious *cassoulet*. MEALS C–F. Shut Sunday, Monday; Christmas, New Year.
La Jonque du Yangtse, boul. Griffoul-Dorval (61.20.74.74). On canal du Midi; the 'junk' is a converted grain barge, chefs are

Eastern, the cooking is excellent Chinese. MEALS C (lunch) –F.
Shut Sunday, Monday lunch.

La Frégate, 1 rue d'Austerlitz (61.21.59.61). On corner of place
Wilson among trees. Toulousian bistro. Genuine local *cassoulet*.
Good-value menus. MEALS B–G. Shut Saturday lunch, Sunday;
26–30 December.

Lourdes

[HAUTES-PYRÉNÉES, MAP 6, page 256]

A Scottish guidebook writer described Lourdes in 1840 as a city of shabby houses and narrow dirty streets. Now it is one of the leading tourist sites of the world, attracting over four million Catholics annually, claimed to be more pilgrims than go to Rome or Mecca. It is a very rich town.

The miracle came in 1858 when a fourteen-year-old peasant girl, a shepherdess named Bernadette Soubirous, claimed that the Holy Mother had appeared to her no less than eighteen times in the grotto of Massabielle above the Gave de Pau river. When Bernadette scratched the floor, a spring appeared.

The water of the spring was believed to cure the sick. Bernadette was examined by church authorities, her visions were declared genuine and pilgrimages to the spot authorized. Bernadette became Sister Marie-Bernard at the Convent of St Gildard in Lourdes. She died in Nevers in 1879, aged thirty-five, and in 1933 was made a saint by Rome.

In 1889 the Basilica of Rosaire was built in front of the grotto in a pseudo-Byzantine style. This and the grotto are the focal point of the Religious City built inside the bend of the Gave de Pau. There is a vast processional esplanade, a huge statue of the Virgin, two big hospitals and two other churches. One was built in 1876 in an extraordinary fake thirteenth-century style and contains some equally extraordinary ex-votos left by pilgrims. The third church is the Basilica of Pope Pius X, built underground in 1958, with space for 20,000 people under a single span of pre-stressed concrete. It is the second biggest church in the world after St Peter's in Rome.

The crowds are at their height between mid-August and

Basilica at Lourdes

mid-September, with tens of thousands filing along the esplanade and big torchlight processions at night. Though Lourdes ranks third in France for the number of its hotels, getting a bed in high summer is very difficult.

Some visitors are, of course, curious tourists, many I have met have been old, devout Catholics wanting the spiritual experience of the pilgrimage before they die. Many have saved for years for the journey. It is a sort of last holiday on their way to paradise. But it is sad to see the very sick, the disabled and the terminally ill arriving in faith and hope and leaving as they came. I am told that all claimed miraculous cures are investigated by a medical commission and that sixty-four have been declared genuine.

The commercialism of Lourdes is appalling. Religious shrines have always attracted touts, villains and charlatans preying on ingenuous pilgrims. In medieval times the routes to the tomb of St James at Santa Compostela, to Jerusalem, to St Peter's in Rome, to Canterbury Cathedral were littered with touts selling 'holy relics', such as enough pieces of the 'True Cross' to build a wooden palace, and pewter medallions of saints guaranteed to give protection or cure. There are plenty of shops in Rome selling holy pictures, statues and insignia, some rather cheap and nasty. But Lourdes goes far beyond this. Even that devoted Roman Catholic writer Hilaire Belloc, whose faithful works won him the rank of Knight Commander of the Order of St Gregory from the Pope, was bitterly outspoken about Lourdes at the turn of the century. The *Blue Guide to France* advises non-Catholics to avoid Lourdes entirely.

It is far too interesting to avoid. But unless you have a cynical sense of humour I would avoid the two main streets selling tawdry religious trinkets and souvenirs and try to avoid the hordes of professional photographers. Selling plastic bottles to take home holy water is one thing – selling them in the shape of the Virgin and selling Virgins you can wind up is going too far. I saw them last time I was there. Try to avoid pickpockets, too. They operate mainly at night.

You can visit the house where Bernadette was born, and a museum, Pavillon Notre-Dame, which shows a film of her life (shut Tuesday in winter). Her father was a miller. Hollywood made a film about her in 1942, too, called *Song of Bernadette* – a typically sickly Hollywood production of the time. Her Saint's Day is 15 February, and 15 August is the main annual pilgrimage. Her body in nun's habit with wax masks on her visible hands and face is displayed rather gruesomely in a glass case in Nevers convent where she died.

Centuries before the miracle, Lourdes was important as the main town of the Bigorre. Its medieval fortress, high on a rocky outcrop above the town, still looks formidable. It was enlarged and altered later, and in the seventeenth century became a prison, then a barracks. You reach it by a lift, by 131 steep steps or by a long ramp. It has about 1000 metres of fortifications, a drawbridge and a fourteenth-century keep. Since 1922 it has contained a museum of the Pyrenees (shut Tuesday in winter), showing life in the mountains in the past and present, very well presented, with fine costumes, scenes of domestic life, and souvenirs of Pyrenean mountaineers, including Count Henry Russell (1834–1906) and Charles Packe (1826–96). Russell was an Irishman who lived in France and became an eccentric mountaineer (*see* Gavarnie, page 163). Packe was squire of Stretton Hall in Leicestershire, a scientist, classics scholar and mountaineer who set out to make the Pyrenees as popular as the Alps. His *Guide to the Pyrenees* was written for mountaineers.

The Moors came over the Pyrenees to take Lourdes in the eighth century, and held it against all attacks. Charlemagne could not take it, so organized a long siege. As the Moors were about to surrender through lack of food, a bird dropped a solitary fish into the castle. The Moorish commander sent it as a present to Charlemagne to prove that he was getting in secret supplies. This fishy story tells of another miracle. The Bishop of Le Puy claimed to have had a dream telling him to suggest to the Moors that they should not surrender to Charlemagne but to the Church of Notre-Dame du Puy. Then their lives would automatically be spared. They agreed, their leader became a Christian and took the name of Lorus, so the town around the castle became Lourdes.

A cable-car on avenue Francis Lagardère to the south of the town takes you to Le Béout (791 metres) with a fine panorama of the town, mountain peaks and valley (open Easter-mid-

October). A cable railway from N21 at the south of Lourdes takes you to Pic du Jer (948 metres) with a wide panorama of the mountains and Lake Lourdes in a lovely setting (open all year). There is sailing, windsurfing and pedal boats on Lake Lourdes (3km NW).

TOURIST INFORMATION 1 place du Champ-Commun
(62.94.15.64)
FESTIVALS Easter – Religious music and art

HOTELS

Albret et Taverne de Bigorre, 21 place Champ-Commun (62.94.75.00). Small, well kept, central, good value; very good regional cooking. ROOMS C–D. MEALS B–F. Shut mid-November–mid-December, January. Restaurant shut Sunday evening, Monday low season.

Relais de Saux, at Marreau de Saux, 3km N by N21. (62.94.29.61) Charming old inn, quiet rural setting, only eight rooms. Not cheap but good cooking. ROOMS G. MEALS F–G.

Impérial, 28 avenue du Paradis (62.94.06.30). One of several hotels *traditionnels de bon standing*. Faces Gave de Pau and mountains. ROOMS E–G. MEALS C–F. Open all year.

RESTAURANTS

L'Ermitage, place Mgr Laurence (62.94.08.42). Lourdes is short of really good restaurants. This is one of the few. Seasonal dishes from regional products. MEALS C–F. Open 1 May–mid-October.

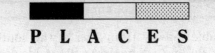

PLACES

AÏNHOA
[Pyrénées-Atlantiques]

A truly beautiful Basque village, 8km SE of Cambo-les-Bains, Aïnhoa has fine seventeenth-century Basque houses with flowered balconies, outer walls repainted every year in white with red-brown half-timbering, and painted shutters. Many have the family name and building date carved in the woodwork. One has a note saying that it was built with money sent home by a son from the Indies. The interesting old church has a two-floor gallery. The village is near the telecommunications centre at Artzamendi, from which there is a superb panorama over the Nive valley. Though it has only 500 people, Aïnhoa has hotels and restaurants because it is a touring centre for the Basque country.

HOTELS

Ithurria (59.29.92.11). Historic monument, seventeenth-century inn used by pilgrims on a road to Compostela. All this and a Michelin star for cooking. Real Basque dishes, including *ttoro* fish soup, super *piperade*. Big rooms with mountain country views. Pool. ROOMS E–G. MEALS D–G. Open mid-March–mid-November. Restaurant shut Tuesday low season.

Argi-Eder (59.29.91.04). Quiet, restful, rooms modernized in Basque style. Good classic regional cooking. ROOMS G. MEALS D–G. Open 6 April–15 November, except Sunday evening and Wednesday low season.

Oppoca (59.29.90.72). Another pilgrims' relais (seventeenth century). Very pleasant. ROOMS D–F. MEALS C–F. Shut mid-November–early April. Restaurant shut Tuesday low season.

AIRE-SUR-L'ADOUR
[LANDES]

Historic town where N124 meets N134, 31km SE of Mont-de-Marsan. Aire was founded by the Romans. A busy market town for ducks and geese. It was the seat of bishops from the year 500 until 1933, when the seat was moved to Dax. The cathedral remains, built in the twelfth century as the church of a Benedictine monastery. The apse was rebuilt in the eighteenth century, but it is worth seeing. So is the other church, Ste Quitterie, on a small hill in the SW corner of the town. In the crypt is a fifth-century marble sarcophagus showing biblical scenes; Jonah and the whale, Daniel in the lion's den, Adam and Eve, Lazarus are all featured, and a scene which I was told depicts the drunkenness of Noah. Poor Noah! The *smell* and noise of all those animals would have driven a saint to drink. It seems that Ste Quitterie was a Visigoth princess martyred here for becoming a Christian in 476. The present church, originally built in 1092, was remodelled in 1309.

Aire's town hall is the former bishop's palace.

You can rent canoes for exploring the Adour river.

TOURIST INFORMATION 1 place de Gaulle
(in season – 58.71.64.70)

MARKET Tuesday

FESTIVAL End of June – fêtes and gala, with procession
of flowers

HOTELS

Commerce, 3 boul. des Pyrénées (58.71.60.06). Traditional hotel with regional cooking. Good value. ROOMS B–C. MEALS A–F. Shut Monday (restaurant); Sunday evening. September–June, 2–15 January.

Domaine de Bassibé, at Ségos, 9km S by N134, D260 (62.09.46.71). Jean-Pierre Capelle, formerly with Guérard at Eugénie-les-Bains, has restored an old country mansion and its estate beautifully, and cooks with great talent. Regional cuisine with modern adaptations. Expensive. ROOMS G. MEALS F–G. Open early April–30 November.

ALDUDES
[Pyrénées-Atlantiques]

S from St Étienne-de-Baïgorry the D948 runs through a valley alongside the Nive des Aldudes, tributary of the river Nive, to Aldudes village and on to the Spanish frontier. A wooded valley, it was the scene in old days of fights between the people of Baïgorry and those of the Erro valley in Spain.

Aldudes is a typical little mountain village with a galleried church. Pays Quint, along the frontier, was always claimed by the Spaniards, and under the Treaty of Bayonne in 1856 was recognized as being Spanish but leased to the people of Aldudes valley in perpetuity. The people of Pays Quint, called Quintoars, come from about thirty families. As their pastures are technically in Spanish territory, they are called 'French citizens abroad'. Until very recently they refused to change their clocks for French summer time! Urepel, the village which leads to Pays Quint, has an interesting Basque-style church with a cupola.

HOTEL
St Sylvestre (59.37.58.13). Simple Logis de France. ROOMS B. MEALS A–B.

AMBÈS
[Gironde]

Downstream from Bordeaux where the Garonne meets the Dordogne, opposite the town of Bourg, Ambès is an industrial centre for petrol, petro-chemical and allied industries.

AMOU
[Landes]

Charming little market town in the heart of important farming and fruit region, south of Eugénie-les-Bains.

TOURIST INFORMATION Syndicat d'Initiative, La Mairie
(58.89.00.22)
FESTIVAL Easter Course Landaise. (Cow-baiting rather
than bullfighting. A team of acrobatic jumpers and
dodgers cavort round the ring avoiding the horns of an
angry cow, which is not wounded or killed.)

HOTEL

Commerce, place de la Poste (58.89.02.28). Big old-style country
inn with super dishes of local produce, cooked traditionally.
Generous portions. ROOMS D–E. MEALS A–F. Shut Monday low
season; 10–30 November; 14 February–1 March.

ANDERNOS-LES-BAINS
[GIRONDE]

With 4km of beach along the NE side of the Arcachon basin,
Andernos has been a very popular little summer resort for
generations and has more charm than some of the newer resorts
on this coast. Lively in summer, it has a casino and a lot of fêtes,
a yachting marina and plenty of water sports.
TOURIST INFORMATION Esplanade du Broustic
(56.82.02.95)
FESTIVALS May – Spring Fête; July – Oysters;
International Jazz; August – Sea Festival

HOTEL

Coulin, 3 ave d'Arès (56.82.04.35). Simple, comfortable. Regional
specialities. ROOMS D. MEALS A–E. Shut Monday low season; 20
December–31 January.

ANGLET
[PYRÉNÉES-ATLANTIQUES]

A town which almost joins Bayonne and Biarritz and which
keeps its Basque-style architecture even for newer houses. The

changing course of the Adour river changed its history, but it became in Napoleon III's time a fashionable place for richer citizens of Bayonne and Biarritz to hide on weekends, and still is. It has 4km of sandy beach and 70 hectares of the Chiberta forest with footpaths, bridle paths, a lake and golf course. Of old Anglet, the sixteenth-century church with seventeenth- to eighteenth-century furnishings and a traditional wooden Basque gallery survives.

The beach is bordered by dunes, the land beyond planted with pines. It is a sporting centre for riding, golf, surfing, sailing from its marina, and even ice-hockey on its international-size ice-rink.

Behind one of its beaches, Plage de la Chambre d'Amour, is a cave called Chambre d'Amour where two lovers were so entranced with each other that the rising sea poured in and drowned them. A walk round the Pointe St Martin from here takes you to Biarritz's Plage Miramar.

TOURIST INFORMATION 1 ave Chambre d'Amour
(59.03.77.01)
FESTIVALS Early August – Festival de Dessin
Humoristique (cartoons); early September –
International Ice-hockey Tournament

HOTELS

Château de Brindos, route l'Aviation, off N10 SW 3½km, almost in Biarritz (59.23.17.68). Beautiful old manor in quiet grounds beside a private lake among lawns and trees. Delightful, very expensive Relais et Châteaux. ROOMS over 1000F. MEALS 400F upwards. Open all year.

Ibis, 64 ave d'Espagne N10 (59.03.45.45). Uninspiring but useful, near station, autoroute and airport of Biarritz. Cheap meals. ROOMS E. MEALS A–D. Open all year.

Chiberta et du Golf, 104 boul. des Plages (59.63.88.30). Modern but superbly situated by the lake and golf course. Expensive. ROOMS G. MEALS C–G.

Villa Clara, Chiberta, 149 boul. des Plages, 9km N by D260, D5 (59.63.83.68). Former villa of Dubonnet family, then the Duke of Windsor, now 'hotel residence'. Separate restaurant. 200 metres from beach. ROOMS and APARTMENTS D–G.

ARAMITS
[PYRÉNÉES-ATLANTIQUES]

Village SW from Oloron-Ste-Marie on D919 road where it joins the beautiful D918 up to Mauléon-Licharre. Dumas named one of his 'Three Musketeers' Aramis. The man may have actually lived as lord of the manor at Aramits, or he could have been absentee-abbot of the abbey which was here. Aramits is now a speleologists' centre for caves in the whole mountain area.

ARCACHON
[GIRONDE]

The Bassin d'Arcachon cuts a triangular watery hole in the straight Atlantic coast between the Gironde estuary and the Spanish border at Hendaye. A fine shallow lake at high tide, it empties quite quickly, revealing vast mudflats beloved by water fowl and seabirds. There is a bird sanctuary at Le Teich in the SE corner and on the island in the middle, Île aux Oiseaux, and many oyster beds with their pens showing at low tide. Arcachon oysters were famous when Rabelais praised them in the sixteenth century, but the natives were destroyed by disease in the 1920s and were replaced by Portuguese stock. These in their turn caught the dreaded Aber disease which spread down from Brittany, and were replaced by Japanese and Canadian stock.

At low tide you can also see stakes sticking out of the water with what seems to be black grapes growing on them. They are small, delicate mussels – *moules bouchots*. *Bouchots* means wooden posts, and it was Irish sailors who taught the French to cultivate them this way in the thirteenth century. Arcachon's shellfish business employs 25,000 people.

In this rather unlikely setting is one of the leading holiday areas of France. In summer especially, the roads around the Bassin and down to the water are crammed with cars, the tamarisk-lined boulevards are thick with people, and 1800 yachts fill its marina. The town of Arcachon is a higgledy-piggledy mix of tourist shops, restaurants, shellfish bars, balconied hotels and apartment blocks. The mixture of architectural styles from Eastern pagoda style to Louis XIV, French Empire and son-of-Corbusier concrete would make a town planner change his vocation. There are two casinos, a *parc d'attractions*, night clubs and discos and a lot of noise and good humour.

The resort of Arcachon is on the SW tip of the basin but the waterside is built up almost entirely from Pyla-sur-Mer which guards the south of the entrance from the sea right round to Andernos-les-Bains (*see* page 110) near the top to Cap Ferret opposite Pyla. And in fact the buildings continue from Pyla a little way down the Atlantic coast to Pilat-Plage and the sand dune of Pyla, 7km S of Arcachon. At 114 metres, this is claimed to be the highest sand-dune in Europe and it is still growing. There are lovely views of sand, sea and pines from the top.

The building of Arcachon started with the arrival of the railway in the 1850s. The railway came first to La Teste, just inland from the Bassin, but the Bordelais who now arrived for weekends started to build villas by the water and the railway was extended to catch the custom. The resort grew very quickly. By 1857 it was a town. In 1859 Napoleon III arrived and Arcachon immediately became fashionable. The railway company decided to spread the season through the winter. They built a winter resort (Ville d'Hiver) back among the trees, starting with the Moorish casino.

Royalty came – Spanish kings, anyway, and Queen Victoria's daughter Princess Louise. Those two great visitors to seaside resorts, the writer Alexandre Dumas and the composer Debussy arrived, too.

Arcachon has survived the air-package rush to Spain and is still popular. It does not look exciting, but it is great fun. It is still fashionable to sit outside the Café de la Plage taking an aperitif.

La Teste is now virtually a suburb of Arcachon. It was called La-Teste-de-Buch for it was capital of Buch, a region of old Gascony, whose rulers were called Captals de Buch and were fierce fighters supporting the English against the French.

Arcachon's Aquarium and Museum has collections of birds, reptiles and fish with a good section on oysters (open Easter to end September). From June to September flat-bottomed boats

will take you to the oyster parcs, Île des Oiseaux, Cap Ferret, or
to the Atlantic Ocean (tel. 56.83.06.62).

TOURIST INFORMATION place Franklin-Roosevelt
(56.83.01.69)
MARKET daily
FESTIVAL 15 August – Sea Festival

HOTELS

Dozens of good hotels.
Arc, 89 boul. de la Plage (56.83.06.85). Modern, very expensive.
Pieds en l'eau. Big rooms, well furnished. Pool on terrace facing
sea. No restaurant. ROOMS F–G. Open all year.
Nautic, 20 boul. de la Plage (56.83.01.48). Good, well kept, fairly
priced, near marina. No restaurant. ROOMS E–F. Open all year.
Bayonne, 9 cours Lamarque (56.83.33.82). Good restaurant with
bedrooms. ROOMS D–E. MEALS B–E. Restaurant shut Monday
off season.

RESTAURANTS

Chez Boron, 15 rue Professeur-Jolyet (56.83.29.96). Well known
in France for shellfish, bouillabaisse, fish *pot-au-fer*. MEALS D–F.
Shut Wednesday low season; mid-January–mid-February.
Chez Yvette, 59 boul. Général-Leclerc (56.83.05.11). Excellent
classical cooking of local fish. Try lamprey (eels) in red-wine
sauce. MEALS C–G. Shut 2 January–2 February.
Patio, 10 boul. Plage (56.83.02.72). Good restaurant. MEALS
E–F. Shut Tuesday except mid-summer; February.
Boucanier, 222 boul. Plage (56.83.41.82). Outstanding fish restaurant. MEALS D–G. Shut Monday lunch; 20 November–
20 December.

ARETTE
and
ARETTE-PIERRE-ST-MARTIN
[PYRÉNÉES-ATLANTIQUES]

The village of Arette on the attractive D918 south of Aramits (*see* page 112) had to be rebuilt after an earthquake on 13 August 1967. A beautiful but zig-zagging mountain road D132 joins it to Arette-Pierre-St-Martin at 1650 metres, the westernmost ski resort in the Pyrenees and a summer centre for mountain walkers and pot-holers. Right on the Spanish border is the world's deepest pot-hole, Gouffre de-la-St-Martin (or Gouffre Lépineux). Its entrance is blocked up to prevent the public killing themselves. It was discovered only in 1950 by a Belgian Dr Max Cosyns and the great French speleologist Georges Lépineux. With another great caver, Marcel Loubens, he found an underground river at 450 metres. Alas, Marcel Loubens was killed there in 1952. But later expeditions discovered vast chambers as deep as 1760 metres. You actually have to cross the Spanish border, very temporarily, on the D132 to see the cave entrance. The Pierre-St-Martin Pass to Spain is normally open only mid-May to mid-October.

Every year on 13 July a group of French mayors from this area of France, Basse Soule, meets a group of Spanish mayors from Roncal in Navarre at the Spanish border at Col de Pierre-St-Martin, 3km S of the ski resort. They come to commemorate with a handclasp at the frontier post a treaty of 1375 which agreed a free zone in which French and Spanish shepherds could graze their flocks. The French used to pay the Spanish three heifers. Alas, they now pay in money. The long-distance footpath GR10 runs along the frontier here. It used to be a mule track used by smugglers – even in the Second World War, when escaped prisoners were taken across.

6km down the D132 towards Arette at Col de Labays, a forest road D441 leads right through the Forêt d'Issaux of oaks and pines to Col de Hourataté (11km). The road is drivable in summer.

TOURIST INFORMATION In Pierre-St-Martin
(59.66.20.09) (also Centre International de Spéléologie)

HOTEL
Salies, 8 place de l'Église (59.34.61.03). Simple, very cheap.
ROOMS B. MEALS A–C. Shut 15 November–10 December.

ARGELÈS-GAZOST
[HAUTES-PYRÉNÉES]

Started in the last century as a little watering spa 13km S of
Lourdes, on the road to Cauterets, it is very popular now, with
many hotels and retirement villas. The surrounding scenery is
superb, with a particularly splendid view from Mendaigne tower
over the Thermal Centre park to the mountains. The old town
up the hillside overlooks le Gave de Pau.

The spa treats respiratory problems. It is a very interesting
centre for touring and exploring. At the N end of the town is
Château de Vileuzac, home of Bertrand Barère (1755–1841).
5km S at Arcizans-Avant are the ruins of a château of the Black
Prince.

The D921 runs through the fertile valley of Gave de Pau.
4 km S above it is St Savin (*see* page 229). The D100 goes to
Artalens on what is called Route du Hautacam. Artalens still has
five little windmills of the type used a lot in Bigorre last century.
After the hamlet the route enters the mountains with lovely
views, passing the tiny ski resort of Hautacam. Hautacam peak
(1764 metres) is reached by a formidable path to the left. There
is a viewing table up there.

TOURIST INFORMATION 1 place Mairie (62.97.00.25)
MARKET Tuesday
FESTIVALS 21 April – Ronde du Hautacam;
early August – Course du Hautacam (a mass mountain
run); early September – Fête de Monton

HOTELS

Miramont, boul. des Pyrénées (62.97.01.26). Pleasant, flower gardens, quiet area. Good value; demi-pension preferred high season. ROOMS C–D. MEALS B–E. Shut 25 October–22 December. Monday in winter.

Cimes, place Ourout (62.97.00.01). Quiet. Good value. Logis de France. ROOMS C–D. MEALS A–E. Shut 10 October–18 December.

Chez Pierre d'Agos, 5km NE at Agos-Vidalos (62.97.05.07). Simple, good value. ROOMS C. MEALS A–E.

ARREAU
[HAUTES-PYRÉNÉES]

Attractive little town which was once capital of the Four Valleys where the rivers Aure and Louron meet and the D918 meets D929. It is 32km NW of Bagnères-de-Luchon and 38km SE of Bagnères-de-Bigorre. Both roads pass through gorgeous scenery. D918 from the west over Col d'Aspin needs care but is a rewarding drive. D929 from the north is easier. If you don't mind zig-zagging mountain roads there is lovely scenery around here.

Arreau has some fine sixteenth-century houses, especially Maison du Lys near the covered market. The thirteenth-century church has marble coronettes. This is an area of Pyrenean marble. At the little industrial town of Sarrancolin, 7km N on D929, they quarry the famous red marble with yellow and grey veins.

TOURIST INFORMATION 1 place du Monument
(62.98.63.15)
MARKET Thursday

HOTEL

Angleterre, route Luchon (62.98.83.04). Unusual 'three-turret' Logis de France – sign of good cooking. ROOMS C–D. MEALS A–E. Shut 10 October–26 December; after Easter–1 June; Monday in winter.

ARTALENS
[*See* Argelès-Gazost, page 116]

ARTHOUS ABBEY
[*See* Hastingues, page 169]

ARTOUSTE LAKE
[*See* Gabas, page 163]

ASCAIN
[PYRÉNÉES-ATLANTIQUES]

Though almost met by the outskirts of St Jean-de-Luz, 7km away on the winding N618, Ascain has kept its Basque atmosphere and is a very pleasant place to stay, just inland, with the brooding mountain of La Rhune looking down on it. In August each year the townspeople organize a run up that mountain and back – a sort of Basque marathon. Fields almost reach the delightful main square, which is surrounded by real Basque houses, a fronton for playing the great Basque game of *pelota* (*see* page 68) and a big but simple village church, with a side door once used by *cagots*, the luckless outcasts descended from lepers. Inside it is a true Basque church, with three tiers of galleries, and behind the altar a huge gilded retable. In the cemetery are interesting old graves, some with the Basque 'swastika'.

Outside the village on the lower slopes of La Rhune is Château d'Asotia, built in 1575 as the summer residence of the Bishops of Bayonne. The river Nivelle runs almost alongside the road to St Jean-de-Luz and it was here in 1813 that Wellington defeated Napoleon's General Soult, whose armies he had chased out of Spain. Soult stayed in one of those old Ascain mansions during the battle.

The Battle of the Nivelle was of great importance in the Napoleonic Wars. It gave the British a real foothold in France. The struggle for the Rhune mountain was vital and the French beat off tired Spanish troops under General Girons until a young British staff officer named Havelock, bringing a message to the Spaniards, led the exhausted troops up the slope, pinning the French to the very pinnacle, where they held out during the night only to be outflanked by the British in the morning.

The 43rd Regiment of the Light Division took Ascain, then the Division broke through the French lines, and the French were rolled up division by division from Ascain to the sea. They lost 50 guns, 5000 men. Most important they had to abandon a sort of Maginot line of entrenchments which they had spent months making. And a month later the British crossed the Nive at Cambo.

During the battle the British used an invention by a Major Shrapnel of explosive shells. Back in 1640 the French fighting the Spaniards on La Rhune ran out of ammunition, so fixed their knives to the barrels of their muskets, charged and routed the enemy. So was invented the bayonet. And the ridge on La Rhune where they did it is still called La Bayonette.

I wonder still how the Spaniards fought their way up La Rhune, which is 900 metres high. When I was young and fit I walked up it on the footpath starting about 100 metres from the church and I must have taken nearly three hours. Better to take the funicular from Col de St Ignace along D4, but it runs only weekends except in July, August, September and Easter. There are views of the sea to Saint Sebastian in Spain, the Landes forests and the Pyrenees from up there – one of the best views in the Pyrenees. Inevitably there is now a TV transmitter up there, too.

Pierre Loti stayed in Ascain to write his great novel about the Basque country *Ramuntcho*, his best work beside *Pêcheur d'Islande*. He stayed at Hôtel La Rhune, which is still there, next to the church and fronton.

TOURIST INFORMATION Mairie (59.54.00.84)
FESTIVAL 15–17 August – Fête with Basque dancing
and Course à la Rhune mountain run

HOTELS

La Rhune (59.54.00.04). See text. Has annexe (Oberena) in quiet gardens with pool. Fair prices. ROOMS D–E. MEALS B–D. Shut 15 January–15 March; Monday in winter.

Parc (59.54.00.10). The former Trinquet, named after the indoor court for playing a form of pelota. ROOMS D–E. MEALS B–F. Shut 1–20 December; January.

ASSON
[PYRÉNÉES-ATLANTIQUES]

A zoo 25km SE of Pau on D37 in exotic gardens with lovely birds, chimps, gibbons, and lemurs from Madagascar. Open daily. (Tel. 59.71.03.34.)

AUCH
[*See* Major Towns, page 61]

AUDENGE
[GIRONDE]

Little family resort on Bassin d'Arcachon, where oysters are cultivated.

AUDIGNON
[LANDES]

Once a halt on the Compestela pilgrim route, this hamlet 5km SW of St Sever has an interesting church with a medieval tower which became the church bell tower in the fourteenth century. Primitive statues of St Peter and St Paul are surmounted with coquilles St Jacques, the pilgrim symbol.

BAGNÈRES-DE-BIGORRE
[Hautes-Pyrénées]

A handsome spa 682 metres up in an amphitheatre of hills to the east of Lourdes, it has become much busier since electrical and other light industries came to it, while keeping its leisurely mountain-resort atmosphere. The river Adour flows past on its way down from the mountains which you can see to the south. Bagnères was a favourite with the British in the mid-nineteenth century. Viscount Alanbrooke (1883–1963), Churchill's wartime Chief of Staff and strategic adviser, was born there. Its fourteenth- to fifteenth-century church has five tiers of arches on its façade. Like most spas, it has a casino. Some houses are faced in marble.

Southward along the west bank of the river you come after 4km to the Château de Médous and the Grottes de Médous, caverns with stalactites and weird rock formations discovered only in 1948. They are lit up and you can take a punt on the underground river (June to September).

To the west of the spa a one-hour walk on woodland paths takes you to the Bédat viewpoint. The town has been known for 150 years for its folklorique singers 'Chanteurs Montagnards' and holds a Mountain Singers' Festival in August. Good excursion centre.

Tourist Information 1 place Lafayette (62.95.01.62)
Market Saturday.
Festivals August – Flower Festival; Mountain Singers

HOTELS

La Résidence, Parc Thermal de Salut (62.95.03.97). Relais du Silence among trees and lawns. Pool. Rooms E. Meals C–E. Open 1 April–15 October.

BARBOTAN-LES-THERMES
[Gers]

A spa hidden way E of Mont-de-Marsan and set in a semi-tropical park with palms, lotus plants and banana trees, it treats ailments of the limbs and rheumatism (season: April to November). A twelfth-century church at the entrance to the park has a porch belltower which was once part of the town's fortifications. South is Lac de l'Uby, a small lake made by damming the river Uby. It has a leisure beach with boats, tennis and a campsite.

TOURIST INFORMATION place d'Armagnac
(62.69.52.13)

HOTELS

Bastide Gasconne (62.69.52.09). Expensive Relais et Château hotel in seventeenth-century manor house; pool. Excellent restaurant. ROOMS F–G. MEALS F–G. Open Easter–early November.
Cante Grit, ave des Thermes (62.69.52.12). Old mansion in greenery. Very good restaurant. Good value. ROOMS C–E. MEALS C. Open mid-April–31 October.

BARÈGES
[Hautes-Pyrénées]

The sickly Duke of Maine, son of Louis XIV and Mme de Montespan, stayed here three times between 1675 and 1681 with his governess Mme de Maintenon, and the place was made. So was Mme de Maintenon, whose care for Louis' children got her into Louis' bed in place of her old friend de Montespan. Barèges (38km SE of Lourdes) has remained a spa for treating wounded and victims of accidents. It gets a number of these from its ski-slopes, no doubt. A military hospital here since the eighteenth century has become a centre for parachutists learning about mountains and skiing. A cable-car runs to the ski-runs from Lienz plateau (1600 metres). The skiing forms a complex with the modern resort of La Mongie. A cable railway climbs up the mountain to a station from which there are interesting views over the Néouvielle massif and pic du Midi de Bigorre. A footpath leads up to le Pic d'Ayre at 2422 metres. You need the right footwear and at least two hours to spare. High up in the massif de Néouvielle is Refuge Packe, named after the Leicestershire scientist and mountaineer who did much to make Pyrenean climbing popular (*see* page 105).

TOURIST INFORMATION Mairie (62.92.68.64)

HOTEL

Europe (62.92.68.04). Logis. ROOMS D–E. MEALS A–E. Shut 14 April–1 June; 24 September–24 December.

BARRAN
[GERS]

W of Auch, a charming thirteenth-century bastide (*see* page 9). The main gate in the old fortified walls passes through a fine square tower into an arcaded main square with a delightful wooden market hall. The interesting golden stone church has an octagonal fortified tower, and there is a moat with fish in it. Nearby are several windmills and the Château of Marères (fourteenth to seventeenth century).

BARSAC
[GIRONDE]

Capital of Barsac sweet wine area with Sauternes Appellation (*see* Wine, page 49); beside the Garonne, it has a curious sixteenth-century church with three naves.

HOTEL

Hostellerie du Château de Rolland, on N113 (56.27.15.75). Quiet, attractive hotel among the vines. Good, pricey meals. ROOMS F–G. MEALS E–F. Shut Wednesday lunch; 1–15 March.

BASSOUES
[Gers]

One of the most delightful little architectural gems in the SW. A little bastide of 1360 (*see* page 9), 35km W of Auch on D943, it has only 500 inhabitants, and one street. A wooden covered market straddles one end of the main street like a bridge. The old village well is beside it. Old timbered houses supported on wood piles form an arcaded street, which leads to the donjon (tower) of the ruined fourteenth-century castle of the Archbishop of Auch. The square keep still stands 37 metres high and has three floors. You can climb the stairs and see the original vaulted arches of the rooms. The last steps are planks leading to the top platform from which you can see a vast panorama over the Pyrenees, just as the sentinels did in medieval days. In the churchyard is a basilica rebuilt in the nineteenth century – the burial place of St Fris, who helped his uncle Charles Martel to drive the Moors out of France but was killed in a final skirmish.

HOTEL

Hostellerie du Donjon (62.70.90.04). Nice village inn. ROOMS B–C. MEALS A–F. Shut 15 January–15 February. Restaurant shut Saturday.

BAYONNE
[*See* Major Towns, page 64]

BAZAS
[GIRONDE]

A charming old Roman town on D11, 15km from Langon, standing high above the Beuve valley, Bazas was important until the fourteenth century. It was ruled by its bishops, so the former cathedral is still the focus of the town. The basilica of St Jean-Baptiste was started in 1233 but rebuilt between 1576 and 1635 after damage in the Religious Wars by the Protestants who were bribed not to destroy it completely. It ceased to be a cathedral at the Revolution. It is spacious and rather reminiscent of Auch, but dark because of its red-and-blue stained-glass windows. It keeps some superb Romanesque portals with rich sculptures and bas-relief carvings of the Expulsion from Eden, Cain and Abel, life of St Peter, and the Last Judgement. There were originally 286 statues. The church is lit at night. Across the attractive square from the church is rue Fondespan with late medieval houses. It leads to the town gates left from the ring of ramparts which surrounded the town until the Revolution.

The fine old 'Alchemist's' house in the square is now the Tourist Office. From the terrace garden by the church are lovely views of the Beauve valley.

Bazas now has some light industry. It still has an important cattle market. Bazadais beef is claimed by gourmets to be the *only* beef for *entrecôte bordelaise*. The steers are fattened on hay, rye, barley until five years old and on Jeudi Gras (Thursday before Shrove Tuesday) there is a parade through the streets. The cattle must have a *'cul panoramique'*, which means horizon-to-horizon hindquarters!

TOURIST INFORMATION 1 place Cathédral
(56.25.25.84)
MARKET Saturday

HOTELS

Relais de Fompeyre, route de Mont-de-Marsan (56.25.04.60). Swimming-pool. ROOMS E. MEALS A–E.
Relais Bazadais, 2km W on D932 (56.25.25.59). ROOMS C–E. MEALS C–F.

BEAUMARCHÉ
[GERS]

Where D946 meets D3 S of Plaisance, a little bastide built in 1240 by King Philippe le Bel. It has a fourteenth-century Gothic church with massive, unfinished clock tower, a stud with mostly Anglo-Arab horses, windmills, and fine views of the Pyrenees. Candlelit concerts are held in mid-summer.

BELHADE
[LANDES]

Hamlet on the little river Petite Leyre in one of the eleven communes in the Parc Naturel Regional des Landes, set up in 1970 and covering an area of 202,000 hectares shared between Landes and Gironde. The little tributaries of the Leyre, which flows into the Bassin d'Arcachon, begin NW of Mont-de-Marsan, and are bordered by splendid trees – mostly oak, chestnut and alders.

RESTAURANT

Chêne Pascal (58.07.72.53). MEALS A–D.

BELIN-BÉLIET
[GIRONDE]

A village on the N10 just before A63 finishes, it is becoming more important as an administration centre of the Landes Regional Park. Eleanor of Aquitaine was born here in 1123.

HOTEL
Aliénor d'Aquitaine (56.88.01.23). ROOMS C–D. MEALS B (Dinner for residents). Open 1 March–1 December.

BELLOCQ
[PYRÉNÉES-ATLANTIQUES]

15km NW of Orthez. The oldest bastide in Béarn, fortified in the thirteenth century. On the Gave de Pau river. The ruined fourteenth-century château by the river was built in a series of round towers to try to avoid projectiles. It belonged to the Dukes of Béarn.

BÉRAUT
[GERS]

Just SE of Condom, bastide built for King Edward I of England in 1286. He built many of the first bastides. Béraut is in an area of ruined châteaux. You can still see Château de Lasserre (sixteenth century).

BÉTHARRAM, GROTTES DE
[PYRÉNÉES-ATLANTIQUES]

Spectacular caves and underground passageways W of Pau beside Gave de Pau and D937. They were discovered by shep-

herds in 1819. An underground river has cut out of the rock a series of descending galleries and eroded shapes. The inevitable stalagmite pillars. Very popular with visitors. The 3km tour includes a short boat trip. A small train takes you to a cable-car to save you from climbing back to the top (open Easter to mid-October).

BEYCHEVELLE, CHÂTEAU DE
[GIRONDE]

The great wine château (*see* Wine, page 41) is a charming white manor house rebuilt in 1757 and bought by the Achille Fould family. The son Armand, Oxford educated, was Minister of Agriculture before taking over the château. The old château had been owned in the seventeenth century by the Duc d'Éper-non (*see* Cadillac, page 141). He was Grand Admiral of France, and ships passing dipped their sails in salute – *baisse-voile*. This became corrupted to the name Beychevelle. (Open Monday to Friday, early June to end September.)

BIARRITZ
[Pyrénées-Atlantiques]

Biarritz may have lost some of its glamour as one of the great fashionable resorts of Europe but it still has charm and a certain elegance even when crowded in mid summer. In the middle of the nineteenth century it was a little fishing port, much less important than St Jean-de-Luz, and its great beaches were known only to local people from Bayonne. But in 1838 a young girl from Spain called Eugénie came there on holiday with her mother, the Countess of Montijo. In 1853 that girl married the Emperor Napoleon III of France. She missed her native Spain so much that she wanted to be as near to it as possible. She chose Biarritz for holidays, and surprisingly Napoleon liked it too. He built a holiday home, Villa Eugénie. Of course, little Biarritz became fashionable. The Royals, the rich, the famous and the hangers-on went there.

Then Napoleon III lost a war to the Prussians in 1870 and fled to Chislehurst in Kent, where his house still stands as clubhouse for a golf course. But Biarritz stayed in fashion. Queen Victoria went there in 1889 and that brought the British. Her son Edward VII loved it. He stayed in the Hôtel du Palais, which was the former Villa Eugénie. It is still one of the Grands Hôtels of France. In 1908 Asquith was appointed Prime Minister there. Edward VII was not the sort of monarch to hurry back to England from his holiday just to let a new Liberal Prime Minister kiss his hand. The Grand Dukes of Russia and the Belgian royal family went there, too.

La Belle Époque finished in 1914, but between the World Wars Biarritz remained fashionable. After the end of the season in Deauville, fashionable Paris moved to Biarritz. Theatre stars and opera singers were seen there. So was the Prince of Wales, especially after he abdicated and became Duke of Windsor.

After the Second World War Biarritz had a fashion revival –

American film stars and directors, Paris fashion moguls, the Windsors again, British Dukes and Duchesses, international millionaires were all seen at the Palais Hotel, the old Miramar and the casinos. Ex-King Farouk of Egypt had a villa there. I once opened my wardrobe at the Miramar to find it crammed with fur coats – mink and the lot – left behind by an English girl who shortly after married a Marquis.

The rich still stay at the Palais, in their own holiday apartments, or at the new, modern Miramar, where they take seawater 'cures', fitness and beauty treatments, and have a choice of diets or gourmet meals. Many Spaniards come for the gambling. It still has two casinos, four golf courses, several heated indoor swimming-pools, gourmet restaurants and sophisticated nightlife. But it also has hotels, holiday flats, simpler restaurants and bars for the families who sunbathe and play on those three magnificent beaches. And it has become one of Europe's top surfing centres, with international championships held there. Grande Plage remains most fashionable, and has some surf. Plage des Basques is the surfers' beach, and above it on the promenade are superb mountain views. The small Plage du Port Vieux is sheltered by the harbour.

There are wonderful views of sea and mountains from the terrace of the Musée de la Mer, which has an unusually good aquarium and an aviary. A small footbridge connects this with Rocher de la Vierge, amid turbulent breakers and with more glorious views of rocks broken by sandy coves.

The humpy path and steps back from the Rocher follows the cliffside to the delightful old Port des Pêcheurs (fishermen's port) with a little harbour, red-roofed buildings, tables outside the cafés and a backdrop of steep cliffs covered in hydrangeas, magnificent in July when they are in blue and pink blossom. What a pity that so many cars line the harbour wall on the land side.

Biarritz has a full programme of fêtes, galas, firework displays and sports championships including tennis, showjumping, surfing, sailing, golf. It is a resort which you grow to like more and more. It keeps calling you back. *See also* Bidart (page 133), Guéthary (page 167), Anglet (page 110) and Bayonne (Major Towns, page 64).

TOURIST INFORMATION place d'Ixelles (near bus
station) (59.24.20.24)
MARKET Daily
FESTIVALS Full programme. Main fêtes: 15–16 August
– Nuit Féerique (fireworks gala), Fête de la Mer;
November – Fête de Biarritz

HOTELS

Hundreds of hotels and pensions of all types.

Palais, ave de l'Impératrice (59.24.09.40). Truly grand, elegant
and tastefully luxurious. Classical and Basque cuisine. All splendid and very expensive. Three restaurants. Poolside lunch service in summer. Open 1 March–30 November.

Miramar, ave l'Impératrice (59.41.30.00). Another elegant,
luxurious and very expensive hotel. Seawater treatment (*see*
text).

Windsor, Grande Plage (59.24.08.52). Good value, middle-
priced. ROOMS E–G. MEALS B–D.

Fronton et Résidence, 35 ave Mar.-Joffre (59.23.09.36). Friendly,
modest, comfortable, good value. ROOMS E. MEALS A–C. Shut
17–31 March; 21 October–25 November.

Auberge du Relais, 44 ave Marne (59.24.85.90). Good-value restaurant with rooms. ROOMS B–E. MEALS B–F. Shut February.

RESTAURANTS

Café de Paris, 5 place Bellevue (59.24.19.53). Great classical cooking. Very expensive and very good. MEALS G. Shut Monday low
season; 1 December–30 March.

Alambic, 3 place Bellevue (59.24.53.41). Next door to Café de
Paris, same direction. Good simple dishes. Excellent value.
MEALS B–E. Shut 31 December–30 March.

Chez Albert, Vieux Port des Pêcheurs (59.24.43.84). Superb fresh
fish. Highly animated. MEALS E–F. Shut Wednesday low season;
15 December–6 March.

BIDACHE
[Pyrénées-Atlantiques]

Village overlooking the valley of the Bidouze between Béarn
and Navarre which was, from the fourteenth century, an
independent fiefdom of the powerful Gramont family who were
its sovereign princes until the Revolution. One became a
Marshal of France. In 1643 he received Mazarin at his château
and later went to Spain to demand the hand of the Infanta
Marie-Thérèse for Louis XIV. Another member of the family,
Comte Philibert de Gramont (1621–1707), a soldier, was banished from the court of Louis XIV for scandalous affairs and
found more congenial surroundings in the more licentious court
of Charles II in England. Forced to marry Elizabeth Hamilton,
one of his mistresses, he returned with her to France and at age
eighty wrote his amusing and scandalous memoirs of the amorous intrigues in Charles' court.

There is enough left of their ruined château at Bidache to be
interesting (open early March to end October, except Tuesday.
son et lumière 13 to 31 July). Bidache has some fine old Navarrais
houses in its single street.

Château de Guiche (7km NW) rebuilt in eighteenth century,
also belonged to the Duke of Gramont (open same days as
Château de Bidache). From Miremont Ridge (6km W) are fine
views over the Pyrenees and Adour valley.

BIDARRAY
[Pyrénées-Atlantiques]

Village in the Nive valley on the D918 between St Jean-Pied-de-
Port and Cambo-les-Bains, has a humped bridge (the French call
them *en dos d'âne* – ass's back) which leads to a medieval church
which started life in 1132 as part of a priory on the pilgrims'
Compostela road. Bidarray is a little resort with several small
hotels.

HOTEL

Pont d'Enfer (59.37.70.88). Very good regional dishes. ROOMS B–E. MEALS C–E. Open Easter–1 November.

BIDART
[PYRÉNÉES-ATLANTIQUES]

A delightful little old fishing village just S of Biarritz, with its houses perched on cliffs, this has long been a resort for people avoiding Biarritz crowds. Its beaches are nearly a mile down from the hotels, so are often uncrowded and very pleasant. Its small square is typically Basque, especially the Mairie, with overhanging eaves, steep roof and carved balconies, the fronton where pelota tournaments are held, and the whitewashed church. Over the church nave hangs a model of a sailing barque and outside in the churchyard are many Basque wheel-shaped tombstones – some commemorate Basque Republican soldiers who were wounded fighting Franco's Fascists in the Spanish Civil War, and who died in the hospital set up for them by their French Basque cousins.

TOURIST INFORMATION 1 Grande Plage (high season – 59.54.93.85)

HOTEL

Bidartea, on N10 (59.54.94.68). Great Basque chalet; regional furnishings; balconies; pool. Good cuisine. ROOMS E–F. MEALS A–F. Shut mid-January–mid-February. Restaurant shut Sunday evening, Monday in winter.

RESTAURANTS

Les Frères Ibarboure, 4km S by N10, D655 (59.54.81.64): moved from Guéthary to huge, comfortable manor in a park in the forest. Outstanding cuisine using regional, classical and original dishes. Family own Bribentania Hotel, Guéthary (*see* page 167). MEALS E–G. Shut 15 November–1 December; part February; Wednesday.

Elissaldia, place Église (59.54.90.03). Good value. MEALS B–C.

BIELLE
[Pyrénées-Atlantiques]

Old Béarn village by the Gave d'Ossau river on D934 SE of Oloron-Ste-Marie. A tributary of the river flows through it. Once the capital of an independent valley, it has kept a certain importance though it has only 450 inhabitants. Some sixteenth-century houses survive between the church and the main road. The château was built in the eighteenth century by the Marquis de Laborde, banker to Louis XV.

BIRAN
[Gers]

Spectacular hilltop fortified village on D374, off N124 18km NW of Auch. Town gate, belfry, and ramparts, remains of a fortress and three Romanesque churches are still there.

BIRIATOU
[Pyrénées-Atlantiques]

Charming photogenic village 5km SE of Hendaye with a little square with a fronton, auberge and church, views of wooded mountain slopes, and the river Bidassoa which marks the Spanish frontier. You can climb up to Choldocogagna at 479 metres, part of the range of hills which the French Napoleonic General Soult tried vainly to fortify against Wellington in 1813 (*see* Hendaye, page 170).

HOTEL
Bakéa (59.20.76.36). Michelin-starred restaurant with fifteen bedrooms in big Basque chalet. Splendid traditional cooking. Shady terrace overlooking the valley. ROOMS B–F. MEALS D–F. Open 1 May–1 October.

BISCARROSSE
and
BISCARROSSE PLAGE
[LANDES]

Biscarrosse, an old town on the shore of a lake – Étang de Biscarrosse et Parentis – is growing now. For a long time it has been a centre for flying boats (hydro aviation) and has a flying-boat museum (open afternoons in summer, weekends rest of the year). Just as this industry seemed to have died, an aerospace testing station has opened between the lagoon and the sea. It is called CEL (Centre d'Essais des Landes). The town has two sixteenth-century manor houses, a fortified fourteenth-century church and an elm tree said to be 600 years old. Round the lake to the SW is the little naval station of Hourtiquets from which you can take boat trips on the lake. The south of the lake and its south-east shores are a forest of oil derricks centred on Parentis-en-Born (*see* page 204). Just north of Biscarrosse is another lake, Étang de Cazaux et Sanguinet. The two roads joining Biscarrosse with its seaside resort Plage are very attractive, the northern one skirting Étang de Cazaux. The Plage has a dozen hotels, campsite and casino, and superb beach. Alas, much of the coast and land southward to Mimizan Plage is used by the French Forces and closed to the public.

TOURIST INFORMATION 19 terrace ave Plage
(58.78.20.96)
FESTIVALS Many fairs and fêtes

HOTELS

Auberge Régina, 2 ave Libération (58.78.23.34). At beach. Good value. ROOMS B–E. MEALS A–E. Open 25 March–30 September.

La Caravelle, Baie d'Ispes (58.78.02.67). Two-star Logis. ROOMS D–E. MEALS A–F. Restaurant shut Monday low season; 1 November–mid-February.

BLAYE
[Gironde]

Perched high above the Gironde where it opens out to an estuary 10km wide, Blaye is capital of a wine area once more important than the Médoc across the water (*see* Wine, page 40). It was always an important defensive position against anyone trying to attack Bordeaux from the sea, especially pirates. It changed hands several times between French and English in the Hundred Years War. Ruins of the twelfth-century château Rudel remain within the later Vauban castle. Jaufré Rudel was a troubadour poet known for his songs of 'love from afar' (*amor londhana*). The story was that he fell in love with the Norman Countess of Tripoli simply by hearing stories of her beauty. He sent her love songs without having seen her. Then at last he made his way to Tripoli but was taken ill on the journey and died in her arms. But she was not his only love, for one poem tells of how he was caught in bed with a girl and vowed in future to

Farmhouse at Blaye

pursue a higher love. In 1689 Vauban, Louis XIV's famous military engineer, cleared the town away to build a massive wall and moated citadel which is still there, with streets, houses and shops, some crumbling, some restored and containing craft shops. There is a quiet vineyard between the inner and outer walls, a small museum, a campsite, a restaurant and hotel, and a seventeenth-century convent, recently restored. At the western side, where there is a cliff running sheer from the river, is the Tour de l'Aiguillette, from which there are fine views of the Gironde and beyond. You can see from here the other two defence forts – Fort Pâté on an isle in mid-stream and star-shaped Fort Médoc on the south bank, recently restored.

Roland, hero of the eleventh-century Chanson de Roland, was said to have been buried in the medieval castle. Nephew of Charlemagne and the ideal of a Christian knight, he is said to have fallen at the massacre of Charlemagne's forces in the pass at Roncesvalles. In the song, the knights were attacked by 300,000 Moors. In fact they were slaughtered by a few hundred Basques who trapped them and hurled rocks down on them.

The volatile, lively and fun-loving Duchess of Berry (1798–1870) was imprisoned in the Vauban castle. Her husband the Duke was in line for the French throne but was assassinated by a Bonapartist. She was already pregnant and gave birth to a son, Comte de Chambord. Her father-in-law, King Charles X, was so ineffectual that in 1830 the people of Paris forced him to abdicate and the royal party fled to Holyrood House in Edinburgh. Louis Philippe, the 'citizen king', took the crown instead of the young Comte de Chambord, and the furious Duchess returned secretly to France to stir up revolution but got very little support. While troops hunted for her in Nantes, she, her handsome young lawyer and two supporters, a man and a woman, hid behind a fireplace. In the night the guards got cold and lit a fire. The dresses of the hidden ladies caught alight. To use the Duchess's own words, the gentlemen put out the flaming skirts by 'dispensing with ceremony'. But it happened again next morning and the gentlemen failed in their duty, so the four frizzling fugitives had to come out, to be arrested.

In Blaye prison, the Duchess gave birth to a daughter. She had, she claimed, married secretly the Neapolitan marquis

Lucchesi-Palli, but in the drawing-rooms and cafés of Paris nobody believed that story. She was discredited and released as being of no further danger. Her son the Comte showed little interest in being king and spent his life quietly in 'blameless inertia'.

A hero of Blaye is the cook of the Maréchal de Plessis-Praslin. In 1649 he served his master's guests sweetmeats which are still called *praslines* and are exported far and wide from Blaye.

In the hills behind Blaye are the vineyards producing the underestimated Blaye wines. For information the Maison des Vins is at 11 cours Vauban (57.42.12.09).

Ferries run to Lamarque in Médoc. For information tel. 57.42.04.49.

TOURIST INFORMATION Cours Vauban (June–October
– 57.42.12.09)
MARKET Wednesday, Saturday

HOTELS

Citadelle, in the citadelle (57.42.17.10). Modern; good views. ROOMS D–E. MEALS C–G.
Château La Grange de Luppé, 1½km N on D255 (57.42.80.20). No restaurant. Quiet nineteenth-century château in park. ROOMS D–E.

RESTAURANT

Caneton d'Argent, 31 rue St Romain (57.42.81.00). Little restaurant, classic cooking, fair prices. MEALS C–E. Shut Sunday evening. Monday except July, August; 15 December–15 January.

BOMBANNES
[GIRONDE]

Sport and leisure centre among pines on Lac d'Hourtin-Carcans, SW of Lesparre-Médoc. Good watersports. Picnic spots (open April to October). In a wooden house is a museum of arts and traditions of the people of Landes (visits afternoons mid-June to mid-September).

BORDEAUX
[*See* Major Towns, page 72]

BOUILH, CHÂTEAU DE
[*See* Cubzac-les-Ponts, page 153]

BOURG
[GIRONDE]

The old fortified town of Bourg stands on a limestone cliff high above the Dordogne river, reached by steps or the winding rue Cahoreau from the port on the Dordogne river. Just downstream the Dordogne joins the river Garonne to form the wide Gironde. Long ago Bourg was actually beside the Gironde, but the deposits brought down by the Dordogne have gradually extended the river. The remains of the fortifications in the upper town are from the thirteenth century. The Château de la Citadelle, old summer palace of the Archbishops of Bordeaux, was rebuilt in the eighteenth century, burned by the Germans in 1944 but restored again. From its terrace the views over the Gironde countryside and rivers must have been beautiful once. Now they are less spectacular. You see mainly oil refineries. The citadel park is very pleasant. In the rocks under Bourg is a maze of long gallery caves, most of which are used as wine cellars. Bourg red wine, once more highly rated than Médoc, has had a major resurgence in quality and is now very good value (*see* Wine, page 56). The vineyards are mostly to the north.

6km east are the prehistoric caves of Pair-non-Pair, which some experts believe to be 5000 years older than Lascaux in Périgord. There are line-drawings of horses, mammoths, bison and ibex, and evidence of habitation by Aurignac man (Stone Age period: 27,000–30,000 BC).

BRASSEMPOUY
[LANDES]

A Roman camp, later an unusually shaped bastide fortified by the English in the thirteenth century. But it is known for its prehistoric caves. Here in 1893 was found the celebrated prehistoric carving in ivory of a woman's head, dating from 23,000 BC now displayed in the National Antiquities Museum of St Germain-en-Laye in Paris. The small museum in the village is open July to August, afternoons only. The village street is almost completely taken over by a Roman-Gothic church with a fine fifteenth-century spire.

Château de la Brède

BRÈDE, CHÂTEAU DE LA
[GIRONDE]

Here in the Graves wine country, Charles Montesquieu, philosopher and jurist, was born in 1689 (*see* History, page 24). His descendants still live there. Both the château and the park, which he had laid out in the English style, remain much as they were in his day. His library of 7000 books in grille-fronted bookcases lining a vaulted room is intact. His travelling trunks are still in the hall.

Sometimes written as one word, Labrède, the castle was built in the thirteenth to fifteenth centuries in rather austere Gothic style, relieved by dunce-cap towers and its reflection in the wide moat.

Montesquieu also produced wine on his estate and exported it to England. He boasted once that the fame of his books had helped his wine sales! And, talking of his wine-cellars, he said: 'I like being at La Brède because here my money is under my feet.' His descendants still produce a good white Graves. (Visits daily except Tuesday in July, August, September; weekends rest of year.)

CADILLAC
[GIRONDE]

Originally an English bastide, built in the thirteenth century, this attractive little wine town on the right bank of the Garonne river still has part of its ramparts but is dominated by the Château of the Dukes of Épernon. The château was built between 1598 and 1620 by the larger-than-life friend of the Protestant leader Henri of Navarre, Jean Louis Nogaret de Lavalette (1554–1642). When Henri became Catholic to claim the throne as Henri IV, the Duke refused to follow and to avoid trouble from him Henri gave him the right to build the château and a series of appointments; he became Governor of the Guyenne, Colonel-General of the infantry and Admiral of France (*see* Château de Beychevelle, page 128).

Partly destroyed during the Revolution, the château's stone was taken to build local mansions. For over a hundred years it was a women's prison and cells remain. More recently it has been restored. It still has some lovely decorations that were saved by being covered, including lovely painted ceilings, eight huge carved ornamental marble fireplaces and Aubusson tapestries. It is now the headquarters of the Connétable de Guyenne and the local white wines Premières Côtes de Bordeaux and Cadillac can be tasted in the west wing (château shut on Monday).

The Chapelle des ducs d'Épernon had a magnificent mausoleum of the Duke designed in 1597 by the sculptor Pierre Biard and destroyed in the Revolution. Some fragments are in the château, one great statue is in the Louvre in Paris.

Château de Benauge, 6km NE by D11, was from the twelfth century the residence of the Comtes de Benauge, but was taken away by Henri III when the Count rebelled and later belonged to the Épernons. They rebuilt it in the seventeenth century. It is ruined but still has a long curtain wall and two massive towers.

FESTIVALS June – Chapter of the Connétable de Guyenne; September–October – Fête of the New Wine

CAMBO-LES-BAINS
[PYRÉNÉES-ATLANTIQUES]

A well-tended spa on a little promontory above the Nive river, 20km SE of Bayonne, with a gentle climate all the year. The older Basque village is down by the river. There are fine views from the upper town to the Basque coast and Pyrenees foothills, and plenty of hotels and good restaurants. It is a good touring centre for the Basque country. Along the river is a delightful park and all round are lovely trees, including fruit trees, and flowering shrubs.

The poet and playwright Edmond Rostand, who wrote *Cyrano de Bergerac*, visited Cambo in 1900 and fell in love with it. In 1910 he built a big villa in the Basque style called Arnaga on a spur with fine views just to the NW on the Bayonne road. Here he lived until his death in 1918. He wrote *Chantecler*, the play in verse, here and the sketches for the original performance can be seen among other souvenirs in the house (open daily early May to end of September, afternoons in April and October). Habitués of the spa included the actress Sarah Bernhardt, Napoleon III and his Empress Eugénie.

TOURIST INFORMATION 1 parc St-Joseph (59.29.70.25)

HOTELS

Relais de la Poste, place la Mairie (59.29.73.03). Charming little hotel with garden and terrace. ROOMS B–E. MEALS D–F. Shut Sunday evening, Monday except July–August; 3–31 January.
Bellevue, rue Terrasses (59.29.73.22). Nice views; good value. ROOMS B–E. MEALS A–F. Shut Monday off season; 1 December–31 January.
Chez Tante Ursule, Bas Cambo (59.29.78.23). Simple, cheap, welcoming; excellent-value meals. Basque specialities, including game, local trout, salmon. ROOMS B–C. MEALS A–C. Shut Tuesday.

CAMPAN
[HAUTES-PYRÉNÉES]

South from Tarbes and Bagnères-de-Bigorre, this little town beside the Adour in the green Campana valley has a charming group of buildings with a sixteenth-century covered market, a typical sixteenth-century mountain church, a fountain and sixteenth-century houses.

The town's most famous man was Sergeant Gaye Mariole, Napoleon's *premier sapeur de France*, such a giant that at Tilsit he is said to have presented arms to his Emperor not with a musket but with the 1.60 metre long barrel of an 84mm cannon.

HOTEL

Beauséjour (62.91.75.30). Good-value simple Logis. ROOMS B. MEALS A–C. Shut 15 November–15 December.

CAPBRETON
[LANDES]

It looks to be part of Hossegor, for they share the same harbour which in old times was the port of Capbreton, but they prefer to live separate lives. Both are very pleasant little resorts, built round a series of inland lagoons. Until 1310 the river Adour flowed into the sea here and Capbreton was an important port. A great storm blocked the channel with sand and diverted the Adour 20km north at Port D'Albret. The sailors of Capbreton were already exploring the world, mainly in search of whales, and they had given the name of their home port, Cap Breton, to the island at the mouth of the St Lawrence river in Canada long before Columbus 'discovered' America. Sailors used the church tower, which carried a light, as a navigation mark from the fifteenth century, and venerated the Pietà in the church porch. The church was largely rebuilt in the nineteenth century after damage in the Revolution. Many good boat trips in season.

The resort has a good beach, a big pleasure-boat marina where the Bourret and Boudigau rivers meet, and many apartments and villas to let.

TOURIST INFORMATION 1 ave Georges-Pompidou
(58.72.12.11)
MARKET Wednesday
FESTIVALS Mid-June – Fête de la Mer; mid-June–
September – Fête d'Eté; 24 December – Feux de la
Tourelle

HOTELS

Atlantic, ave Lattre de Tassigny (58.72.11.14). ROOMS C–E. MEALS D–E (evening only). Hotel open 31 May–30 September; restaurant open 2 June–15 September.
Miramar, front de Mer (58.72.12.82). Simple; beside beach. Balconies with sea views. ROOMS C–E. MEALS C–E (evening only). Open 24 May–24 September.

RESTAURANT

Le Regalty, quai Pêcherie (58.72.22.80). One of the best restaurants along the Landes coast. Excellent fish. MEALS F–G. Shut Monday; 15–30 November; 15–30 January.

CAP FERRET
[GIRONDE]

Bathing resort on point at entrance to Bassin d'Arcachon. Luxury villas and hotels among the pines and sand dunes. Good for sailing and oysters. Splendid views over coast and basin from top platform of the lighthouse which is 52 metres high with a light that carries for 50km. You must climb 258 steps.

A little railway runs across the cape from Bélisaire on the Bassin to the Atlantic beach.

TOURIST INFORMATION 1 place du Marché (56.60.63.26); (Note: 15 June–15 September – 12 ave Océan, 56.60.63.26)

HOTEL

Dunes, 119 ave Bordeaux (56.60.62.73). ROOMS C. Shut 25 September–25 April.

CAPVERN-LES-BAINS
[HAUTES-PYRÉNÉES]

Small spa with springs rich in magnesium and calcium sulphate. 20km NE of Bagnères-de-Bigorre. From its terrace are beautiful views to the Pyrenees and to the ruins of Mauvezin castle, 4½km S by D80. This fortress, built between the tenth and fourteenth centuries, was used by the English Black Prince and later by Gaston Phoebus, a poet who was a violent and bellicose Comte de Foix. The donjon, which still stands, is 36 metres high and has six rooms containing a folklorique museum (open daily May to September, Sunday rest of year). The mountain views from its platform are magnificent.

TOURIST INFORMATION, rue Thermes, Thermes (15
April–22 October – 62.39.00.46)

HOTEL

Le Laca, route Mauvezin (62.39.02.06). Modern, quiet, near-
thermal establishment. Hydrotherapy, solarium, sauna, gym-
nasium. Heated swimming-pool. Good food. ROOMS D–F.
MEALS C–E. Open mid-April–October.

CASSAIGNE, CHÂTEAU DE
[*see* Condom, page 151]

CASTILLON-LA-BATAILLE
[GIRONDE]

The defeat here in 1453 of General Sir John Talbot, Earl of
Shrewsbury, virtually ended English rule in Aquitaine (*see* History, page 18). A very old man with a string of successes in battle
and a reputation for courage, he had returned to Gascony to
save Bordeaux and the English territories when the French
army were rolling the English back. He was fed a false report
that the French were retreating, left his position to pursue them
and fell into a trap. He was killed. The spot is marked by a small
monument by the Dordogne river, 2km E from the town along a
minor road. It is now a busy little town on the Bordeaux-
Bergerac road. The battle is re-enacted with *son et lumière* in
August.

TOURIST INFORMATION Mairie (57.40.00.06)
FESTIVAL *See* text

HOTEL

Bonne Auberge, 12 rue 8-Mai 1945 (57.40.11.56). Good regional
cooking. ROOMS B. MEALS A–E. Shut Saturday lunch, Monday;
1–21 November.

CAUMONT, CHÂTEAU DE
[*See* Cazaux-Savès, page 148]

CAUTERETS
[HAUTES-PYRÉNÉES]

In the sixteenth century, the childless princess Jeanne d'Albret was brought to Cauterets near the Spanish frontier by her mother, Marguerite of Navarre, poetess, wit and writer of the somewhat bawdy tales *Heptameron*. The waters were believed to cure sterility. In due course the princess became pregnant, which changed French history, for the child became the great King Henri IV.

The curative power of the waters was known from the tenth century. The town has prospered on them, praised through history by Gaston Phoebus, Baudelaire, Victor Hugo, George Sand, Châteaubriand and Flaubert. More recently it has become popular, too, for skiing, climbing, camping and mountain walking.

It is still a delightful town, surrounded by superb scenery, with cable-cars, lifts, footpaths and mountain roads leading to peaks, lakes and waterfalls close to the borders of Spain.

The Gave de Cauterets river runs through the town to Lourdes, 30km N, although place Clemenceau is built over it. There is all the entertainment of a spa and winter-sports centre – casino, cinema, theatre, disco, nightclub and indoor swimming-pool.

A lovely excursion is southward on D920 to the waterfalls of Lutour, Cerisey and Pont d'Espagne along Val de Jéret and then on foot to the deep-blue Lac de Gaube in a bowl surrounded by mountains (1½ hrs walk return). Near Pont d'Espagne is a monument to the hotelier who virtually founded the ski resort, Alphonse Meillon. He built Hôtel d'Angleterre in 1879. The Cauterets museum of flora and fauna of the mountains is also the centre of the Western Pyrenees National Park.

TOURIST INFORMATION 1 place Mairie (62.92.50.27)

FESTIVAL July – motor race

HOTELS

Trois Pics, ave Leclerc (62.92.53.64). Very good for summer or winter. Includes fitness club, pool, squash. ROOMS D–E. MEALS B–D. Shut May; 1 September–mid-December.

Etche Ona, 20 rue Richelieu (62.92.51.43). Logis with good cooking. ROOMS C–E. MEALS A–E. Shut mid-April–early May; 25 October–20 December.

Pont d'Espagne, at Pont d'Espagne, 8km by D920 (62.92.54.10). Tranquil mountain hotel. Ten rooms. ROOMS C. MEALS A–D. Open 15 June–20 September. Restaurant 1 April–10 October; Christmas; part February; weekends January–March.

CAZAUX-SAVÈS
[GERS]

Château de Caumont, overlooking the Save valley 2km N of the village, SE of Gimont, is one of the great large-scale Gascon châteaux. It was built on the site of a twelfth-century fort in 1530 for a member of the Nogaret de Lavalette family whose grandson became Duc d'Épernon and lived here (*see also* Cadillac, page 141). Set in a park, it has three battlements around a fortified courtyard, four pepper-pot towers and six watchtowers in different sizes. Inside are some fine decorations, including tableaux, a picture of the battle of Lutzen (1813) by Van Loo and portraits, including one of François, Duc de la Rochefoucauld, a writer whose love affairs got him into terrible trouble at the court of Louis XIV, especially the one with a member of Louis' family, Mme de Longueville. His memoirs were so racey that he had to deny that he had written them. The old kitchens are interesting. (Visits to Château Caumont mid-July to end August, afternoons.)

CIBOURE
[Pyrénées-Atlantiques]

Ciboure faces St Jean-de-Luz across a harbour and virtually the same port. I heard an Englishman describe them as 'like Brighton and Hove', but they are hardly that – they are both working fishing ports, and their history is of fights and quarrels. In the sixteenth century Ciboure challenged St Jean's right to levy harbour dues on ships entering port. Their hostility led to cross-accusations at the notorious witchcraft trials of 1609 and a pitched battle took place on the little isle between the towns. To calm their fury, Franciscan monks built a monastery on the isle, with a church dedicated to Our Lady of Peace. The towns then fell out over who owned the island!

The isle is joined now to the banks of the Nivelle river, the monastery is now the customs house.

Like St Jean, Ciboure was the lair of pirates in the seventeenth and eighteenth centuries. They lived in the area called, quite inappropriately, Croix Rouge, uphill to the ruined tower and abbey of Bordagian. The people of this area had been accused of witchcraft in 1609. Two hundred women from the two towns were burned alive.

In 1813 when Wellington's army took the town, camp followers and gypsies swarmed in from Spain and took over this quarter. They intermarried with the 'Cagots', the outcast descendants of lepers left from the medieval pilgrimages to Santiago (see St Étienne-de-Baïgorry, page 218), and stayed until 1880, living apart under their own 'king'.

The church of St Vincent (sixteenth century) is a fine example of Basque architecture, with the usual three-tier gallery and huge gilded altar. It has some good stained glass and treasures from the Franciscan church. Nearby on quai Ravel, with a good view of the harbour ships, is a Dutch-style house, No. 12, where Maurice Ravel, composer of *Bolero*, was born. There are fine old Basque houses in rue Pocalette, parallel to the quai. A 3km walk along the quay, past a narrow bathing strip, is the fortress of Socoa, built by Henri IV in the seventeenth century and strengthened by Vauban. Here there is another little harbour with good views of St Jean-de-Luz from its break-water. It is used by yachts.

From Socoa a road (D912) climbs to the clifftop along the Basque corniche, following the cliff edge to the border town of Hendaye (*see* page 170) – a lovely run. The N10, an old main road which was the only way to Spain along this coast, crosses the bridge between St Jean and Ciboure. This used to be a hellspot for traffic and is still crowded in summer but much relieved by the A63 motorway. (*See also* St Jean-de-Luz, page 219, for Ciboure information, festivals and hotels.)

RESTAURANTS

Chez Dominique, 15 quai Maurice Ravel (59.47.29.16). Superb fish bistro serving only fish landed that morning. MEALS F–G. Shut 16–22 April; October; Monday, Sunday (except summer).
Arrantzaleak, ave Jean Poulou (59.47.10.75). Lovely fish from quayside grilled before your eyes. Good non-fish dishes, too. Summer terrace beside Nivelle river. 'Rugby teams assured a good welcome,' says the owner. MEALS D–F. Shut Monday evening, Tuesday except summer; mid-December–mid-January.

CONDOM
[GERS]

A true Gascon town which grows on you very fast and a true centre of Armagnac brandy. The river Baïse which runs through it was canalized here mostly to take Armagnac brandy to the Garonne and Bordeaux, and although the spirit goes by road these days, the quays look neat and ready for the boats to come back. A few pleasure boats use them.

Condom is a charming place to stay to taste the spirit of Gascony in both senses, and the right spot for a Museum of Armagnac which you will find in rue Ferry off place Voltaire (shut Monday, also Sunday in winter). Round the corner is the old Bishops' Palace, now the town hall, and the Cathedral of St Pierre, built in 1506–13. During the Wars of Religion the Pro-testant General Montgomery took the town but was bribed heavily not to destroy the cathedral. It has a heavy square tower and two enormous flying buttresses. Its cloisters are lovely. It is floodlit on weekends in summer. Next to it is the old Chapel of the Bishops.

The town is built on a hill above the river. There are famous Armagnac caves, including Janeau near the station on D930. The town's name can cause some embarrassment or hilarity in both English and French but the sheath was actually named after its French inventor Jean Condom.

The grapes for Armagnac were originally grown just around Condom and some still are. The many châteaux around here were centres of vineyards and brandy distilling. You can soon reach them by taking D931 SW from Condom and turning on to side roads. First is Château de Cassaigne, 6km from Condom, originally thirteenth century. It became the country residence of the Bishops of Condom. Its kitchens are particularly interesting, with sixteenth-century bread-ovens, pans and crockery. One room shows how the brandy is made and in the cellar the Armagnac is ageing in wood. From the terrace you can see the vineyards. Cassaigne produces one of the very best Armagnacs, called Monluc (visits daily).

Take D229 for 4km, turn right and there is Château du Busca-Maniban – two storeys with a huge courtyard, a monumental staircase and two ancient kitchens with equipment and utensils (visits early April to mid-November afternoons except Monday).

From Cassaigne take D142, then D42 left to Château Monluc, a medieval fortress called St Puy, fought over by the French and English, but renamed for Blaise de Monluc, a fanatical Catholic leader in the Wars of Religion who commanded in the south-west and committed appalling atrocities, mass murdering women and children in towns he took. He then wrote his unrepentant memoirs and is solemnly called in the green Michelin 'Maréchal of France and Man of Letters'. The château has interesting old Armagnac-making items and now *pousse-rapière* is made there – a liqueur made from fruit macerated for a long time in Armagnac. It is often drunk topped with sparkling dry white wine. (Visits daily except Sunday, open Sunday afternoons in July, August.)

Among vineyards 5km W of Condom is the superb little thirteenth-century village of Larressingle, like a miniature fortified city. Its gateway and some of its outer walls are still there. You enter by a bridge over the moat and although the fortress tower is ruined, you can climb three storeys. The fortified Romanesque church is dedicated to Sigismond, King of the Burgondes, martyred by a son of Clovis, King of the Franks, around AD 520.

TOURIST INFORMATION 1 place Bossuet (62.28.00.80)
MARKET Wednesday (good street market)
FESTIVAL Second Sunday in May – Fête de Bandos
(lively festival of music played in the street)

HOTELS
Continental, 20 ave Mar-Foch (62.28.00.58). Pleasant, comfortable hotel by the river, looking across to the town. Gascon dishes, grilling over wood. ROOMS B–F. MEALS A–E.
Logis des Cordeliers, rue des Cordeliers (62.28.03.68). Pleasant, tranquil hotel. Separate from Table des Cordeliers restaurant (*see* below). ROOMS D–E.

RESTAURANTS
Table des Cordeliers, 1 rue des Cordeliers (62.68.28.36). Superb regional dishes in a sixteenth-century chapel. Back at the top after some problems. Independent of hotel (*see* above). MEALS C–G. Shut January; Sunday evening, Monday except 1 June–30 September.

CONTIS-PLAGE
[LANDES]

Small resort S of Mimizan. Little streams link up to produce the Contis *courant*, a fast river running into the sea. Three seasonal hotels. Campsite.

HOTEL
Le Neptune (58.42.85.28). No restaurant. ROOMS B–D. Open 1 June–30 September.

CRÉON
[GIRONDE]

Thirteenth-century bastide with arcades on three sides of its square, capital of Entre-Deux-Mers and a pleasant, important market town; located among hills and valleys, it is called Petite Suisse (Little Switzerland). 3km E is an abbey church, La Sauve Majeur, built in the eleventh to thirteenth centuries, partly ruined but still with an impressive octagonal tower and capitals showing biblical scenes including the beheading of John the Baptist, fabulous beasts and sirens. The eleventh-century church of St Pierre nearby contains thirteenth-century wall paintings.

MARKET Wednesday

RESTAURANT

Prévot, 1 rue Dopter (56.23.08.08). MEALS C–F. Shut Tuesday evening, Wednesday; 30 August–6 September.

CUBZAC-LES-PONTS
[GIRONDE]

Before they built the A10 motorway into Bordeaux in 1974 and its new bridge over the river Dordogne, I used to get caught in a monumental traffic jam in a place called St André-de-Cubzac, waiting to cross a narrow bridge on the N10. The only other way was to go miles SE to cross at Libourne. Called Le Pont Route, it was a viaduct 1046 metres long, and was one of the historic bridges of France. It was built in 1882 by Eiffel of the Paris Tower fame, and looked as if it was. Not many vehicles use it now. A third bridge, Pont Fer, just upstream, 2325 metres long, carries the railway. The three bridges together make quite a sight.

Just N of St André on the tiny D115 road is Château de Bouilh (*see* Vineyards, page 57), historic home of Comte de Feuilhade-de-Chauvin. It was designed by the great Bordeaux architect Victor Louis in 1787 for the Marquis de la Tour du Pin after he had finished the Bordeaux theatre. Alas, the Revolution came and Bouilh was never finished. The Marquis was very rich and powerful. His son married the beautiful Henrietta-Lucy Dillon, whose Anglo-Irish ancestor had raised a regiment and come to France to serve the exiled James II of England. The Dillons had married into the highest French aristocracy. Lucy's trousseau cost a fortune; the gifts she received were worth a royal ransom. She became a friend of the Queen at court. She was at Versailles when the Revolutionaries marched on the palace and took the King and Queen prisoner. Louis XVI said to Lucy's husband, 'You are in complete charge. Save my poor Versailles for me.' Her father-in-law actually became Minister of War under the Revolution. Inevitably, under the Terror, he was arrested. Lucy and her husband got away to Holland, then she returned to protect her property and had another baby while she was being hunted. She fled from Bouilh to a house hidden in the Haut-Brion vineyards for the birth. She fooled the Revolutionary guards sent to hunt the house and went to face the fearsome Tallien, the man running the Terror in Bordeaux, in his office. Then she recalled her husband from Holland and actually persuaded Tallien to give them a passport under the name Citizen Latour and his wife. They escaped on a little ship of 150 tons lying in the river to America. She became a true pioneer-American farmer's wife, but she still stamped the butter which she sold with her family coat of arms because that helped to sell it!

They returned to Bouilh but her husband was in trouble again for hiding the Duchess of Berry there in 1835 when she was plotting to overthrow King Louis Philippe, so they had to sell it. (Visits with wine tastings 1 May–1 October, Thursday, Saturday, Sunday.)

DAX
[LANDES]

The Romans called it Aquae Tarbellicae, and its hot springs were already famous. Ever since then its waters and mud baths have brought relief to rheumatic sufferers. The little town on the Adour river has spread in recent years, but the old centre on the south bank with narrow streets and little squares is still the most interesting part. At the corner of place Borda is Fontaine Chaude, the Roman hot bath, a pool surrounded by white arcaded walls. The hot mineral spring has been pumping out water at 64°F for more than 2000 years. The pool has become something of a tourist attraction now, and several more modern thermal establishments, using the same water, now offer the 'cure'. Some are in hotels.

Dax was part of England's Aquitaine Empire after Eleanor married Henry Plantagenet in 1152, and remained English for 300 years. The Gothic cathedral they built was pulled down to make way for the seventeenth-century classical building you see now, but I wonder why the French bothered. The new one is dull.

Dax has pleasant parks and riverside walks but it is not elegant or beautiful like so many spas.

The remarkable Saint Vincent de Paul was born in a nearby hamlet in 1580. As a priest he was captured by corsairs and sold as a slave in Tunis. There he converted his master, a renegade Savoyard, back to Christianity and they escaped back to France. He formed an association for helping the sick from St Lazare priory in Paris, an orphanage, a nursing order and the Sisterhood of Charity. The house where he was born is by the church at Berceau St Vincent-de-Paul 7km NE. The house was reconstructed last century.

TOURIST INFORMATION place Thiers (58.74.82.33)
MARKETS Friday, Saturday
FESTIVAL Mid-August – Fête

HOTELS

Du Lac, over river at St Paul-les-Dax, Lac du Christus

(58.91.84.84). Big, with pleasing modern architecture. Pool, club disco. Good value. ROOMS C–E. MEALS C–E. Open all year.

Grand, rue Source (58.74.84.58). Has its own thermal establishment. Big. Rooms C–E. MEALS B–E.

Miradour, ave E. M. Lacroix (58.74.98.86). Modern with garden by river. Cheap. ROOMS C–D. MEALS C. Shut three weeks in March.

RESTAURANT

Bois de Boulogne, allée Bois de Boulogne (58.74.23.32). Delightful woodland setting. Excellent grills. MEALS A–D. Shut Monday; October.

EAUX-BONNES
[PYRÉNÉES-ATLANTIQUES]

Béarnais troops wounded in the Battle of Pavia in 1525 were brought home to be treated in the sulphurous waters of this little spa at 750 metres. It is in beautiful mountain surroundings on D918, 6km from Laruns and 40km S of Pau. It has a twelfth-century church and is a good centre for local walks and excursions. Some shepherds around here use a language of whistles which can be heard up to 200 metres away. A short way SE along D918 is the impressive twin waterfall of Le Cros Hêtre. 8km up the valley lies the ski resort of Gourette (1400 metres), oldest ski resort in the Pyrenees. Then the narrow road climbs round the Col d'Aubisque (1709 metres) on its way to Arrens and Argelès-Gazost (*see* page 116) before joining N21 to Lourdes.

TOURIST INFORMATION (Mid-May–end September – 59.05.34.02)

HOTELS

Poste (59.05.33.06). ROOMS C. MEALS A–D. Shut mid-April–mid-May; 1 October–20 December.

Pene Blanque (59.05.11.29), Gourette Inter-hotel. ROOMS D. MEALS A–E. Shut Easter–early July; 1 September–20 December.

EAUZE
[Gers]

Under the Romans, this little town (pronounced A-ouse) SW of
Condom was capital of Novempopulania, almost predecessor of
Gascony and was then Armagnac's main ecclesiastical centre
until sacked by the Moors. It calls itself Capital of Armagnac, but
that means Armagnac the drink, for it produces some of the
best. The main square is called place d'Armagnac and has some
fine sixteenth-century arcaded houses of brick and timber. The
fifteenth- to sixteenth-century church was made mainly from
the stones of the Roman town, which has disappeared. Marquis
de Caussade distillery, route de Cazauban, puts on a *son et
lumière* show in its Armagnac caves in July and August.

The great Armagnac Marquis de Montesquieu is made
along the same road (visits – mornings, tel. 72.09.82.13). Main
centre of the Armagnac aperitif Floc is Maison des Producteurs,
9 place Armagnac. Floc is made of a blend of Armagnac and
grape juice, as pineau is made from cognac. It is also said to go
well with melon, *foie gras*, strawberries and gateau. The July Fête
lasts a week and includes balls, bands, operetta, ballet, corrida,
fishing and flying contests.

TOURIST INFORMATION 1 place Mairie (62.09.85.62)

MARKET Thursday

FESTIVALS Mid-May – Secondhand Fair; early June –
Armagnac brandy Fair; July – fête (*see* text)

HOTEL

Armagnac, 1 boul. St Blançat (62.09.88.11). Simple, convenient.
Super cheap menus. Try *pintade fermier* (guinea fowl marinaded
with vegetables, wine and Armagnac). ROOMS A–B. MEALS
A–F. Shut Sunday; 1–15 March.

ESPELETTE
[PYRÉNÉES-ATLANTIQUES]

They used to run iron-mines and make porcelain in this village of winding streets on D918 SW of Cambo-les-Bains. Now they grow the famous fiery red peppers (*piment*) essential to Basque cooking, and breed pottoks, attractive little semi-wild Pyrenean ponies. It is on the Laxa, a tributary of the river Nive, and its houses always seem to be nicely painted in white. In summer they are decked with flowers. In October garlands of red peppers are hung around them. That is when the Fête du Piment is held. Piments de l'Espelette are greatly sought after.

The pony fair is in January. These were sold as pit ponies in the old days – mostly exported to Britain. Imagine being born and bred in the freedom of the Pyrenees then being imprisoned in a dark dank pit for the rest of your life; worse than being a human miner. Happily they are now becoming popular in France for children to ride. Until that happened they were all sold for meat.

The village is dominated by a seventeenth-century church with three tiers of balconies inside. Facing it is the château of the Barons of Espelette, now the town hall.

HOTEL
Euzkadi, rue Principale (59.29.91.88). A fine old inn, modernized inside; renowned for true Basque dishes. ROOMS C. MEALS A–E. Shut Tuesday off-season, Monday; 15 November–15 December; part February.

RESTAURANT
Relais du Labourd, route St Jean-de-Luz D918 (59.29.90.70). Regional cooking in an old farmhouse among fields. MEALS B–F. Shut Sunday evening, Wednesday; 15 January–15 February.

EUGÉNIE-LES-BAINS
[LANDES]

King Henri IV relaxed in its sulphuric waters from the river Bahus, a tributary of the Adour, but it was named after the Empress Eugénie, wife of Napoleon III. The countryside is beautiful but the spa was disappearing into insignificance when Michel and Christine Guérard took over the marvellous mansion in lovely gardens which the Empress Eugénie loved, and made it into a shrine of modern cuisine called Les Prés d'Eugénie. Michel offered the very best of nouvelle cuisine, then he gave us 'cuisine minceur', proving that slimming can be a gastronomic experience – if you have the money. You can improve your fitness, take cooking lessons, learn a lot about wine, slim in refined luxury or enjoy his superb modern-classical cuisine douceur. The hotel has been called 'the most sophisticated slimming club in the world'. It is inevitably very expensive and an experience to remember for life.

TOURIST INFORMATION Tourist Office (58.58.15.37)

HOTELS

Prés d'Eugénie (58.51.19.01). Relais et Châteaux hotel (see text). Rooms over 1000F. Meals over 400F. 'Minceur' slimming meals for residents only. Shut early December–15 February.

Relais des Champs (58.51.18.00). Down to earth, modern, comfortable, pleasant; pool. ROOMS D. MEALS A–D. Shut 31 October–1 March.

FLARAN, ABBAYE DE
[GERS]

Founded in 1151 near where the rivers Baïse and Auloue meet, it is now on the D930 south of Condom and is used as a sort of exhibition centre from time to time, though you might arrive and think that it was deserted. It is actually only closed on Tuesday. Originally it was Cistercian. Built in biscuit stone with a red roof, it is small and simple. It was sold to a private buyer after the Revolution and devastated by fire in 1970. The cultural authorities have restored much of it. The twelfth-century church is worth seeing and there are remains of a fourteenth-century chapter house and cloisters.

FLEURANCE
[Gers]

The little bastide on the Gers river which was named for the wild flowers which grew around it is now a busy town on the N21 north of Auch. But the road to it is lined with bowls of growing flowers, and flowers decorate the delightful old arcaded market square. The fine arcaded covered market with the town hall above it is from a later date but fits beautifully into the scene. The bastide was authorized by King Philippe of France in 1272 but within twenty years had passed to the powerful Albret family, who were friends of the English. The Gothic church with an octagonal tower is fourteenth century. It has some lovely sixteenth-century stained-glass windows by Arnaud de Moles. The town is a centre for horse riding and show-jumping.

TOURIST INFORMATION Mairie (62.06.10.01)
FESTIVALS June – Show-jumping; August – Horse-racing

HOTEL

Fleurance, route Agen N21 (62.06.14.85). Comfortable, modern hotel with outstanding restaurant *Cusinato* (62.06.07.70). ROOMS C–F. MEALS A–E. Shut mid-December–mid-January. Restaurant also shut Sunday evening, Monday except in July, August.

FOURCÈS
[GERS]

By a little medieval bridge over the river Auzoue on the D114
west of Condom you reach a most attractive little bastide founded by Edward I of England in 1287. Beside the slow river
where lilies bloom is a fifteenth-century château, then the circular bastide – a most unusual design. Its half-timbered arcaded
houses are grouped round the circular market-place which is
shaded with plane trees. A very photogenic and seductive place.

FRONSAC
[GIRONDE]

A little village only 3km from Libourne, its wines have missed
out in recent times to the more famous St Émilion and Pomerol,

though once they were much sought after. The town is dominated by the Tertre de Fronsac on which stands Château de Fronsac, owned by seigneurs of this name since Charlemagne. You can drive through the gates to see a splendid view of the Dordogne valley, Libourne and surrounding vineyards. A Wine Fair is held in the village in May and another on or around 12 September. (*See also* Château la Rivière Wine Visits and Tastings, page 55.)

GABAS
[Pyrénées-Atlantiques]

A superb place for exploring high mountains and lakes, but on most excursions guides are essential. You need time and proper clothing. Furthermore, hotels and accommodation are very scarce. Camping may be the best bet.

The Maison du Parc National is open for information in the afternoon from 15 June to 15 September, or you can telephone at other times (59.05.32.13).

The most impressive peak is Pic du Midi d'Ossau at 2884 metres – a pointed bare rock often just appearing through a cloud. Around it live rare, shy animals which have survived for centuries up here, like the isards, a sort of chamois, small browny-gold coloured creatures and, wisely, very shy indeed. It takes about ten to eleven hours to climb Pic du Midi up the marked path GR10. There is a night shelter (refuge CAF de Pombie) to break the journey. You must have a guide. The views at the top, they say, are truly breathtaking. So, I should think, is the climb, although not classed as very difficult. The ascents begin from Lac Bious Artigues, reached from Gabas by a lane D231, which ends there. There are paths round the lake and GR10 path continues up to Lac Ayous at 1960 metres, which is overshadowed by Pic d'Ayous at 2288 metres. The ascent takes about two and a half hours, the descent one and a half hours, and there are grandiose views from the refuge up there.

A much easier excursion is to drive on D934 and round Lac de Fabrèges to the ski resort of Sagette. Take the cable-car up to

Pic de la Sagette at 2031 metres and pick up the little mountain train to Lac d'Artouste at 1989 metres. This is a superb area. Both lakes are used to supply electricity. The barrage de Fabrèges is very impressive. The D934 southward leads to Spain through Col du Pourtalet (open June to November). Gabas itself is a pleasant little place where mountain waters of the rivers Bious and Brousset meet to form Gave d'Ossau. It has a chapel from 1121 – once part of a hospice to shelter pilgrims to Compostela. Cheese is made from the milk of the sheep taken up the mountains in summer. The whole Ossau valley is known for lovely wild flowers.

HOTEL

Vignau (59.05.34.06). Very simple. ROOMS A–B. MEALS A–D. Shut 15 November–15 December.
You may have to stay at Laruns (12km) or Eaux-Bonnes (a small spa, 16km, *see* page 156).

GAVARNIE
[HAUTES-PYRÉNÉES]

Possibly the finest area of the Pyrenees. A walking, climbing and skiing centre in one of the most beautiful areas of France, only 50km south of Lourdes by a good road which climbs through wilder and wilder country after it leaves Luz-St-Sauveur. From Gavarnie a much lesser road winds to the Spanish border and to the spectacular Cirque de Gavarnie.

Although it has an interesting fourteenth-century pilgrims' church, the village itself is now mainly a mountain centre with a few hotels and houses belonging mostly to mountain guides or people connected with skiing, and it can get very crowded. It has a statue of Count Henry Russell, the eccentric Franco-Irishman who did much to open up the Pyrenees to climbers and who dug his own caves to live in when the mood took him.

You can see the Cirque de Gavarnie from here. You can reach it by a stiff walk, though the traditional way has always been to ride a mule or a horse. They stand patiently in a row at

Cirque de Gavarnie

the end of the village like horses in a Western film. You pass through gorgeous scenery gurgling with mountain streams to the Pont de Neige, the centre of the vast amphitheatre of glacial mountains which rise in vertical faces to three terraces and surround you on three sides. Victor Hugo said, 'It is a mountain and a wall, the most mysterious edifice of the most mysterious of architects.'

In late spring waterfalls pouring down make white lines on the grey rock. The vertical line of the summit is broken by several peaks, some rising to 3000 metres. The Grande Cascade is a most dramatic waterfall, plunging over 400 metres – the highest in Europe. When the mountain snows are melting there is a single fall. After July there are two.

TOURIST INFORMATION Mairie (62.92.49.10)

HOTELS

Cimes (62.92.48.13). ROOMS D. MEALS A–F. Shut November.
Taillon(62.92.48.20). Simple ROOMS B–C. MEALS A–C. Shut 1 November–20 December.

RESTAURANT

RESTAURANT

La Ruade (62.92.48.49). Mountain style. Very cheap. MEALS A–B. Open 15 June–9 October.

GÉAUNE
[LANDES]

King Edward II of England founded it as a bastide in 1318 and for centuries it has been a centre for Tursan wine, of which the red is most interesting, while the white is full of flavour and drunk very young. You can try it all at the Tursan Co-operative (tel. 58.44.21.25). The fifteenth-century church has a large bell-tower porch. It is near Aire-sur-l'Adour, SE of Mont-de-Marsan.

GÈDRE
[HAUTES-PYRÉNÉES]

Just 8½km north of Gavarnie (*see* page 163) on the beautiful D921 where the Gave de Héas river meets the Gave de Gavarnie, this charming village is the centre for reaching Cirque de Troumousse. It is smaller but wilder than Cirque de Gavarnie, and reached by a more winding route. You can drive for 15km then walk up a zig-zagging climbing path for about half an hour. You must pay a toll for this exertion. There is a monument to the Virgin on top at 2801 metres. The path is usually closed by snow from December to April.

HOTEL

Brèche de Roland (62.92.48.54). Good views from restaurant. ROOMS D. MEALS A–B. Open 1 June–1 October; French school holidays; weekends 26 December–20 April.

GIMONT
[Gers]

On N124 E of Auch, Gimont was built as a bastide in 1265 on a
ridge overlooking the river Gimone by the Abbot of Planselve
and the Count of Toulouse for the French. It has a superb
wooden covered fifteenth- to sixteenth-century market hall. Its
Wednesday market is one of the most important in Gers,
especially for ducks, geese, *foie gras* and pâté. It is regarded as a
gastronomic town.

The Gothic church dates from 1506. A kilometre upstream
from the village of Cahuzac on the opposite side of the river are
the ruins of twelfth-century Cistercian Gimont Abbey.

Château de Larroque in Gimont is a favourite of mine. It
was built during Napeoleon III's Empire by a local mayor who
had just spent a lot of money giving the town its hospital. Alas he
spent too lavishly and went bankrupt before he could live in the
château. It was stripped, empty and decaying when the Fagedet
family bought it twenty years ago and miraculously revitalized it
as a hotel. It is worth going there if only to see it and to take a
drink on its great terrace overlooking its park and delightful
fields and woods.

MARKET Wednesday
FESTIVAL First Wednesday of Lent – Salted Meat and
Confit Fair

HOTELS

Château de Larroque, route de Toulouse N124 (62.67.77.44). *See*
text. Not expensive for a Relais et Châteaux hotel. Excellent
cooking. ROOMS F–G. MEALS D–G. Shut 1–20 January; Sunday
evening, Monday lunch in winter.

Coin du Feu, boul. Nord (62.67.71.56). Another Fagedet family
hotel. Meals excellent value. ROOMS C–D. MEALS A–F.

GUÉTHARY
[Pyrénées-Atlantiques]

An old fishing port hidden in a creek on the Basque coast between Biarritz and St Jean-de-Luz, it is now a bathing resort with its main town on top of the cliff beside N10 and very near A63 motorway. With its steep lanes winding down to the harbour, it looks like a fishing village in Cornwall. There are beaches on either side of the harbour and another 2km away – Plage de Cenitz. Its fronton in front of the Mairie is famous for producing good *chistera* players – the ones who play *pelota* with the claw-like wicker basket on the right hand. The church has a seventeenth-century Pietà and a monument to a local lad, Monseigneur Mogabure (1850–1910), who was the first Archbishop of Tokyo.

The main railway Paris–Madrid runs through the town, but is fairly well hidden. There are sculptures by Swiecinski in the museum.

Tourist Information 1 place Mairie (59.26.56.60)
Festival Summer fête with Basque dancing and
Courses des Vaches

HOTEL
Pereria (59.26.51.68). Lovely garden. Rooms A–D. Meals B–D. Open 1 March–30 October.

GUÎTRES
[Gironde]

An old town with old houses and alleys on the right bank of the river l'Isle, 16km NE from Libourne. It is a joy to lovers of steam trains. In the old station is a museum with old rolling stock and locomotives. The locos include one of the fastest steam trains used on SNCF, the French national railways – La Mountain 9, built in 1947 and still in very good shape. During the summer (May to October) a 1924 steam loco pulls trains from Guîtres to

Marcenais westwards. (For information and timetables tel. 57.69.01.47.)

TOURIST INFORMATION Syndicat d'Initiative (in season, afternoons only – 57.69.11.48)

HAGETMAU
[LANDES]

This busy modern town 29km SW of Mont-de-Marsan is a centre for grain and pork from the Chalosse farms, manufactures chairs and is a lively cultural centre for theatre, music and pottery. Many exhibitions are held and the fête in July is renowned for processions, dances, Courses des Vaches and corridas. I expect there were a few celebrations when Wellington stayed here after winning the battle of Orthez. It is a *village fleuri* – flowered village.

St Giron's crypt, 2km W, remains from a vanished abbey church. It has been a place of pilgrimage since the ninth century and is still regarded as one of the important sites of Gascony. It has well-preserved, beautifully sculpted Romanesque capitals and is supported by fourteen columns. The staircase is tenth century. St Giron converted this area to Christianity in the fourth century. There are a number of farmhouses offering beds and meals around here. Ask at the Syndicat.

TOURIST INFORMATION Syndicat d'Initiative, place République (shut afternoons except July–August – 58.79.38.26)
MARKET Wednesday
FESTIVAL Last week of July – Fête

HOTELS

Auberge Lacs d'Halco, Les Lacs (58.79.56.56). Very quiet, in countryside; good cooking, warm welcome. ROOMS B–C. MEALS B–D.
Jambon, 27 rue Carnot (58.79.32.02). Only eight rooms, but very good cooking. ROOMS B–C. MEALS C–E. Shut January; hotel, not restaurant, shut Sunday night, Monday.

HASPARREN
[Pyrénées-Atlantiques]

East of Cambo-les-Bains. Its name in Basque means 'at the heart of the oaks', but its forest, long since disappeared, was used for its tanning industry. It is a shoe-making town, and also has an engineering plant. One of the most industrialized of Basque towns.

7km SE are Grottes Isturits and Oxocelhaya, which you can reach through the village of St Esteben. They are quite interesting, but mostly to experts. Isturits has traces of human occupation showing man's evolution. Oxocelhaya's chambers are decorated with stalactites, stalagmites, columns and shining 'draperies' formed of translucent ice.

HASTINGUES
[Landes]

A tiny bastide built by John Hastings, Lord Lieutenant of Gascony, in 1289 for Edward I of England. It is on a spur above the south bank of the Gave de Réunis west of Peyrehorade, and is one of the best preserved bastides in the area. A lot survives – the gatehouse, part of the fortified walls, the central square and cellars, the Governor's house and the justice house. 4km SE is the abbey of Arthous, whose abbot helped to build the fortified town. The isolated abbey and chapel date from the twelfth century. It was yet another stop on one of the routes to Compostela. Later it was used as a farm and was very dilapidated when major restoration work started. The monastery buildings contain an archaeological museum, prehistory and Roman (shut Tuesday, except in July and August).

HENDAYE
[PYRÉNÉES-ATLANTIQUES]

Many people are so busy going back and forth between France and Spain that they do not notice that Hendaye is a pleasant resort with an enormous beach backed by magnolias, palms and mimosa, a pretty promenade, boulevard de Mer, and a corniche road along the coast to St Jean-de-Luz. Winston Churchill knew. He chose it for a holiday in 1945 after Hitler's death and the Allied victory in Europe. Its climate is mild. There are really three areas – the beach, the town rising on the banks of the river Bidassoa which forms the frontier with Spain, and the less interesting area around the very important frontier railway station where roads and rail cross the river. Since the A63 motorway was built to bypass the town Hendaye has become less crowded and more attractive.

Upriver is Île des Faisans, a mudflat where once kings and leaders met and history was altered. Here François I of France, captured at the battle of Pavia, was exchanged for his two sons, who went as hostages for his ransom. Their father left them in Spain for quite a time while he spent money building châteaux. The long, extremely complicated negotiations for the Treaty of the Pyrenees were carried out here in 1659 by Cardinal Mazarin, who had succeeded Richelieu as power behind the throne in France. The treaty fixed the frontiers, with France getting Roussillon, the Cerdagne and Artois, Spain keeping Catalonia. Young Louis XIV was more or less ordered to marry the Infanta of Spain, Maria Theresa, eldest daughter of King Philip IV of Spain. He was in love with Mazarin's niece, Marie Mancini. The treaty was signed in a beautifully decorated pavilion set up on the muddy island. It was designed by the great artist Velazquez. He died soon afterwards from a chill caught out on the mud.

In rue des Pêcheurs in Hendaye the great writer of the sea, Pierre Loti, died in 1923. 4km upstream is the frontier village of Behobie and the road twists to the very Basque hamlet of Biriatou, where the Black Prince had a fortress. The auberge, fronton and church make a charming group. The church is believed to have been the chapel of the Prince's castle.

In 1813 Wellington's troops crossed the Bidassoa at low tide on a broad stretch of sands and attacked and took Hendaye in a fierce and important action.

TOURIST INFORMATION 12 rue Aubépines
(59.20.00.34)
MARKETS Wednesday, Saturday
FESTIVAL August – Fête Basque

HOTELS

Gitanilla, 52 boul. Leclerc (59.20.04.65). Only seven rooms but good restaurant. ROOMS B–C. MEALS C–D. Shut 15 October–30 November; Sunday evening, Monday except July, August.

Pohoténia, route Corniche (59.20.04.76). ROOMS D–E. MEALS C–E. Shut January.

Chez Antoinette, place Pellot (59.20.08.47). In town. Regional cooking, but open only 15 June–15 September. ROOMS B–E. MEALS C.

Biriatou.

Bakéa (59.20.76.36). Best restaurant for a long way. Good value. Quiet, shady terrace with views. ROOMS B–E. MEALS C–F. Open 1 May–30 September.

L'HÔPITAL ST-BLAISE
[PYRÉNÉES-ATLANTIQUES]

Tiny hamlet on D25 E of Mauléon-Licharre, its name came from a hospice on a pilgrims road and it still has a curious twelfth-century church with a centre tower. It also has two hotels and has its devotees among visitors – probably for the fine scenery and the peace and calm away from the D936 Oloron–Bayonne road.

HOTEL

Touristes (59.66.53.04). ROOMS A–B. MEALS A–C. Shut 25 February–15 March; Monday except July, August.

HOSSEGOR
[LANDES]

A bright, pleasant resort, lively in summer, which owes its charm
to a salt lake left behind when the river Adour changed course.
Its name derives from the British Horse Guards who were
encamped here during Wellington's campaign in 1813. The lake
is joined to the sea by a canal, so you can choose sheltered
beaches on the lakeside, or great long fine sands on the Atlantic,
both backed by trees. There is a delightful harbour where
fishing and pleasure boats mix. It shares the harbour with the
twin resort of Capbreton (*see* page 144), so there is a great choice
of beaches, shops, bars, cafés and restaurants which are alive
and happy daytime and evening. But there are many villas and
bungalows, mostly high quality, hidden away in the forest
behind, and these are nearly all let to visitors in summer, so it is
easy to find peace when you want it.

The lake makes it a good family resort, though you must
watch children on the Atlantic beaches where great waves roll in.
It is splendid for watersports, with lake and sea sailing, surfing,
windsurfing and good fishing.

Oysters are farmed in the lake and served by excellent fish
restaurants around the lake and harbour. Hossegor retains a
certain elegance lost to so many seaside resorts in Europe. President Mitterand has a private house nearby at Latche.

TOURIST INFORMATION place Pasteur (58.43.72.35)
FESTIVALS Hossegor shares with Capbreton a Fête of
the Sea in mid-June and almost non-stop fêtes, regattas
and firework displays throughout summer

HOTELS
Les Huitrières du Lac, 1187 ave du Touring Club (58.43.51.48).
On east side of lake, superb seafood with oysters from their own
park in the lake. Restaurant opens on to terrace above the lake.
Only nine rooms, so book well ahead in season. ROOMS C–D.
MEALS C–G. Shut December–end February; Wednesday off
season.
Beauséjour, ave Tour-du-Lac (58.43.51.07). Attractive fin-de-

siècle mansion converted with modern comfort. Pool, garden (season only). ROOMS F–G. MEALS F. Shut November–late April. *Neptune*, 1053 ave du Touring Club (58.43.51.09). Simpler hotel with good regional cooking on lakeside. ROOMS B–D. MEALS A–D. Shut 15 November–1 March.

HOURTIN
and
LAC HOURTIN-CARCANS
[GIRONDE]

Hourtin is the only town around the wild lake hidden in the middle of marshland and forest, and the main holiday resort. Although on the D3 road, it has a port on the lake for sailing and pleasure boats and is a canoeing centre.

Hourtin-Port is a new resort making a play for families with its slogan '*Les Enfants d'Abord*' – 'Children above all'.

The lake is 19km long, bordered by marshy land with streams and canals running through (*marais*) to the north and much of the east. Woods and dunes 60 metres high separate it from the sea to the west – protected forest. There are several pleasant little beaches round it and at a few you can find self-catering villas.

Hourtin-Plage is being developed fast. It has a good marina, lakeside apartments and Apartotel called Espacotel.

Carcans in the south has a beach on the Atlantic coast, Carcans-Plage, also being developed, with another Espacotel. It is an enormous beach typical of this whole coastline.

Maubuisson is another growing little resort with new villas. Here you can pick up boats which cruise this canal as far as the National Marine centre at Le Contaut in the north and through Canal de Jonction which joins the lake to Lac de Lacanau (*see* page 178).

A road from Hourtin past Mimizan to Hossegor is called Route des Lacs. You cannot actually see the lakes most of the way, but little connecting roads go down to the water and to little beaches.

Tourist Information Hourtin, 1 place l'Église
(56.41.65.57); Maubuisson, route de l'Océan
(56.03.31.16)

HOTELS
Hourtin
Dauphin, 1 place Église (56.09.11.15). ROOMS D–E. MEALS B–E.
Open 1 May–1 October.
Espacotel (56.09.17.51). 196 rooms and apartments. No prices
available. Open 1 April–30 October.
Maubuisson
Lac (56.03.30.03). Thirty-six rooms, good views. ROOMS C–E.
MEALS C–D. Open end March–end September.

HUCHET, COURANT D'
[*See* Léon, page 182]

HUME, LA
[GIRONDE]

Near La Teste on Bassin d'Arcachon, La Hume has a family
beach and mid-June to mid-September a 'medieval village'
where blacksmiths, jewellers, leather-workers and other craftsmen dressed in medieval costume work in the original way in
front of visitors. To add a little confusion, it has a small museum
of automation.

L'ISLE DE NOÉ
[GERS]

A little fishing town where the Grande and Petite Baïse rivers
meet, on D939 S of Condom and N of Mirande (*see* page 191);
seventeenth-century château.

HOTEL

Auberge de Gascogne, rue Président Wilson (62.64.17.05). Simple inn. Very cheap meals. ROOMS B. MEALS A. Shut Wednesday; 3–10 July; November.

L'ISLE-JOURDAIN
[GERS]

The old pilgrim route from Bordeaux to Jerusalem (now GR65 long-distance footpath) and the river Save wander through this old bastide on N124 Toulouse road E of Auch. There are remains of two arcaded markets, a superb *halle* (covered market) and an old town hall. Its classic church, mainly eighteenth-century, has a fine fifteenth-century clock tower. St Bernard, Bishop of Comminges, died here in 1123. It became a bastide in 1230. Known for its fêtes, it has several each year.

TOURIST INFORMATION Town Hall (62.07.25.67)
FESTIVALS Spring – Musical; summer – Carnival with
Corso Fleuri; early November – one week fête of
St Martin

HOTEL

Hostellerie du Lac, 1km W on N124 (62.07.03.91). Superbly situated on lakeside. Yachting, swimming-pool. ROOMS C–D. MEALS A–F. Shut part February.

ITXASSOU
[PYRÉNÉES-ATLANTIQUES]

A charming and very Basque village sited quietly just off the beautiful but important D918 from Cambo-les-Bains to St Jean-Pied-de-Port, so it lures quite a lot of visitors from the time that the cherry trees blossom in spring. About 1300 people live here and it has nine hotels, but remains a tranquil country village – a good place for a couple of nights rest after seeing the more crowded places. The Basque-style church with galleries inside is very pretty. The steep little D349 beside the Nive is most attractive as far as Bidarray where it joins the equally attractive but busier D918 to St Jean. The Pas de Roland on D349 is said to have been made by the horse of Charlemagne's heroic knight Roland cutting a way through rock with his hoof. Another attractive little road branching right takes you to Artzamendi, where from the telecommunications centre you get superb panoramic views of the Nive valley and to the hills of the valley of Bidassoa at the Spanish border.

HOTELS

Chêne (59.29.75.01). Big, old Basque house on edge of village made into peaceful hotel among lush greenery, with views of green mountainsides. The owner, Geneviève Salaberry, is also the chef. Nice regional dishes. ROOMS B–C. MEALS A–E. Shut 1 January–1 March; Monday evening, Tuesday except in July, August.

Du Fronton (59.29.75.10). Typical traditional family-run hostelry with three 'chimneys' from Logis de France. True Basque dishes. Good-value meals. Terrace for summer meals has good mountain views. ROOMS B–E. MEALS C–F. Shut 1 January–15 February; Wednesday late season.

LABASTIDE-CLAIRANCE
[PYRÉNÉES-ATLANTIQUES]

A typical bastide of the early fourteenth century built by the Béarnais. It is in the valley of the delightfully named Joyeuse river 8km NE of Hasparren, and has typically Basque houses painted white and red, and a galleried church.

LABASTIDE D'ARMAGNAC
[Landes]

One of the most charming of the bastides, built in 1291 by
Bérnard IV, Count of Armagnac, 15km SE of Roquefort. It was
the model for Henri IV's Place des Vosges in Paris at the beginning of the seventeenth century. It has a Gallo-Roman villa with
mosaics. Around the attractive place Royale are old arcaded
houses of stone and wood decked with flowers in summer. The
church in the village is Romanesque and on the route Cazaubon
outside the village is a chapel dedicated to Notre-Dame des
Cyclistes, with a wooden bell tower.

This is wine country and there is a little wine museum,
Armagnac brandy cellars and a fête at picking time.

FESTIVALS September – Fête des Vendanges and Fêtes
Folkloriques, with costume parade and candlelit dinners
under the arcades

LABOUHEYRE
[Landes]

Small town on N10 where D626 branches off to Mimizan-Plage.
The N10 skirts most of it. It grew from a Carmelite Convent of
1150 which ministered to pilgrims. Pleasant forest area with
tracks SE to Marquèze, where a little train takes you to Sabres
(see page 214). Westward the path goes to Mimizan.

HOTEL
Unic, route de Bordeaux (58.07.00.55). Logis. ROOMS B–D.
MEALS A–C. Shut mid-December–1 February; Sunday evening,
Monday.

LA BRÈDE
[See Brède, Château de La, page 141]

LACANAU-OCÉAN and LACANAU
[Gironde]

Seaside resort backed by sand dunes and pines used for tapping resin 5km W of the top of Lac de Lacanau. Huge beach of fine sand. It became popular for summer villas at the turn of the century and has grown in recent years into a well-equipped resort, still expanding. Its watersports facilities are good. The big Lac de Lacanau, joined by a canal to Lac Hourtin-Carcans (*see* Hourtin, page 173) is famous for windsurfing. Le Moutchic is the base. Lacanau itself on the east side of the lake is a little market town set in the pine forest, with a lovely eighteenth-century church. The lake, 8km long, has excellent fishing for pike, perch and eels. A stretch is set aside for water-skiers.

TOURIST INFORMATION, Lacanau-Océan place Europe (56.03.21.01)
FESTIVALS Lacanau-Océan: June – Festival of the Sea; August – International Surfing Championships.
Lacanau ville: June – Wine and Regional Food Fair

HOTELS
Lacanau-Océan
Étoile d'Argent, place Europe (56.03.21.07). Logis de France. ROOMS C–D. MEALS D–F. Shut 1 December–25 January.
Golf, Domaine de l'Ardilouse (56.03.23.15). Quiet. ROOMS E–G. MEALS A–F. Shut January.
Lacanau ville
Commerce, place Église (56.03.54.40). ROOMS C–D. MEALS A–C. Shut January.

LACQ
[Pyrénées-Atlantiques]

In 1951 one of the most important reserves of natural gas was found just west of Pau at a depth between 3500 and 5000 metres. Since then it has been producing nearly a third of

France's gas consumption. Industrial plants here also produce petroleum products and chemicals derived from petrol and sulphur including aluminium.

At the petrol station on the nearby Pau-Bayonne main road is a museum devoted to the activities of the Elf organization at Lacq.

The gas discovery changed the economy of the south-west and brought in many people. A new town of Mourenx, across the Gave de Pau river, houses most of the 10,000 technicians and office workers from the plant in high-rise apartment blocks. But the Lacq reserves are beginning to run out, and production is due to cease by the end of the century.

Lacq looks most extraordinary here in the Pyrenees, with its network of brightly coloured pipes. At night, the flames from the wells can be seen for miles, like a city in a bombing raid.

LANGON
[GIRONDE]

On the south bank of the Garonne, the Graves wine town of Langon is also an administrative and commercial centre and one of the great gastronomic towns of south-west France. From here you can explore the vineyards of Sauternes, Barsac, Premières Côtes de Bordeaux and Entre-Deux-Mers quite easily. It is joined to Macaire by a new bridge.

TOURIST INFORMATION 1 allées Jean-Jaurès
(56.62.34.00)
MARKETS Tuesday, Friday

HOTELS

Claude Darroze, 95 cours Gén-Leclerc (56.63.00.48). A member of a famous family of restauranteurs and a brilliant chef. Great variety of dishes from Grandma's recipes of Aquitaine to his own inventions. He hunts the best ingredients like a sleuth. Pricey. Rooms of style and comfort. ROOMS D–F. MEALS F–G. Shut mid-October–early November; part January.

Mary Lou, 38 cours Sadi-Carnot (56.63.09.32). Simple, cheap.

Regional dishes. ROOMS A–B. MEALS A–C. Shut 1–15 July;
15–31 August; Wednesday.

RESTAURANT

Grangousier, 2 route d'Auros (56.63.30.59). Claude Darroze has
a hand in this one too. Local specialities. MEALS A–F.

LARRESSINGLE
[*See* Condom, page 152]

LAVARDENS
[GERS]

Village on a hilltop below a massive half-ruined seventeenth-
century castle which was built on the site of one knocked down
by order of Henri IV to prevent the Counts of Armagnac using
it as a base for insurrection. The present castle was built around
a rock. There are lovely panoramic views from it. It has been
partly restored and is used for exhibitions and concerts. Next to
it is a square tower with pointed spire which formed part of the
original castle but is now a rather incongruous porch to the little
village church.

Lavardens is 18km NW of Auch just off the D930. There are
pleasant little roads to Auch and to Condom northwards.

LECTOURE
[GERS]

One of the oldest towns in this part of France. It was the capital
of the Lactorate tribe and in Gallo-Roman times the centre of
the cult of Cybele (the Grande Mère) with sexual rites.

About a hundred sarcophagi have been found, along with
hundreds of other finds including Gallic wells. It rated a bishop
in the fifth century but was sacked by the Visigoths.

It was in an important position above the Gers river which comes down from Auch, an equally old town, and continues to join the Garonne, so almost inevitably it was rebuilt in the tenth century to make it even stronger. Its château became the capital of the powerful Counts of Armagnac from 1325. When Louis XI of France took it from them in 1473, killing Jean V, the tyrannical Count, Armagnac lost its independence. Louis butchered the population of Lectoure.

It is a pleasant town, still enclosed by ramparts and with fine old houses, as well as towers, a thirteenth-century fountain of Diana and the remains of the château. The most charming part of the town is the Promenade du Bastion, a walk shaded by chestnut trees, with a bandstand and great views of the Pyrenees. The viewing table helpfully points to neighbouring towns and villages and to such useful spots as Peking, New York and Moscow!

The belfry of the attractive Gothic church nearby rises to 50 metres but until 1792 it rose proudly to 90 metres. It was not a victim of the Revolution but of a bishop who either could not be bothered or could not afford to maintain it. The church was originally the cathedral of St Gervais and St Protais and was built in the thirteenth century on the site of a pagan temple. It has been reconstructed or altered several times and now looks rather like two semi-detached buildings. The late fifteenth-century Gothic nave is 21 metres high. The choir is Flamboyant, opening on to nine chapels. A collection of bull-sacrifice altars was found on the site during fifteenth-century alterations. They are now in the museum in the town hall, which is in the old Bishops' Palace.

In the centre of the town are arcaded stone houses with big doors to delightful private courtyards.

Hidden among trees on Promenade du Bastion is a memorial to Jean Larmes, born here in 1769. He joined the army in 1792 as an ordinary soldier and showed such authority and courage that he was a general three years later! In 1804 he was made a Marshal of France, then Duke of Montebello in 1808. In 1809 he was mortally wounded at the battle of Essling.

TOURIST INFORMATION cours Hôtel-de-Ville
(62.68.76.98)

MARKET Friday
FESTIVALS Second Sunday in August – Fête de Melon;
first Saturday/Sunday in September – Lace Fair.

HOTELS

Bastard, rue Lagrange (62.68.82.44). Imposing eighteenth-century house. Terrace, garden. ROOMS C–E. MEALS B–G. Hotel shut February. Restaurant shut 24–30 December; Friday evening, Saturday lunch; Sunday evening in winter.

LÉON and COURANT D'HUCHET
[LANDES]

Very likeable little town beside a lake which is joined to the sea by a channel Courant d'Huchet. The old main square with the town hall, the timbered houses beside the church, and two welcoming inns becomes lively in summer and on weekends it is crowded with people and market barrows. There is a good, largish campsite between the lake and the square. We used to take our children there. Both the lake and the Courant are surrounded by vegetation, some semi-tropical and so lush that in places you could believe that you were in a jungle. It is virgin forest. The boat journey along the Courant, which takes four hours, is quite enchanting. At first the trees overhead almost touch and the route is rich in flowering shrubs. In August the flowering hibiscus is beautiful. Giant ferns and great cypresses give way to fields and vines and then jungle again until you reach the sand dunes and beach. The boats run from Easter to the end of September (tel. 58.48.75.39).

Professional fishermen take an enormous haul of *anguilles* (eels) some nights from the Courant. The shallow lake at Léon is good for swimming, canoeing, sailing and fishing. It has a beach, restaurants, cafés and boats for hire. It is an old estuary, blocked over centuries by sand, and when the crowds have gone, a haven for wildfowl. Many species of mushrooms grow round here.

TOURIST INFORMATION Mairie (July, August –
58.48.76.03)

HOTELS

Centre, place Église (58.48.74.09). True old inn in main square with old-style cooking. Remarkably cheap menu. ROOMS D–E. MEALS A–E.

Commerce, place Église (58.48.73.04). Very cheap menu. ROOMS C. MEALS A–E. Open 15 March–30 September.

Du Lac, at the lake 1½km NW (58.48.73.11). Overlooks lake; lovely position. Book. Good regional cooking. ROOMS B–C. MEALS A–C. Open 1 April–1 October.

LESCUN
[Pyrénées-Atlantiques]

Hamlet with beautiful views about it, loved by mountaineers and walkers. It is perched in a sweep of mountains above the vallée d'Aspe just off the beautiful N134 as it sweeps down to Spain from Oloron-Ste-Marie. It is up a winding little dead-end road which zig-zags on another 6km of hard driving to the refuge of Labérouat at 1450 metres. The GR10 footpath will take experienced mountaineers to the Pic d'Anie at 2504 metres. There are, I am told, absolutely superb views from there. Lescun has some fine old houses. The N134 through marvellous scenery enters the Parc National des Pyrénées and continues through Col du Sumport (1632 metres) to Spain. This is the only pass of the Central Pyrenees normally open in all seasons. The Roman legions used it; so later did the pilgrims to Compostela.

HOTEL

Pic d'Anie (59.34.71.54). Quiet, good views, good cooking. ROOMS C–E. MEALS A–E. Open 1 April–20 September.

LESPERON-LE-SOUQUET
[LANDES]

Lesperon was a bastide built by the English in 1325. It is divided from Le Souquet by the N10. By 1325 the Château Souquet was the headquarters of a brigand gang who were the curse of France in the Hundred Years War, fighting wherever they could get loot and roaming the countryside looting, killing, robbing, raping and burning. They preyed, too, on the Compostela pilgrims.

Lesperon is about 30km S of Labouheyre, 2½km W of N10 in the Vignac valley. There are several hotels round here.

HOTELS

Auberge du Souquet, on N10 (58.89.60.30). High-standard Logis de France. Good value. ROOMS A–D. MEALS A–D. Shut 1–31 December; Wednesday.

Chez Darmaillacq, in village (58.89.61.45). ROOMS B–C. MEALS A–F. Shut 15 September–10 October, Monday off season.

LÉVIGNACQ
[LANDES]

Very pleasant village between N10 and the coast NE of Léon in a valley of the Vignac river. Next village off N10 to Lesperon (*see* page 184). It has traditional half-timbered Landais houses and an unusual fourteenth-century fortified church with a Renaissance doorway. Inside the church wooden vaulting is decorated with naïve eighteenth century religious paintings. Before the phylloxera struck the vines last century, this area produced a lot of wine.

LIBOURNE
[GIRONDE]

Roger de Leybourne from the County of Kent founded this bastide in 1265 at the meeting of the Dordogne and Isle rivers, and the French claim that it still has an atmosphere of England.

It has become more industrialized in recent years, bigger and busier while retaining a lot of charm. It still has its truly lovely fourteenth-century waterside gate with a pointed tower (Tour du Grand-Port on the quai de l'Isle). Grand-Place is arcaded though most of its houses are sixteenth to nineteenth century. The town hall is fifteenth century but was badly restored in 1910. Where ramparts once stood are tree-shaded avenues and down by the water are wide quaysides with benches where you can sit to enjoy the river views.

In the Middle Ages Libourne rivalled Bordeaux as a wine port, sending St Émilion, Pomerol and Fronsac wines to England and Holland. However the Bordelais won privileges from the English, then from the French, which gave them tax concessions and the right to tax goods passing the port, so Libourne gradually lost the trade war, though wine was still shipped to England until around 1914. It is still an important wine town. Château de Fronsac (*see* page 162) is only 2½km W.

It was believed in the Middle Ages that whoever held Libourne held Aquitaine, for it is at the tidal limit of the river, the meeting point of two rivers then vital for transport, and was then a major crossing place of the Dordogne which had few bridges. The Black Prince wisely strengthened it as a fortress. He signed a treaty here with Pedro the Cruel of Castile and Carlos II of Navarre.

The 220-metre stone bridge, Grand Pont was built by Napoleon. Crossing this and turning W you come, in 7km, to Vayres, with a fine Renaissance château built in the sixteenth century by Louis de Foix on the remains of a medieval castle. You can see excellent Empire furniture in the Grand Salon (open Sunday afternoons; every afternoon in July and August).

TOURIST INFORMATION 1 place Abel-Surchamp
[Grand-Place], (57.51.15.04)
MARKETS Tuesday, Friday, Sunday morning

HOTELS

Loubat, 32 rue Chanzy, opposite station (57.51.17.58). Traditional, recently renovated. Bordelais cooking, good wine list. Best in town. ROOMS D–E. MEALS C–E.

Gare, 43 rue Chanzy (57.51.06.86). Cheap, very adequate. ROOMS B–C. MEALS A–B. Shut November. Restaurant shut Sunday.

Ripaille, 2 rue Treilles (57.25.02.52). Grill rooms. Logis. ROOMS C–D. MEALS A–D.

LICQ-ATHÉREY
[PYRÉNÉES-ATLANTIQUES]

Hamlet popular with Pyrenean connoisseurs as a centre for seeing some of the most dramatic scenery. It is in the Haute Soule in the Saison valley, south from Mauléon-Licharre by D918 then right on D26. Southward the valley splits into two parts – the valleys of the Larrau river and the Uhaïtxa. There are great sharp rocks and cracks running down the mountainside. One road, D113, leads to the famous Gorges de Kakouetta but you may not be able to reach it (*see* Ste Engrâce, the shepherds' village, page 232). Another road D26 leads to Col d'Erroymendi with magnificent views and on to Port de Larrau into Spain.

From Licq-Athérey in September they hold the great hairy Rally des Cîmes in the mountains – originally for Land Rover-style vehicles, now four-wheel drive essential. There is hang-gliding too, good fishing and lovely walks.

Touristes (59.28.61.01). ROOMS B–E. MEALS A–E. Shut
Christmas.

LOMBEZ
[GERS]

Lombez is 3½km from Samatan by the river Save, on D632
between Tarbes and Toulouse. The river runs through part of
the town and the octagonal tower of Lombez's handsome red-
brick cathedral dominates the river valley. The tower is 43
metres high and has twelve bells. The cathedral is among winding narrow streets of the old quarter, flanked by an eighteenth-

Cathedral of Ste Marie at Lombez

century Bishop's residence. The elegant tower has five storeys. Inside are relics of St Majan, a wanderer who settled as a hermit near here and who with St Clair and St Prim, converted the region. The town can become flooded after heavy winter rains in the mountains swell the river Save. (*See also* Samatan, page 234.)

FESTIVALS 1 June – Fête of St Majan; third Sunday in August – Fête

LOUPIAC
[GIRONDE]

Wine village in a lovely position near the right bank of the Garonne, known for its white wines (*see* Vineyards, page 52). Upstream from Cadillac (*see* page 141). In a vineyard a Roman villa has been excavated with mosaics indicating that it belonged to the Roman poet and wine-grower Ausonius.

LOURDES
[*See* Sites, page 102]

MARCIAC
[GERS]

Another thirteenth-century bastide which is known now for its Jazz Festival, the largest in SW France, attracting American and English bands and performers. It is at the crossing of D3 and the beautiful D943 coming down from Montesquiou and Bassoues. Its large market square is still arcaded. It has a château, water-mills and two notable churches, one fourteenth century, the other a fifteenth-century convent chapel with an octagonal tower. Nearby is a lake with watersports and cafés.

FESTIVAL Mid-August – Jazz Festival

MAUBUISSON
[*See* Hourtin, page 173]

MAULÉON-LICHARRE
[PYRÉNÉES-ATLANTIQUES]

Once two separate towns divided by the Saison river (Gave de Mauléon), Mauléon-Licharre is situated in a wide valley on D918 which runs through gorgeous scenery all the way to near Lourdes and joins the D26 through more superb scenery to the Spanish border. Mauléon is capital of Soule, one of three French Basque provinces, and French capital of espadrilles, the rope-soled canvas shoes. They make other footwear here, too, from sandals to boots, and they make cheese and conserves. The ruins of the fifteenth-century castle overlook the town.

Château Andurain, a Renaissance manor built around 1600 for the Bishop of Oleron, has some fine seventeenth- to eighteenth-century furnishings. The town has several beautiful buildings and arcades around the market square. It was ceded to the Black Prince in 1261 and not reconquered from the English until 1449 by Comte de Foix. Mauléon is a very good centre for touring superb mountain scenery.

TOURIST INFORMATION 10 rue J. B. Heugas
(59.28.02.37)
MARKET Tuesday

HOTELS

Château, 25 rue Navarre (59.28.19.06): charmingly Basque, including the cooking. Cheap. ROOMS B–C. MEALS A–C. Shut 15 January–1 March.
Bidegain, 13 rue Navarre (59.28.16.25). Delightful, family-run. Shady garden. ROOMS D. MEALS A–F. Shut 15 January–15 February.

MAUVEZIN
[Gers]

An English bastide built in 1275 at the old frontier of Aquitaine and Narbonne. It is 12km N of Gimont in the Arrats valley where D654 from Fleurance meets D928. The people are very proud of their huge arcaded main square, bigger than the Capitole in Toulouse and decorated freely with flowers. It has a stone-columned market hall and thirteenth-century belfry. From the upper terrace of the church there are lovely views over the valley. The narrow streets are intriguing. Among the old houses is Maison Jeanne d'Albret. She was Queen of Navarre, a poetess, mother of Henri IV of France and a most fervent Protestant. Mauvezin was very much a Protestant town and still has a Protestant temple of the nineteenth century.

FESTIVAL Third Monday in August – Garlic Fair

RESTAURANT
La Rapière, rue des Justices (62.06.82.08). Excellent value; family cooking by the Fourreau family. **MEALS B–G.** Shut 25 June–1 July; Tuesday evening, Wednesday.

MIÉLAN, LAC
[*See* Mirande and Miélan, page 191]

MIMIZAN and MIMIZAN-PLAGE
[Landes]

Before the planting of Les Landes, the ancient city here was mostly buried by the encroaching dunes in the eighteenth century. The town today is dull but some pleasant modern villas have been built in the surrounding woods. Just N is a shallow lake, Étang d'Aureilhan, with a very attractive walk through colourful shrubs and flowers. Towards Mimizan-Plage the tower of a thirteenth-century abbey remains from the old town.

Mimizan-Plage has been the site of a coastal holiday development plan and is a lively, quite noisy place in summer, but the plan has not progressed quite as fast as expected. There are all the usual resort facilities, with water sports. Beside the rather strange Château de Woolsack near the beach is a monument to the first Frenchmen to fly the Atlantic. They landed here in 1929. Mimizan is known internationally for producing paper. Alas, if the wind is in the wrong direction, you can smell it.

TOURIST INFORMATION 38 ave M. Martin (58.09.11.20)

FESTIVALS 1 May – Festival of Flowers of the Sea, Mimizan-Plage

HOTELS

Au Bon Coin, by the Étang, 1½km from the town (58.09.01.55). Expensive; pleasant big bedrooms, delicious cooking. Lakeside garden, punts, pedaloes. ROOMS G. MEALS C–G. Shut February; Sunday evening, Monday except July, August.

Côte d'Argent, 4 ave M. Martin (58.09.15.22). Modern. Sixth-storey restaurant has superb sea views. ROOMS F–G. MEALS D–F. Hotel open 1 May–30 September. Restaurant open 1 June–20 September.

Mermoz, 16 ave Courant, Plage (58.09.09.30). Three-chimney Logis de France. Good value. ROOMS C–E. MEALS A–E. Hotel open Easter–mid-September. Restaurant open 1 June–10 September. No lunches served.

MIRANDE and MIÉLAN
[GERS]

Only 25km SW of Auch on the N21, Mirande is a useful centre for seeing lovely Gers countryside to the west and north-west. It is a very pleasant agricultural town, quite lively, with a market for ducks and geese. This is bastide country and inevitably Mirande is one, founded in 1281 by a bishop. It still has an impressive main square with stone arcades, shady plane trees, and flowers in summer. Several old buildings survive, including

a watch-tower, Tour de Rohan, the château of the old Counts of
Asturac, a pilgrims' hospice and convent. The fifteenth-century
Gothic church of Notre-Dame is in Languedoc style, with an
unusual bell tower called by the locals 'Arc de Triomphe'. The
Musée des Beaux Arts, next to the church in rue de l'Évêché, has
interesting seventeenth- to eighteenth-century costumes and
Italian and Flemish paintings which please most amateurs but
are dismissed as being third rate by experts. *The Head of a Fawn*
attributed to Rubens is dismissed by pundits as very dubious.
(Museum shut Tuesday.)

11km down N21 is Lac de Miélan, a popular little summer
recreation and holiday spot. It was man-made by damming the
river Osse, which was thereby considerably slimmed. Miélan
village is yet another bastide, built by the French in 1284,
knocked down by the English in 1370, then rebuilt and recap-
tured by the French in 1450.

TOURIST INFORMATION, Mirande 13 rue de l'Évêché
(62.66.68.10)
MARKETS Mirande; Monday. Miélan; Thursday

HOTELS
Mirande
Pyrénées, 5 ave d'Étigny (62.66.51.16). Modest inn recently
improved. Good regional, modern cooking of local ingredients.
ROOMS B–E. MEALS A–F. Restaurant shut Monday in winter.
Europ, 2 ave d'Étigny (62.66.51.42). Comfortable for its price.
Regional family cooking. ROOMS B–C. MEALS A–F. Restaurant
shut Saturday low season.
Miélan
Lac (62.67.51.59). Beside lake with dining terrace overlooking
water. Simple ground-floor rooms in park with fishing, ped-
aloes, bathing. Popular with holiday-makers. High-standard
cooking. Big choice of menus. ROOMS C–D. MEALS A–F. Open
all year.

MONGIE, LA
[Hautes-Pyrénées]

From this large modern ski resort 1800 metres above the Campan valley you can take a cable-car past La Taoulet to the Pic du Midi de Bigorre at 2865 metres for one of the finest views in the Pyrenees. There is a TV transmitter and an observatory set up in 1880. The valley below is extremely beautiful. It is also possible to drive up to the Pic on a hairy toll road from Col de Tourmalet 4km W from La Mongie on D918. La Mongie is south of Bagnères-de-Bigorre by D935 and D918.

With Barèges (*see* page 122) on the other side of the Tourmalet it offers forty ski lifts and cable-cars. One problem with La Mongie is that most hotels shut in summer.

Taoulet, a village at 2340 metres above La Mongie, is a good mountain walking centre, with Garet waterfall and Lake Gréziolles nearby.

TOURIST INFORMATION Office de Tourisme
(62.91.94.15)
MARKET Monday

HOTEL
Pic d'Espade (62.91.92.27). Logis de France, at least opens part of summer – but not its restaurant. ROOMS D–E. MEALS A–B. Open 15 December–15 April; 1 July–30 August (except restaurant).

MONTALIVET
[Gironde]

My wife and I used to take our children to a campsite beside this enormous beach which we shared with the naturists from the big camp almost alongside. Now it is much more organized, especially the naturist centre. When this opened in the early 1950s it claimed to be the first naturist holiday village in the world. Called Centre Hélio Marin (or CHM to dedicated strippers), it is on the Gironde coast on D102 and it now covers 170 hectares of pine forest alongside the beach, has open-air theatre, cinema, disco, dance floor, restaurants and, of course, swimming-pool, sauna and shops – even a beauty parlour. You can hire a wooden bungalow, caravan or tent-pitch. It stays open all the year and takes over 2000 people (tel. 56.09.30.47).

MONT-DE-MARSAN
[LANDES]

A strange town, known for bullfights and horse-racing, the resin industry and military aircraft research. It is also the prefecture for Les Landes. The old town is interesting and attractive and is divided from the modern factories by the beautiful Jean-Rameau park with walks through lovely flowers and trees. The magnolias are gorgeous.

The old town centres around the meeting over weirs of the Midou and Douze rivers to become the Midouze. From the bridge crossing the Midou are lovely views of this meeting of the waters. There are pleasant old buildings here, especially the old mill buildings and an old semi-circular lavoir, still fit to be used by anyone whose washing-machine breaks down.

On the 'island' between the two rivers the old theatre in place de Gaulle has been turned into Les Halles, a covered market. There is another old covered market off place St Roch, south of the Midouze. Mont-de-Marsan is also an agricultural market centre, handling maize, fruit, chickens, geese, ducks, pâtés and *foie gras*. It regards itself as a gastronomic centre but Michelin seems not to have noticed.

In the arena they hold both *courses landaises*, in which cows are tormented into fury, and the bloodier Spanish *corridas*, in which bulls are killed.

The huge racecourse can stable 300 horses and stages many events, from show-jumping to pony-trotting, jumps and races on the flat, finishing with an international Grand Prix in September. Many fêtes are held, too.

There are several museums, from Musée Dubalen, devoted

to prehistory and natural history in a Romanesque chapel, to the Musée Despiau-Wiérick, devoted to the sculptures of Charles Despiau (1874–1946), including some fine female busts and nudes, and of Robert Wiérick (1882–1944), a local man who designed the equestrian statue to Maréchal Foch in the place Trocadero in Paris. There are other works by Bourdelle and Gauguin. This museum is in the fourteenth-century Donjon Lacataye, the tower which is all that remains of Gaston Phoebus's castle. There is a fine view from the top of the tower. (Museums shut Tuesday.)

Mont-de-Marsan was built up around a fort built by the Emperor Charlemagne when he was trying to hold down the Gascons after the massacre by the Basques of his army rearguard under Roland at the pass of Roncevalles. It was destroyed several times by the invading Norsemen, and rebuilt in 1141.

TOURIST INFORMATION 22 rue Victor Hugo
(58.75.38.67)
MARKETS Many; main market Tuesday
FESTIVALS Many; biggest is Fête de la Madeleine in
mid-July

HOTELS

Richelieu, 3 rue Wiérick (58.06.10.20). Traditional; town centre. Good regional cooking. ROOMS B–D. MEALS A–F. Shut 10–20 January; Saturday except high summer.

Siesta, 8 place Jean-Jaurès (58.06.44.44). Town centre; comfortable, nice atmosphere, regional cooking. ROOMS C–D. MEALS A–E.

Midou, 12 place Porte-Campet (58.75.24.26). Pretty, rustic dining-room with open fire. Real Landais dishes. ROOMS B–C. MEALS A–E. Shut Sunday evening mid-October – mid-June.

RESTAURANT

Clefs d'Argent, 333 ave Martyrs de la Libération (58.06.16.45). Excellent value. Fish fresh from Bordeaux. Good Landais cooking. MEALS A–E. Shut 15–30 October; 2–9 January; Monday.

MONTESQUIOU
[Gers]

Photogenic hill village overlooking the river Osse on D943 SW
of Auch, with prehistoric tumuli, Gallo-Roman villas and the
ruins of the Montesquiou family castle where Marshal Montesquiou, a son of d'Artagnan, was born in 1645. D'Artagnan's
mother was a Montesquiou.

MONTFORT-EN-CHALOSSE
[Landes]

26km W of St Sever on D32. The Chalosse region covers the
green, hilly southern Landes above the Adour river, very fertile,
with simple-looking old farming villages. The centre of Montfort is a pleasant maze of narrow lanes and stepped alleys. It has
one of the most important markets for ducks and geese in
France on alternate Wednesdays and a big fête on 30 August. It
was an English bastide and has many fine old Gascon houses.
The museum shows peasant life in earlier days.

MARKET *See* above

FESTIVAL *See* above

HOTEL

Touzins, 1½km E on D32, D2 (58.98.60.22). One of the best
Logis de France in SW France. ROOMS D–E. MEALS C–E. Shut
mid-January–mid-February; Monday except July, August.

MONTRÉAL
[Gers]

One of the earliest English bastides, built high on a spur of rock,
and although it was much destroyed in the Revolution it is still a
classic bastide built on the grid system with a central arcaded

square, a château built at the same time – Château Balarin and a twelfth-century Romanesque church, as well as a fifteenth-century Gothic church. It is on D15, 15km W of Condom.

On the edge of the town are remains of the Gallo-Roman villa of Séviac from the fourth century with a lovely mosaic floor, thermal baths and tiles and coins. The wine grown around here is mostly made into Armagnac, including the well-known Montréal Armagnac of Pierre Massartic.

TOURIST INFORMATION 1 place Hôtel-de-Ville (62.28.43.18)

RESTAURANTS
Gare, 3km S on D29 (62.29.43.37). Redundant railway station converted. Delicious regional cooking by young chef. MEALS A–C. Shut 5–31 January; Thursday evening, Friday low season.
Chez Simone (62.29.44.40). Local favourite. Simone Daubin is a true Gascon chef. MEALS A–D.

MORLAAS
[PYRÉNÉES-ATLANTIQUES]

Little town 12km from Pau, built after the Moors destroyed Lescar in 841, and which was capital of Béarn until the twelfth century. Its Romanesque church delights artists, especially for its beautifully carved and fascinating doorway with figures showing many biblical scenes from the Massacre of the Innocents and Flight into Egypt to the Day of Judgement. The apostles look splendidly happy.

HOTEL
Glisia (59.33.41.12). Simple. Good-value meals. ROOMS A–C. MEALS A–B. Shut two weeks in July. Restaurant shut Saturday lunch, Sunday.

MORLANNE, CHÂTEAU
[PYRÉNÉES-ATLANTIQUES]

21km NE of Lannemezan. Built in the fourteenth century by the murderous thug and writer Gaston Phoebus to defend his northern border of Béarn, it was restored around 1971, and refurnished with Louis XVI pieces and fine paintings of Canaletto (*View of Venice*), Fragonard and good lesser artists (open afternoons, March to October). The church with four-teenth century bell tower was also part of the defences.

MUGRON
[LANDES]

A very pretty village overlooking the Adour valley in the Chal-osse region (*see* St Sever, page 230). Lovely views from gardens by the Mairie. An important agricultural centre for the area. Once it was an Adour river port for exporting wines to Holland.

NAVARRENX
[PYRÉNÉES-ATLANTIQUES]

An old town on the right bank of the Gave d'Oloron river, with fine ramparts built by Henri d'Albret, King of Navarre, around 1540. Charles IX attacked it in his battle against the daughter of Henri – Jeanne de Navarre, the Protestant mother of the future Henri IV. La Porte-St-Antoine defending the river bridge is particularly well preserved. From February to August Nav-arrenx is a great fishing centre for trout and salmon. Championships are held in March, April and July. The D947 crosses the river here to join the D936 to Oloron-Ste-Marie (*see* page 200). The little road on the right bank D27 is much prettier.

TOURIST INFORMATION Mairie (59.66.10.22)
MARKET Tuesday

HOTEL

Commerce (59.66.50.16). Rooms B–C. Meals A–E. Shut January; 15–31 October; Sunday evening, Monday except July, August.

NOGARO
[Gers]

The Romans called it Nogarolium (*planté de noyers* – the place of walnuts). Then in 1060 St Austinde, Archbishop of Auch, founded the church, and the town grew as a stopping place for Compostela pilgrims. Two convents were built – St Vincent in 1250 and a Capucin convent in 1620 to minister to the pilgrims. What a splendid tourist business centred around the roads to Compostela!

Now Nogaro, on the N124 20km NE of Aire-sur-l'Adour, is known for Armagnac brandy, its championship cow- and bull-fights, a Grand Prix de Paul-Armagnac race in September for Formula 2 cars, Coupe de Pâques races at Easter for Formula 3, and spring motor-cycle races. Horse-races are held in August. Hang-gliding is popular too.

Its eleventh-century Romanseque church is still there, but only four arches of the old cloisters remain.

Market Saturday

HOTELS

Dubroca, 11 rue d'Artagnan (62.09.01.03). Simple. Good cooking by the patronne. Rooms A–C. Meals A–F. Shut 22 December–7 January; weekends low season.

Otelinn, 1km N on N124 (62.09.12.11). Swimming-pool, quiet, good cheap menu. Rooms D. Meals A–F.

Arènes, place Arènes (62.09.03.33). Gascon family cooking of regional dishes. Simple family atmosphere. Rooms B. Meals A–D.

OLORON-STE-MARIE

[Pyrénées-Atlantiques]

A pleasant touring centre SW of Pau where the Gave d'Aspe and Gave d'Ossau rivers meet at the foot of the Pyrenees to form the Gave d'Oloron. It started as a Roman hillside post, was destroyed by Barbarians but revived in the Middle Ages. Meanwhile a new town had grown up on the west side of the Aspe. Not until the middle of the nineteenth century were they amalgamated, which accounts for the town having two cathedrals. Now it is capital of Haut Béarn, with 15,000 people, makes

Carving in portal, Ste Marie

berets, shoes, sandals and lovely chocolate and holds many fairs
and festivals. The old buildings are in silver-grey stone, the new
are mostly white with grey roofs, so it looks much brighter in the
sun than in winter. New apartment blocks are spreading around
the perimeter. Up a steep hill is Saint-Croix cathedral, started in
1070, with the dome added 200 years later. The Protestants took
it over but it was returned to Catholicism in 1621. It is massive
and called *rude* (meaning crude) by the French architectural
experts because of its rather military-looking tower and
Moorish-Spanish dome. True, Ste-Marie is more harmonious
and attractive and has a much more interesting history. It was
built for Gaston IV, Viscount of Béarn (1090–1131) on his
return from the First Crusade, to celebrate his big part in the
taking of Jerusalem. Its original doorway is absolutely delightful. It is carved in Pyrenean marble. The vision of the Apoca-
lypse shows elders playing the viol and the rebec, instruments of
medieval troubadours. And there are scenes of everyday life
from cheese-making to smoking salmon.

Gaston IV sits on his horse and there are Moors in chains to
show his part also in the reconquest of Spain from the Moors.

In the centre, place Gambetta, there are old houses, some
arcaded. The little old quays of the rivers are delightful. There
is a fine old stone bridge over the Ossau. Fishing is very good,
with a lot of trout and salmon. This is a rich agricultural area,
with vines, orchards and cattle-raising.

TOURIST INFORMATION place de la Résistance
(59.39.98.00)
MARKETS Tuesday; Sunday morning
FESTIVALS 1 May – Cattle Fair; August – Biannual
International Folk Festival draws folk artistes from
many countries.

HOTELS

Le Béarn-Darroze, 4 place Mairie (59.39.00.99). Modernized. Res-
taurant in 'winter garden'. Nice view, good cooking. Excellent
Armagnac. ROOMS C–D. MEALS B–E. Open all year.
Relais Aspois, 5km S by N134 at Gurmençon (59.39.09.50).
Restful charming inn where shepherds stayed on their way to
and from Pyrenean pastures. Rooms now air-conditioned. Calm

and peaceful. ROOMS B–D. MEALS A–E. Shut 15–30 November.
Restaurant shut Monday lunch.

ORTHEZ
[PYRÉNÉES-ATLANTIQUES]

The Viscounts of Béarn acquired Orthez in the twelfth century
and it became their capital, and the notorious Gaston Phoebus
(*see* Pau, page 85) held a brilliant Court there in the fourteenth
century, according to the great chronicler Froissart. When the
Counts of Foix took over, the capital moved eastwards 43km to
Pau. Now Orthez is a large market town known for pigs, calves,
chickens, *foie gras* and especially Bayonne hams, which are called
'Bayonne' only because the salt used for curing comes from
there. The furniture industry has come to Orthez too.

Orthez suffered greatly in the Wars of Religion. Jeanne
d'Albret, the Protestant Queen of Navarre and mother of Henri
IV, had a house there but the Catholics took the town. The
Protestant General Montgomery turned them out and damaged
the town terribly in the process. Comte Gabriel de Montgomery
was originally a Catholic and commanded Henri II of France's
Royal Scottish Guard. In those days, of course, the Scots were on
the French side against the English. It was he who accidentally
killed Henri II in a tournament and he had to flee to London to
avoid the wrath of Catherine de' Medici, Henri's wife. In England he became a Protestant and returned to France to lead
Protestant armies. He was finally forced to surrender a castle in
Normandy when down to a handful of starving men. Catherine
promised him safe conduct but directly he was in her hands she
had him beheaded in Paris.

After Montgomery took Orthez there was an outbreak of
plague in the town, causing more suffering.

In the Napoleonic Wars Wellington approached the town in
February 1814, after chasing Soult's French forces away from
Bayonne.

Soult had 30,000 men in the hills to the north and west.
Wellington attacked strongly and the French were beaten and

driven back towards Toulouse. Général Foy, one of the best French commanders, known as '*héros citoyen*' (citizen hero) was wounded for the fortieth time so deserves the memorial to him on the spot where it happened, 3½km N of the town.

After all these troubles, it is surprising that Orthez still has many old houses and mansions around rue de Bourg-Vieux, including the house of Jeanne d'Albret. The thirteenth-century Pont Vieux in the town centre is a superb hump-backed bridge with four fine arches and a defence tower in its centre. Tour Moncade to the north of the town remains from the castle of 1242 where Gaston Phoebus held his feasts and entertainments.

Jean Froissart, at the castle in 1388, gave a wonderful description of a dinner party there, starting at midnight when Phoebus left his chamber with twelve servants bearing torches in front of him.

On the artificial lake Orthez Biron, rich in fish, you can sail, windsurf, canoe or row.

TOURIST INFORMATION 1 rue Jacobins (59.69.02.75)
MARKET Tuesday (especially ham)
FESTIVALS March – Carnival; last weekend in July –
major fête

HOTEL
Reine Jeanne, 44 rue Bourg-Vieux (59.67.00.76). In old part of town. Old house. English pub! ROOMS D. MEALS A–C. Shut 7–14 February.

RESTAURANT
Auberge St-Loup, 20 rue Pont-Vieux (59.69.15.40). In restored ancient hospice. Good value. MEALS C–F. Shut Sunday lunch (except summer).

OSSÈS
[PYRÉNÉES-ATLANTIQUES]

Quiet little village in Nive valley 10km from the Irouléguy vineyards and 12km N from St Jean-Pied-de-Port by D918, then D8.

HOTEL

Mendi-Alde, place Église (59.37.71.78). Old, traditional Basque house; comfortable Logis. Good hideout in lovely country. Varied, high-quality meals. ROOMS B–C. MEALS A–D. Shut mid-November–mid-December; Monday in winter.

PARENTIS-EN-BORN
[LANDES]

Oil has spoiled Parentis. Oil derricks spread across much of the south end of Étang de Biscarrosse et Parentis (*see* Biscarrosse, page 135) and across the country around the little town, and although some effort has been made to hide them behind pines, they have ruined the area for holiday-makers. Otherwise it is a pleasant place. There is a museum about Landes oil production (open early April to end October).

PAU
[*See* Major Towns, page 85]

PAUILLAC
[GIRONDE]

Not only centre of the wine district which includes Château Lafite, Château Latour and Mouton Rothschild but an oil-refining town and a port on the Gironde for oil tankers, boats carrying chemicals, and passenger boats. It is on quite the most attractive stretch of D2 through the Médoc. Opposite in the wide river is Île Philippe. Pauillac is one of the oldest towns in the Médoc and it even has a beach and little harbour for fishing boats, as well as a pleasure-boat marina. It is a fishing and sailing centre for the people of Bordeaux. There is a Maison du Vin (a wine information bureau) by the quayside which is extremely helpful, telling you which vineyards you can visit and offering maps. It is signposted. (La Verrerie, quai Léon Perrier, tel. 56.59.03.08.)

MARKET Tuesday, Saturday morning
FESTIVALS Whitsun – Fête with sailing regattas;
September – Wine Festival

HOTELS

Château Cordeillan Bages (56.59.24.24). Very attractive. Not well known. Delicious meals. ROOMS G. MEALS D–F. Shut January.
France et Angleterre (56.59.02.31). Old favourite. Good value. ROOMS E–F. MEALS A–F. Shut 22 December–2 January.

PENON
[LANDES]

Brand-new little beach resort just north of Hossegor where a big international surfing championship is held. Mostly self-catering accommodation of flats or villas by the sea, cabins and bungalows in the forest. 2km inland is Étang Blanc, an attractive patch of water. A small road D189 turns off D652 and skirts the lake with pretty views.

PEYREHORADE
[LANDES]

Famous for fish – salmon, pike and pibales from its rivers Pau and Oloron which join to form Gaves Réunis. It holds fishing competitions as well as motorbike and side-car rallies. It is on the N117 between Bayonne and Orthez and over the bridge are Hastingues (*see* page 169) and Abbaye d'Arthous. Smaller roads south and south-west are very attractive. Once, *gabares* (flat-bottomed poled boats) carried merchandise along the rivers and on to the Adour. Now there are pleasure boats at the little quayside.

At the foot of the hill crowned by the keep of the ruined Château d'Apremont is the old village around the sixteenth-century Château Montréal built by the Viscounts of Orthez. This large château is flanked by four round towers. The entrance gates are unusual.

The road to Bayonne D936 rises into the Basque hills with splendid views.

TOURIST INFORMATION 1 place Sablot (58.73.00.52)
MARKET Wednesday

HOTELS

Central, 175 place Aristide-Briand (58.73.03.22). Comfortable for its price. Good country cooking lightened with modern touches. Menus offer cheap and honest meals to gastronomic. ROOMS E. MEALS B–G. Shut 12–18 November; mid-February–mid-March; Sunday evening, Monday except July, August.
Mimi, rue Nauton-Truquez (58.73.00.06). Simple, popular locally. ROOMS A–D. MEALS A–C. Shut Friday except restaurant.

PEYRESOURDE-BALESTAS
[HAUTES-PYRÉNÉES]

Twin ski resorts at around 1600 metres, south of Arreau (*see* page 117). Col de Peyresourde just N takes you on the road to Bagnères-de-Luchon and the major resort of Superbagnères.

PILAT-PLAGE
[*See* Arcachon, page 113 and Pyla-sur-Mer, page 209]

PISSOS
[LANDES]

Although it has only about 800 inhabitants, Pissos has many visitors passing through the Landes Regional Park because of its Maison des Artisans, an exhibition and shop of Landes products from furniture to gastronomic specialities. It is at the meeting of N134 and D43 where N134 crosses Grande Leyre river E of Parentis. Pissos has three windmills and a Romanesque twelfth-century church, and watersports on the Eyre and Leyre rivers.

PLAISANCE
[GERS]

A French bastide which is now a centre for Côtes de St Mont VDQS wines, both red and white, which are worth trying in local restaurants of Gers and eastern Landes. The French built the town in 1322 but twenty-three years later the Black Prince knocked some of it down. It is where D3 meets D946 SE of Aire-sur-l'Adour, on the river Arros. The little winding D37 road NE climbs into some beautiful hill scenery. Just south is another bastide, Beaumarchés, with a notable sixteenth-century bell tower.

Surprisingly, little Plaisance has a Michelin-starred restaurant – Ripa Alta, which was the town's Roman name.

TOURIST INFORMATION 4 rue Ste Quitterie
(62.69.44.60).

MARKETS Plaisance: Thursday. Beaumarchés: Monday
morning

HOTELS
Ripa Alta, 3 place Église, Plaisance (62.69.30.43). In a fourteenth-century house; comfortable rooms. Maurice Coscuella is a very skilled chef who really does follow the market and seasons to produce his own dishes. Try local wine. ROOMS B–E. MEALS B–G. Shut early November–early December; Monday lunch in winter.

D'Artagnan, 4 rue de la Porte, Plaisance (62.69.30.37). Simple, comfortable rooms. Wonderful value, cheap meals. ROOMS C–D. MEALS A–C. Shut Saturday.

POMAREZ
[LANDES]

A renowned centre for *courses landaises*, the 'cow-fights' where a quadrilla of four young men called *sauteurs* (leapers) get in the ring with deliberately infuriated cows and show off their gymnastic abilities in avoiding being gored. Big festivals are held on Whit Monday, the second Sunday after Whitsun, and the week of 15 August.

Pomarez is 11km due S of Montfort-en-Chalosse (*see* page 196) on D7 road towards Orthez.

HOTEL
Auberge du Chalet, route de Dax (58.89.82.16). ROOMS A–B. MEALS A–C.

RESTAURANT
Pecotche (58.89.30.37). Good family meals at bargain prices. MEALS A–C.

PORT DE LANNE
[LANDES]

Pretty little port on the Adour river and N117, 30km NE of Bayonne. Known for salmon and shad, and for breeding racehorses. Boats will take you upriver to Saubusse and Dax (*see* page 155).

HOTEL
Vieille Auberge, place l'Église (58.89.16.29). Attractive early-eighteenth-century inn with its old décor and furniture. Good

salmon and confit. Garden, swimming-pool. Seasonal. ROOMS D–F. MEALS C–F. Open early June–end September.

PRÉCHACQ-LES-BAINS
[LANDES]

Spa on the left bank of the Adour river specializing, like Dax, in the treatment of rheumatism and respiratory problems. It has warm springs rich in calcium sulphate coming out at 63°F and a cold sulphurous spring at 18°F – also mud baths.

TOURIST INFORMATION Syndicat (58.57.21.72)

HOTEL
Les Sources (58.57.21.21). In the thermal establishment. Seasonal. ROOMS B–D. MEALS A–C. Shut 1 November–1 April.

PYLA-SUR-MER
[GIRONDE]

Seaside resort 4km S of Arcachon near to the massive sand dune of Pyla (*see* Arcachon, page 113). Pyla is still growing. It has some high-grade villas in the woods behind. Both Pyla and its neighbour Pilat-Plage are still regarded as high-class little resorts.

TOURIST INFORMATION Town Hall, rond-point du Figuier (56.22.53.83)

HOTELS
Pyla
La Guitoune, 95 boul. Océan (56.22.70.10). Very popular for its setting and excellent fish. Pricey. ROOMS D–G. MEALS F. Open all year.
Beau Rivage, 16 boul. Ocean (56.54.01.82). Large hotel near beach. ROOMS D–G. MEALS C–D. Hotel shut 1 December–12 March. Restaurant shut for lunch Monday, Tuesday, Wednesday in season; Monday evening, Tuesday low season.

Pilat-Plage
Corniche, 46 ave Louise Gaume (56.22.72.11). Small holiday hotel with fine views over Bassin d'Arcachon. Run by well-known family. ROOMS D–G. MEALS B–C. Open late March–late October. Restaurant closed Wednesday except July, August.

RAUZAN
[GIRONDE]

If you take D670 south from St Émilion the road becomes very attractive for a few miles after crossing the Dordogne river. Off to the right is the village of Rauzan which is an important centre in Entre-Deux-Mers. Dominating the valley are the ruins of a château which still looks romantic, though it was built as a castle for defence and lacks the upper storey of its round keep which was once 30 metres high. It was built by one of Edward I of England's commanders in the early fourteenth century but later given by Henry VI in 1437 to Bernard Angevin.

Turn left further down D670 and you reach the ruined abbey of Blasimon, dedicated to St Maurice. The village was a bastide. The twelfth- to thirteenth-century abbey church stands in an attractive valley. It was damaged in the Revolution but attractive decoration survived – the beautiful façade with big bell-gable and a few arcades of the abbey cloisters.

RESTAURANT

Gentilhommière, Rauzan (57.84.13.42). MEALS C–F. Shut 15–30 November; Monday.

RÉOLE, LA
[GIRONDE]

There are some delightful little towns and villages in Entre-Deux-Mers country and among the vineyards across the two rivers. La Réole is one of the most attractive of all. It is on N113 on a balcony overlooking the Garonne river upstream from St Macaire and only 19km from Marmande.

The Romans spotted its strategic value. The Benedictines built an abbey in Charlemagne's reign. The English built a castle there, right on the border of English Gascony and French territory. And the Protestants held it in the Wars of Religion. Through history it was able to ward off many attacks. Now it is a busy but peaceful agricultural town, still with its old houses and attractive, narrow, winding streets.

The twelfth-century Benedictine abbey church of St Pierre was vandalized by the Protestants, restored and somewhat altered in the sixteenth century. It contains good paintings, including *Marriage of the Virgin* by Jean de Batse. The early eighteenth-century monastery buildings, now used as public offices, are a delight. Local craftsmen made the ironwork, such as the elegant wrought-iron cloister gate of 1756. Alas, the castle built by Richard Coeur de Lion was demolished in 1629. You can, however, see traces of old town walls. The synagogue in rue Blandin dates from the twelfth to thirteenth centuries. But the gem is the twelfth-century Romanesque town hall, Maison Communale, one of very few civil buildings which still remain from that time. The ground floor was Les Halles, the market, upstairs was Salle des Échevins (Aldermen's Hall).

There are good views looking south across the river to the Bazas and Les Landes, a lovely view of La Réole across the river. Good river-fishing.

TOURIST INFORMATION 1 place Libération (high season
– 56.61.13.55)
MARKETS Wednesday, Saturday

HOTEL

Du Centre, 42 rue Armand-Caduc (56.61.02.64). Old favourite. Some rooms have good views. Good-value meals. ROOMS B–C. MEALS A–D.

RIONS
[Gironde]

You can enter this little fortified town on the Garonne by its fourteenth-century gateway, Porte du Lhyan. It is in excellent condition. So are sections of the ramparts and a square corner-tower. It is 4km downstream from Cadillac and on the stretch of D10 which is attractive all the way to Bordeaux.

RISCLE
[Gers]

A jolly village on the river Adour, SE of Aire-sur-l'Adour, with lots of fairs and fêtes in summer, cow- and bullfights, fishing contests and watersports.

MARKET Friday
FESTIVALS Easter Monday – Fête des Fleurs; second Sunday in August – Fair of local produce

HOTEL
Paix (62.69.70.14). Simple. ROOMS A–B. MEALS A–D. Shut 27 August–6 September; 1 October–1 November; Monday except July, August.

ROQUEFORT
[Landes]

On D932 where it meets D626 NE of Mont-de-Marsan. It has a historic fortified church founded by Benedictines and taken over by an order of Hospitaliers, Antonins, as a commanderie.

Roquefort was the capital of Pays de Marsan. In 1371 John of Gaunt, Duke of Lancaster, fourth son of Edward III of England, married here Constance, daughter of Pedro the Cruel of Castile, and later claimed the Castile crown, but could not wrest it from a rival. So later he married off his daughter

Catherine to the future King of Castile. When his brother Richard became King of England, John became Duke of Aquitaine. His wedding at Roquefort was a double one. His brother Edmund of York married another daughter of Pedro.

Pedro got the title 'Cruel' for murdering a brother. Another of his brothers had already betrayed him and had him taken prisoner but he escaped and got back his throne. At one stage in the brothers' war, the Black Prince marched into Spain and helped Pedro to defeat the great French commander du Guesclin. But Pedro broke his promises so the Prince marched back to Aquitaine and Pedro finally lost.

HOTEL

Colombier (58.45.50.57). Logis de France. ROOMS A–C. MEALS A–C.

ROQUETAILLADE, CHÂTEAU DE
[GIRONDE]

Imposing feudal château 7km S of Langon built in 1306 by Cardinal de la Mothe, nephew of Pope Clément V, the man who suppressed the Knights Templars, accusing them of murder, immorality, corruption and rape, and moved the Papacy to Avignon in 1308. It formed a double castle with a twelfth-century fort, both enclosed in the same walls. It has six formidable round towers and a square crenellated keep, but is very graceful and looks very well surrounded by woods, vineyards and fields. Like others, it was perhaps over-restored last century by Viollet-le-Duc, the architect responsible for rebuilding the medieval city of Carcassonne and restoring Notre-Dame in Paris.

He was responsible for the vaulted rooms, huge monumental fireplaces and restored frescos. The delightful nineteenth-century kitchen has gleaming copper, iron ranges and stone sinks. (Visits – mornings July, August; afternoons May, June, September; Sundays and holidays, including some school holidays, in February, March, April, October, November.)

SABRES
[LANDES]

Typically Landais. A village in the Landes de Gascogne natural park in the huge maritime-pine plantations which hide hamlets and houses from the main roads. The village itself has a medieval church altered over centuries, but with a beautiful Renaissance doorway and tall arcaded bell tower. But Sabres has become famous now as the only gateway to Marquèze in the Leyre valley, and its Ecomusée which shows you superbly the old traditions and life of Les Landes. From Sabres a little old train takes you along a stretch of line once disused to an 'airial' – a clearing in the forest called Marquèze which cannot be reached any other way. A typical old Landes hamlet has been reconstructed from the superb nineteenth-century house which was here and other buildings which were dismantled and removed here from other abandoned 'airials'. A water-mill with threshing floor is nearby.

The train runs approximately every forty minutes, every day from June to mid-September, on Saturday afternoon and Sunday from end of March to May and mid-September to end of October. No trains run early November to March.

MARKET Sunday

HOTEL
Auberge des Pins, route de la Piscine (58.07.50.47). Big Landaise inn hidden among pines in garden. Comfortable. Regional cooking. ROOMS B–E. MEALS A–F. Shut 2–16 January; 15–30 November; Sunday evening, Monday low season.

ST CLAR
[GERS]

A seductive well-preserved and unusual old hilltop bastide east of Lectoure, with two arcaded central squares, showing how important it was as a market. It still is – especially for garlic. It is called the Garlic Capital of Gers, and has the second largest garlic market in France. In one square, place de la Mairie, is a superb wooden covered market of the thirteenth century, and a nice stone town hall.

St Clar is also an important centre for strawberries, melons, chickens, ducks and sunflowers for sunflower oil. The French call these *tournesol* because the flowers turn towards the sun. St Clar has some lovely old houses, some half-timbered and some in stone.

ST ÉMILION
[GIRONDE]

Even a total abstainer would find this hilltop walled wine town delicious. Before the summer crowds found it and when trees had not yet obscured much of the view from the terrace of the Hostellerie de Plaisance, and as you drank your wine you could see across the crowded russet rooftops to the hills beyond. I was offered an old stone two-up, two-down house for £600. Its cellar alone would be worth more than ten times that now. The Plaisance is much posher now and caters a lot for Americans. But if you can find a place to park near the main church, Église Collégiale, or have worked up a thirst by walking up that steep and demanding hill, the magic of St Émilion is still there.

Round the corner from the Plaisance is the ancient bell tower in a delightful little square called place du Clocher. Here is the cave of the Union des Producteurs de St Émilion where you can taste good wine and buy it. (*See* Vineyards, page 55.)

Next to the church are the beautifully preserved fourteenth-century Collégial cloisters. Down a steep cobbled street is the market square with an old acacia tree planted in 1848 and the little eighteenth-century house turned into a restaurant, Logis de Cadène, where I eat now. Facing into the square is the gaunt monolithic church, carved out of rock by Benedictine monks during the ninth to twelfth centuries by joining together existing caves. Its bell tower looks like the tower of a vanished church. It was stripped of altar, tombs and bones during the Revolution and turned into a gunpowder store, ruining the frescos, of which little remains. It is a sombre place, like a deserted underground ballroom, with two rows of massive rectangular rock pillars and a vaulted roof. Beside it is the thirteenth-century Chapelle de la Trinité, Gothic, with an odd polygonal apse, and also Ermitage de St Émilion, the dark underground cell and oratory of the Saint, and catacombs used for burial.

A steep lane leads to Tour du Roi, the keep of a castle built for Henry III of England in the thirteenth century. From the top of the tower is a fine view of the town and Dordogne valley. From the foot is made the annual proclamation of the Vendange, the wine harvest – the great moment of the year.

St Émilion's Jurade was founded in 1199 by King John of England. Its members control the quality of wine and classify it as Premier Grand Cru, Grand Cru classé, Grand Cru and AOC St Émilion.

TOURIST INFORMATION place Créneaux (57.24.72.03)
MARKET Sunday morning
FESTIVALS May – Fête Chapitre des Vignerons de la
Montagne; June – Fête de la Jurade; September – Fête
des Vendanges

HOTELS

Plaisance, place Clocher (57.24.72.32). Very attractive (*see* text). Bedrooms modernized. Excellent cooking. ROOMS F–G. MEALS C–G. Shut 2–31 January.

Remparts, rue Guadet (57.24.70.43). Totally renovated. No restaurant. ROOMS E–F. Shut 20 December–8 February.

Commanderie, rue Cordeliers (57.24.70.19). Old house, totally renovated. Pleasant cheaper menu. ROOMS C–E. MEALS C–G. Shut December, January. Restaurant shut Tuesday.

RESTAURANTS

La Cadène, place Marché (57.24.71.40). See page 53. Regional family cooking. Super wines from own vineyards (Château de Clotte). MEALS C–F. Shut 25 June–2 July; 3–11 September; evenings October–June; Sunday evening July–September.

Francis Goullée, rue Guadet (57.24.70.49). Good value. MEALS
C–F. Shut August; Monday low season; Sunday evening.

ST ÉTIENNE-DE-BAÏGORRY
[PYRÉNÉES-ATLANTIQUES]

I came upon this delightful Basque village 5km from the Spanish border when I was 'jeeping' round the Pyrenees in the early
1950s researching magazine articles about smuggling. I wanted
lunch. Over the little hump-backed bridge which crosses the
river Nive des Aldudes, jumping with trout, was a little hotel
called Le Trinquet which had been run by the Arcé family for
four generations. On the tree-shaded terrace I had a superb
meal of local Basque specialities, including trout from the river,
and a lot of red wine. Young Émile Arcé was in the kitchen.
There was a lively wedding feast across the terrace. They kept
sending me across red wine; then they asked me to join them.
Around 11 p.m. the bride and groom went to bed. Around
1 a.m. I went to bed. When I left next day at noon the party was
still going on.

I go back regularly. It is one of my favourite hotels in
France. The hotel is now called l'Arcé, it has a Michelin star and
young Pascal Arcé (fifth generation) has joined his father Émile
in the kitchen. But I was still stopped nearby by a customs patrol
recently to see if I was smuggling anything from Spain. The way
into Spain is by Col d'Ispéguy, which has a long smuggling
history. St Jean-Pied-de-Port is 11km away.

St Étienne has a little row of modern shops now, but its old
houses are pure Basque, some with fine front doors and lintel
carvings. The church, altered a little in the eighteenth century,
still has the typically-Basque three-storey galleries inside, and
three altars richly gilded.

Above the more modern bridge, a hump-backed medieval
bridge draped in ivy leads to Château d'Echau, home of a
well-known Basque family. In the eighteenth century the
Vicomte d'Echau and the villagers fell out over the ownership of

a big forge which produced guns and shot for the privateers of St Jean-de-Luz. Finally they agreed to share it fifty-fifty.

Just by the château is a group of houses which belonged to the 'untouchables', the Cagots, who are believed to have been descended from lepers left behind from pilgrimages to Compostela. These unhappy people had to live separately from the community. They could not appear in public places, carry arms, sit with other people in church or, on pain of death, marry or have sexual relations outside their caste. They wore a goose foot as a distinguishing mark. They could own land but whatever food they produced they had to eat themselves and could not sell. So they became craftsmen – carpenters, weavers, masons, iron workers. Their separation from the rest of the community was not broken down until the nineteenth century.

St Étienne (or simply 'Baïgorry' as they call it locally) is the centre for Irouléguy wine, with a Co-operative cave in the village. (Tastings – must phone first; tel. 59.37.41.33.) Whites are rare; orangey-coloured rosés are popular with tourists to the Basque region, and reds are drunk by locals. The reds must contain at least 50 per cent Tannat grapes, the rest being made of a local grape called Fer, Cabernet Sauvignon and Cabernet Franc. The wine is ruby coloured, full of fruit, has a spicy taste but is not so heavy as Madiran. It goes well with *piperade*.

TOURIST INFORMATION place l'Église (59.37.47.28)
FESTIVAL mid-August – Noce Basque (Fête)

HOTELS

Arcé (59.37.40.14). *See* text. New wing with very comfortable rooms. Enclosed sun-lounge style dining room by river. Swimming-pool added. Wonderful cooking with true Basque dishes (*gabure, piperade*). ROOMS F–G. MEALS C–F. Open mid-March–mid-November.

Juantorena (59.37.40.78). Entirely renovated. Village centre. Patron does the cooking. ROOMS B–C. MEALS A–D. Open all year.

ST JEAN-DE-LUZ
[Pyrénées-Atlantiques]

A busy but charming fishing port which is the heart of the French Basque country. It was a whaling port from the eleventh century when there were still whales in the Bay of Biscay and became the world's greatest whaling port under the English until they left in the fifteenth century. Whales had been driven from neighbouring waters and the Luzians pursued them as far as Spitzbergen. They claim that they taught the Norwegians how to catch whales! As whales became scarcer, they turned to cod, which they fished as far away as the banks off Newfoundland.

In the seventeenth century they found a more rewarding way of using their seafaring skills. They took to piracy so enthusiastically that the English Government called St Jean 'this veritable nest of vipers'.

Now it is mostly a tuna-fishing port, with anchovy boats taking over in winter. Tourism is just as important. With its neighbour Ciboure (*see* page 149) it is a very popular and modern resort, but still has old narrow streets and tall elegant Basque houses. Its fine curving beach attracts families and its harbour has made it a yachting centre.

The great open space opposite the harbour is called place Louis XIV in honour of the royal wedding of 9 June 1660. As part of the Treaty of the Pyrenees of 1659 and to try to ensure that the resulting peace between France and Spain would continue, Mazarin, successor to Richelieu as France's powerful first minister, arranged for young Louis XIV of France to marry the Spanish princess, the Infanta Marie-Thérèse. Louis was against it. He was in love with Mazarin's niece Marie Mancini. But he was told to get on with it and do his duty to France. The wedding was a sumptuous party. The bride stayed with the Queen Mother, Anne of Austria, at a house on the harbourside since called La Maison de l'Infante. The whole cortège moved off from there, walking on carpets laid along the streets. Cardinal Mazarin, sumptuously dressed, led the procession, followed by Louis in black with white lace, then the Princess in silver with a violet cloak and wearing a gold crown. The Queen Mother and all the court followed.

They walked to the thirteenth-century church of St Jean-Baptiste where the service took three hours. Afterwards, the door by which the young royal couple had entered the church was bricked up so that it would not be polluted by lesser mortals. They all went back to the Maison de l'Infante where the King and Cardinal threw gold souvenir medals into the crowd. Then the whole court followed the couple to the house where Louis had been staying, belonging to the widow of a shipowner named Lohobiague. They all had dinner there, then the couple were put to bed by the Queen Mother.

Louis must have found the girl very dull, judging by the number of mistresses he had later, although he was also obviously somewhat highly sexed. While waiting for a mistress to finish her toilette, he would bed her lady-in-waiting!

You can see the outside of Maison de l'Infante and you can visit the Lohobiague mansion, now called Maison Louis XIV. It is a superb arcaded château, with four square turrets.

The old Barre quarter where these houses stand is on the strip of land which almost encloses the harbour. Much of it is now a shopping and leisure pedestrian area. Napoleon stayed at No. 2 rue Mazarin, which in 1813–14 Wellington took over when he spent the winter in St Jean-de-Luz.

St Jean has a very full programme of fêtes, carnivals and other lively events throughout the summer. Tourism has brought a lot of large apartment blocks built behind the beach.

TOURIST INFORMATION 1 place Mar-Foch
(59.26.03.16)
MARKET Tuesday, Friday
FESTIVALS end June – St Jean Fête, a great old
traditional festival; July – Tuna Festival; early
September – Ttoro Festival (*ttoro* is a fish, tomato, onion
and garlic stew); September – Ravel Music Festival;
24 December – Noël Basquais in St Jean church.

HOTELS

Grand, 43 boul. Thiers (59.26.12.32). Truly fin-de-siècle 'grand', recently reopened after total renovation. Direct access to beach.

Expensive. Classical Basque cuisine. ROOMS G. MEALS E–G.
Shut 3 January–3 February; restaurant shut Sunday evening;
Monday low season.

Hôtel et Motel Basque, 2km N by boul. Thiers (59.26.04.24).
Luxury modern complex in its own grounds facing sea. Hotel
plus self-catering. ROOMS F–G. MEALS D–F.

La Fayette, 20 rue République (59.26.17.74). Quiet Logis of
character in pedestrian street. Good bourgeoise cuisine in *Kayola*
restaurant at sensible prices. ROOMS D–E. MEALS C–F.

RESTAURANTS

Kaïku, 17 rue République (59.26.13.20). Considered the best in
St Jean. Mostly straightforward dishes; lovely fish. In a 1580
house. MEALS E–G. Shut mid-November–20 December; Monday lunch in summer; Wednesday rest of year.

Vieille Auberge, 22 rue Tourasse (59.26.19.61). Best value. Excellent Basque dishes, generous portions. Highly praised for value
by my *Complete Travellers' France* readers. In little old street.
Beamed rustic room. MEALS A–C. Shut mid-November–mid-
March; Tuesday evening, Wednesday except July, August.

ST JEAN-PIED-DE-PORT
[PYRÉNÉES-ATLANTIQUES]

Since at least the twelfth century, St Jean-Pied-de-Port (meaning
St John at the foot of the Pass) has been catering for tourists, and
making a good living from them. It has not always had its
present reputation for hospitality. The Pass to which its name
refers is Roncesvalles, which was the main route into Spain for
the pilgrims on their way to the tomb of St James in Compostela
at Santiago.

Around 1150 a monk from the great teaching abbey of
Cluny wrote a guide for pilgrims, telling them of places of
interest on their various routes, where they could find hospices
for food and lodging, and a guide to the language and customs
of local people. The Cluny monks must have had a bad time in
St Jean-Pied-de-Port, for he warned pilgrims against muggers.

St Jean-Pied-de-Port

Locals were likely to attack pilgrims with sticks, demanding money; if the pilgrims refused, they would knock them down and take their money anyway. He described the people of St Jean as swarthy, ugly, wicked, debauched, corrupt, drunken, violent, cruel, lacking all good will and full of vice. Perhaps this was a hangover from Charlemagne's disastrous campaign into Spain and the slaughtering of the rearguard of his army and of his best-known warrior Roland in the Roncesvalles Pass in 778. On one of his expeditions to spread Christianity at the point of the sword, Charlemagne invaded Spain, took Pamplona but failed to budge the Moors from Saragossa. During his retreat through the Pass, the local Basques attacked his rearguard by throwing boulders and trees on them when they were trapped in the narrow valley and encumbered with a baggage train which, no doubt, the Basques were after. Roland, Warden of the Brittany Marches, was killed.

The most popular of the medieval *gestes* (romantic ballads) told the story quite differently. In the Song of Roland the attacking Basques became 300,000 Moors! Roland fought heroically and when all was lost tried to break his famous sword on a stone, but the sword split the stone wide open. Then he tried to recall Charlemagne with great blasts on a horn but the strain broke a vein in his neck and killed him. Charlemagne, over thirty miles away, heard the call and returned to avenge his hero. The French always preferred the romantic legend to the facts. When the Norman soldiers were hard pressed at the Battle of Hastings, they chanted the Song of Roland to rally their courage.

The hospice run by the monks for the pilgrims at St Jean-Pied-de-Port was very important because walking over the pass in those days took considerably more energy than pressing an accelerator pedal, and many of the faithful were old, infirm or just worn out after walking for weeks. Some had come half-way across Europe. They usually climbed to Roncesvalles by what is now the long-distance footpath GR65, parallel to the D933, to join the old Roman road. There was a monastery for rest and refreshment at the top of the Pass on Col d'Ibaneta.

St Jean was already very busy when I first knew it in the 1950s. Now it can be very crowded indeed around midday in summer, and particularly around the stalls and souvenir shops from place Floquet to place de Gaulle across the Pont Neuf. The cafés and restaurants near to Porte de France are busy most of the day and evening. But it is an interesting and attractive town and has a great festive atmosphere in summer, with regional singers and dancers seemingly giving shows most days and pelota matches leading to a very festive midsummer championship.

The attractive river Nive cuts the town in two, with a nice view from the Vieux-Pont. St Jean is very well preserved for a medieval town and keeps much of its fortifications. Within fifteenth-century ramparts the old town climbs steeply between red-brick sixteenth- to seventeenth-century houses to the great citadelle which truly dominates the countryside. Below is the medieval hospital now containing a library and a museum of pelota (open July, August only).

The 'new town' is within another wall of ramparts of the seventeenth century. Down there is the great court and wall of the fronton where the pelota matches are played.

St Jean is a popular fishing centre, a winter-holiday resort and a very good centre for exploring the mountain scenery. Its hotels and restaurants have plenty of variety. At Les Pyrénées Hotel, Firmin Arrambide proves just how good Basque cooking can be at its best.

Whichever direction you drive, you will find lovely scenery, but especially if you head SE to the Iraty Forest on the D18. If you don't mind some rather hairy driving, take the left turn on to D19 to Col Bagargui. Very rewarding.

TOURIST INFORMATION place de Gaulle (59.37.03.57)

HOTELS

Pyrénées, 19 place de Gaulle (59.37.01.01). See text. Well worth its prices for superb cooking and pleasant surroundings. ROOMS G. MEALS E–G. Shut 20 November–21 December; 5–27 January; Monday evening, Tuesday in winter.
Etche Ona, place Floquet (59.37.01.14). Excellent value. Very Basque. ROOMS C. MEALS B–E. Shut 5 November–mid-December; Friday except in school holidays.

RESTAURANT

Arbillaga, 19 place de Gaulle (59.37.06.44). Dedicated to Basque cooking. MEALS A–F. Shut Wednesday.

ST LARY-SOULAN
[HAUTES-PYRÉNÉES]

Ski resort and summer mountaineering centre on D929, 12km S of Arreau. Developed in the 1950s, it has become popular since 1976 when the Bielsa Tunnel was opened into Spain about 20km SW. The ski slopes are reached by cable-car to Pla d'Adet

(1680 metres), or by a little mountain road to Espiaube (1600 metres) and La Cabane (1632 metres). A gondola runs S from Pla d'Adet to Soum de Matte (2377 metres).

SW of St Lary, the D929 turns right in a beautifully dramatic drive to Lac d'Orédon, in the spectacular great Massif de Néouvielle, part of the Parc National des Pyrénées. There is a series of lovely valleys to explore from D929 by car or by fairly athletic walking.

Maison du Parc in St Lary offers an audio-visual show on the fauna of the Pyrenees (daily during school terms or by request to Field Director; tel. 62.39.40.91).

St Lary is only 69km from Tarbes and 44km from Bagnères-de-Luchon in Haute Garonne, and is a good centre for mountain exploration.

TOURIST INFORMATION rue Principale (62.39.50.81)
MARKET Saturday

HOTELS

Cristal Parc, route Pla d'Adet (62.99.50.00). Next to a thermal spa. Comfortable modern rooms. ROOMS E–G. MEALS B–G. Shut mid-October–mid-December; mid-April–mid-May.
Terrasse Fleurie (62.39.40.26). Typical mountain hotel. Cheap. ROOMS C–D. MEALS A–C. Open mid-June–30 September; mid-December–mid-April.

ST MACAIRE
[GIRONDE]

This wine town, on a rock alongside the Garonne river upstream from Cadillac, has been described as 'an island in time and space'. Nearby the N113 crosses the river to Langon but just misses the old town, which seems never to have joined the modern world. The new town along N113 is very recent and like a separate place.

Across the river is Sauternes country – a different wine and different world (*see* Wine, page 49). You can see that world through the fortified gates of St Macaire's medieval defences.

The old bastide itself looks inwards to its narrow streets, medieval houses and arcaded square. Only its fine ancient church of Saint-Sauveur looks out to the world from its terrace. Once a priory, it had a history of quarrels between 'rebellious and disobedient' monks and the higher churchmen. The present church is mostly twelfth century. In an old relais of Henri IV's reign is a museum of the PTT – the post and telegrams communications of Aquitaine. The stamps are very interesting (open early April to mid-October except Tuesday).

TOURIST INFORMATION Le Prieure (56.63.34.52)

HOTEL

Arts, allée des Tilleuls (56.63.07.40). Simple hotel with only nine rooms but very good restaurant *Le Gerbaude*. ROOMS C. MEALS A–D. Restaurant shut Sunday evening, Wednesday.

ST MONT
[GERS]

On the Adour river 6km W of Riscle by D946, St Mont is a small hillside town with lovely old Gascon houses, a restored eighteenth-century priory, a village church which is half Romanesque (eleventh century) and half Gothic (twelfth century), and a famous wine Co-operative.

Union des Producteurs Plaimont (tel. 62.69.78.87) is one of the biggest and most lively wine co-operatives in the south-west. Combining growers from St Mont, Aignan and Plaisance areas, it has 1350 wine growers among its members, growing on 2000 hectares and aiming for more. They are *eleveurs*, maturing and blending wines, and are *négoçiants*, too, supplying many British merchants, including Tesco and Lay and Wheeler. They produce Madiran, Côtes de St Mont (VDQS wine, just below AOC rating and a good bargain) and Côtes de Gascogne (Vin de Pays).

ST PALAIS
[Pyrénées-Atlantiques]

St Palais likes to call itself Basque but is technically in Basse-Navarre. It has the liveliness of a Basque village, the dancing, pelota galas, and a big Festival de la Basque which is held on the first Sunday after the 15 August. It is on the river Bidouze NE of St Jean-Pied-de-Port on D933 at the meeting place of two pilgrim routes and it keeps old bridges, chapels and roads from those pilgrim days.

Its charter to hold a market goes back to the fifteenth century.

In the sixteenth century when the Spaniards threw out Jews and gypsies, the Jews settled in Bayonne and many of the gypsies settled around St Jean-de-Luz and in St Palais. They were oppressed by the Basques, who suspected them of being responsible for much of the smuggling. Presumably the Basques wanted this traditional trade for themselves! They were also accused of black magic. The Basques tried to have them deported to the French colonies but they sat tight and took up their traditional trades as weavers, tinkers and charcoal burners, but it was not until last century that they started to mix with the local people.

TOURIST INFORMATION 1 place Hôtel-de-Ville (59.56.71.78)

HOTEL
Trinquet, rue F. de St-Jaymes (59.65.73.13). ROOMS C. MEALS A–E. Shut 1–15 February.

ST PÉ-DE-BIGORRE
[Hautes-Pyrénées]

Pé in Gascon meant Peter and the town 10km W of Lourdes by D937 grew from a Benedictine abbey dedicated to St Peter. It was said to be the biggest and most beautiful religious building in the Pyrenees, but was burned in the Religious Wars and wrecked in an earthquake of 1661. The remains of the old church beside another built in the seventeenth century can be seen from the arcaded main square.

The Gave de Pau river runs through the village and there is a view over the area from beside it.

MARKET Wednesday

HOTEL

Pyrénées (62.41.80.08). Pleasant two-star hotel with views from the restaurant. ROOMS B–C. MEALS A–E. Hotel open 1 February–30 October; restaurant shut mid-November–mid December.

ST PÉE-SUR-NIVELLE
[PYRÉNÉES-ATLANTIQUES]

On the D918, 13km E of St Jean-de-Luz, beside the Nivelle river, St Pée was of little interest when I was younger except to scholars of the Napoleonic Wars. Now it is a small resort, thanks partly to the building of a reservoir nearby. Fishermen have a choice of river or lake waters and you can sail or sailboard on the lake.

Joseph Bonaparte, brother of the Emperor Napoleon, fled here in 1813 to await his brother's orders after his comprehensive defeat by Wellington at Vitoria in Spain. He must have been rather a sorry sight after his previous glories as King of Naples and usurping King of Spain. He had lost his reputation, all his baggage and his money. The orders soon came. He was summarily dismissed to hand over his command to Soult, who was supposed to stop Wellington at the Pyrenees. Joseph returned to his estate at Morfontaine and on his brother's defeat at Waterloo escaped to America and became a US citizen.

I have always found St Pée charming – a fine old village with tall Basque mansions in the main street with dates like 1676 and 1636 on their carved lintels, others with eighteenth-century dates. The Basque church has a gallery facing the choir which was for the local bigwigs. The Nivelle is crossed near the village by 'Roman' bridges. All old bridges are called 'Roman' in the Pays Basque.

Fronton, at Ibarron, 1½km W (59.54.10.12). Pleasant Basque house. Very good cooking. Terrace and winter garden. Lovely local wild salmon in season. ROOMS C–E. MEALS C–F. Shut 1–25 March; Tuesday in winter.
Nivelle (59.54.10.27). 'Three-chimney' Logis de France. Small and friendly. ROOMS D–E. MEALS C–D. Shut February; Monday low season.

ST SAVIN
[HAUTES-PYRÉNÉES]

The Benedictine abbey here on the left bank of the Gave de Pau was one of the biggest religious houses of the Pyrenees, and its abbots were seigneurs of the whole area, including Cauterets and its important healing springs. The Roman governors of Bigorre had a villa here, which was used later by a Christian priest as a base for missionary work. Charlemagne helped him to build the abbey but in 843 the Norsemen burned it to the ground. It was rebuilt in 945 by Raymond I, who gave the monks the land in the valley of Cauterets.

Now the village has only 600 people and although it is only 3km S of the resort of Argelès-Gazost and 16km S of Lourdes, few people see it except those staying there, because it is on an old road and they use the parallel D921. I think it is a delightful spot, with a main square full of old houses and a stone cross dated 1783 and a terrace with magnificent views over the Argelès valley to Pic de Viscos (2241 metres) and Pic Long (3192 metres).

Very close is the Chapelle de Piétat, a Romanesque abbey church, fortified in the fourteenth century – all that remains of the abbey. It has a fine Romanesque door and interesting internal decorations, including a beautiful wooden carved figure of

Christ and two large fifteenth-century paintings on wood, each divided into nine episodes in the life of St Savin.

Above the village is the ruined castle of Arcinas Avant, built by the Black Prince.

HOTEL

Panoramic (62.97.08.22). Rooms vary; all adequate. Lovely panoramic views. ROOMS B–D. MEALS A–D. Shut early October–Easter.

ST SEVER
[LANDES]

Pronounced 'Sevé', this small hilltop town straddles the Adour valley 17km S of Mont-de-Marsan and is a landmark in this part of Les Landes. It was called Cap de Gascogne (Head of Gascony) for its exalted position. It is rich in little architectural gems. The eleventh-century Benedictine abbey church, though extensively repaired, is still a fine Romanesque building, so is the museum next to it. The abbey church has six apse chapels, a nave with five bays and a clock tower. Another fine building is the Convent of the Jacobins founded in 1280 by Edward I of England. This has an elegant cloister. Old abbey buildings are still in use as houses and as the town hall. There are also old mansions, especially in rue General-Lamarque, half-timbered houses, windmills and a Confrerie Gastronomique des Jabotiers which promotes delicacies of Les Landes.

From Promenade de Morlanne you have fine views of the forest and Adour river.

TOURIST INFORMATION 1 place Tour-du-Sol (in season – 58.76.00.10)
FESTIVALS July, August – historic entertainments at the Jacobin abbey

HOTELS

Relais du Pavillon, 2km N by D933 (58.76.20.22). New young chef has joined Jean-Jacques Dumas, and it remains one of the best places to eat in Gascony. A pity that the modern decor lets it down! Comfortable adequate rooms. (Inter-Hotel, Logis de France.) ROOMS D–E. MEALS C–G. Shut Sunday evening in winter.

France et Ambassadeurs, place cap du Pouy (58.76.00.01). Two-chimney Logis. Good value. ROOMS A–C. MEALS A–E.

ST SEVER-DE-RUSTAN
[HAUTES-PYRÉNÉES]

25km NE of Tarbes. St Sever-de-Rustan has kept some remains of its Benedictine abbey including the very Benedictine church, but the cloister has been taken away and reassembled in the Massey Gardens at Tarbes. There it has been joined by capitals from the fifteenth-century collegiate church of Trie-sur-Baïse, 5km from St Sever. Much of that church is now in the Cloisters section of the Metropolitan Museum of Art in New York.

STE CROIX-DU-MONT
[GIRONDE]

A typical wine village on a hill above the Garonne on the right bank between Loupiac and Verdelais. Narrow lanes winding through vineyards take you to the chais on the hill. From the shady church terrace is an agreeable view of the Garonne valley and the Sauternes country over the river. Cliffs and caves nearby are encrusted with oyster shells.

Château de Tastes is superbly positioned on top of the hill, with lovely views, and its vineyards are historic. Alas, very little of its splendid white wine is made today. With Loupiac, Ste Croix-du-Mont makes the best sweet white Bordeaux wines outside Sauternes. Château Loubens is the best producer. Its dry whites are called Fleuron Blanc, its secondary sweet label is Château Terfort. Because of the current unpopularity of sweet wines, much of the crop is now vinified early before it gets sweet, and sold as a Bordeaux Sec. A pity!

STE ENGRÂCE
[Pyrénées-Atlantiques]

Old shepherds' village among wooded mountainsides and gorges along the beautiful little D113 road from the D26 S of Tardets-Sorholus and Mauléon-Licharre (*see* page 189). A track road leads to the narrow Gorges de Kakouetta (*see also* Licq-Athérey, page 186).

The waters emerging at the gorges may be connected to an underground river emerging in the Gouffre de la Pierre-St-Martin 8km E, where pot-holers have reached a depth of 728 metres.

A series of paths which are still used as sheep trails for moving the flocks up and down the mountains in summer and winter radiate southwards from Ste Engrâce towards the Spanish border.

The eleventh- to twelfth-century church of Ste Engrâce, an old pilgrims' church, is regarded as one of the most interesting in the Pyrenees. Most roads and paths are closed in winter.

STE MÈRE
[Gers]

Just over the border from Lot-et-Garonne on the N21 Agen-Auch stretch, this interesting fortified village was once the frontier of English Gascony. It was, in fact, built at the end of the thirteenth century by Géraud de Moulezun but when the English came they seem to have used it as a prototype for their defence posts, called Châteaux Gascons. These castles were built on a hill commanding the surrounding countryside. They had no moat nor defence ditch but were built like a strong keep with two smaller towers at the end. The ground floor was used as a kitchen and to store food. Ladders led to the upper floors and these could be pulled up in time of trouble. The only windows lit one big second-floor room.

The English found these Gascon forts so effective that they

built them on the Scottish borders as defence against the
marauding Scots.

SALIES-DE-BÉARN
[PYRÉNÉES-ATLANTIQUES]

A delightful and handsome old town on both side of the Saleys
river, Salies has been a spa since the Middle Ages. To the lovely
old houses, arcaded squares and terraces, pleasant new buildings and squares have been added with good taste. Salies is on
the D933 between Sauveterre and the N117 just W of Orthez.

The legend of the springs shows a nice variation from the
standard story of a wounded old horse being set free in a forest
to return fit and lively, leading its master to the healing spring.
This time a wild boar was wounded but escaped from its hunters. It was next seen fit and well near a pool but its bristles
sparkled in the sun like white crystals. It was salt. Thus the
hunters found the salt springs.

Even the river is slightly salt but not as clean as it should be
these days. From Pont de la Lune, a little bridge over it, you can
see lovely typical old Béarnaise timbered houses with galleries
overhanging the river, all decorated with flowers in season.

Salt was once produced from the springs to sell for the table,
the kitchen and or especially for salting ham. Perhaps even
today Bayonne ham could be prescribed medicinally!

Now the water and the salt are prescribed at the thermal
establishment for rheumatism, gynaecological problems and to
help broken limbs to mend. Salies has most of the usual entertainments and activities of a spa, including golf (nine holes). One
package offers you hotel, three thermal sessions, including mas-
sage and sauna, and daily green fees. The thermal establishment
is in place du Jardin Publique (tel. 59.38.10.11).

TOURIST INFORMATION 1 boul. St-Guily (59.38.00.33)
MARKET daily
FESTIVAL early September – Fêtes du Sel

HOTELS

Golf, Domaine Hélios, route d'Orthez (59.65.02.10). In a lovely green setting, Francis Barrat offers varied dishes – regional, classical, low calorie. ROOMS D–E. MEALS C–E. Open 31 March–30 September.

Larquier, ave Salines (59.38.10.43). Simple, cheap, good value. ROOMS A–B. MEALS B–C. Open 1 April–30 September.

SAMATAN
[GERS]

19km SW of l'Isle Jourdain, 47km SW of Toulouse at the very eastern edge of Gers. It was a pilgrim halt in the old days, now known for its *foie gras*, geese and duck market, and for its many fêtes and fairs. There are several old châteaux around here, including a Château Latour of the seventeenth century with good furnishings, pictures, chapel and pigeonnier. Nearby is Château Pradel where the writer Belleforest lived and worked. It is said that Shakespeare got some of his plots, including Hamlet, from Belleforest's *Histoires Tragiques*. The French, of course, are fairly certain about this! One young French writer told me that nearly all the best of Shakespeare came from Belleforest.

MARKET Monday

FESTIVALS Fourth Saturday, Sunday and Monday in
August – National Foie Gras Fair; 11 November –
cooking contest

HOTEL

Maigné (62.62.30.24). Very simple cheap rooms. Louis Maigné is famous in Gascony for his gorgeous, no-nonsense, rich, satisfying Gascon meals. Excellent value. ROOMS A–B. MEALS A–F. Shut 20 September–20 October.

SARE
[Pyrénées-Atlantiques]

When I first saw Sare, tucked beneath La Rhune mountain S of Ascain and St Jean-de-Luz, it was a gem of a Basque village, still fairly unknown to tourists, full of old Basque houses and with a true Basque-country atmosphere. It has become something of a resort now and well-heeled people of St Jean have moved in. But it has not lost its Basque atmosphere. All new buildings have to be in Basque style and colours. It still has its shady streets, its fine fronton – where Edward VII watched the game from its tiers of stone seats and where it is played with religious fervour – its arcaded town hall, and its church with three tiers of galleries. But I don't think that Sare goes in for smuggling any more. Once it was the capital of smuggling: sheep, brandy, liqueurs, cattle and, in wars and times of persecution, men. In the 1950s they denied that it took place any longer ('the last old smuggler died last month'), but it did, except that the contraband was radios, car spares and transistor parts. It was all done by a few men, not armed gangs, and was regarded by the Basques as legitimate free trade. Many Allied airmen who had evaded capture with the help of the French after being shot down, passed through Sare to be led over the Pyrenees by smugglers. If it goes on now it will be gangs smuggling drugs or arms to the Basque nationalists in Spain.

Sare has a superb war memorial by Real de Sarte, showing a grenade-thrower in bas relief on the outline of pelota player in the same attitude.

The village is reached from Ascain through the St Ignace Pass, at which the cog-railway runs to the top of La Rhune (*see* Ascain, page 118). Southward very near to the Spanish frontier are prehistoric caves – Grottes de Sare.

Pierre Loti, who stayed in Ascain while writing *Ramuntcho*, set the story in Sare, which he called 'Etchejar'.

HOTELS

Arraya, 1 place de Sare (59.54.20.46). An ancient pilgrims' *auberge*, superbly converted, with ravishing country bedrooms and wonderful cooking, of classical regional dishes, slightly on the light side. Very expensive meals but worth the francs. ROOMS F–G. MEALS G. Open 1 May–1 November.

Fagoaga-Baratchartea, quartier Ihaler (59.54.20.48). Three-chimney Logis. Meals very popular. ROOMS B–C. MEALS B–D. Shut 20 December–1 March.

SAUVE, LA
[GIRONDE]

Once the centre of a great forest, this little village in Entre-Deux-Mers region is now surrounded by vineyards. The trees were cleared by Benedictine monks from an abbey founded by St Gérard in 1079. The ruins are still imposing. On the nearby hilltop is the thirteenth-century parish church with interesting sixteenth-century frescos inside and four fine statues outside. It is on D671 SE of Créon towards Sauveterre-de-Guyenne.

SAUVETERRE-DE-BÉARN
[PYRÉNÉES-ATLANTIQUES]

In a gorgeous position on a spur overlooking the Gave d'Oloron, SW of Orthez on the D933, it looks particularly attractive from along the river bank. From there you can see little but the remains of a twelfth-century fortified bridge, a wooded island, the tower of Château Montréal and the Romanesque twelfth-century bell tower of the church, all framed in trees, with the Pyrenees on the horizon. It is an enchanting little town, lazy and romantic on a hot summer's day. It is easy to believe the story of Sancie.

In 1170 Sancie, widow of Gaston V of Béarn, was accused of killing the baby born to her after her husband's death. Her brother, the King of Navarre, said that she must face the judgement of God. Bound legs and wrists, she was tossed from the bridge into the fast-moving river. The waters brought her gently to the shore. She was judged innocent and restored to her position and rights.

The remains of the castle and keep of Château de Montréal include the large central bell tower and a beautiful doorway.

Château de Laàs, 9km SE by D27, was bequeathed to the French nation by its last owners, named Serbat, to whom we all owe thanks. The large seventeenth-century manor house with parkland is extremely attractive, is sumptuously furnished, and is packed with treasures collected by the rich art connoisseur and his wife. Much of it came from Hainault and the north. Among all these treasures, I liked the wood decorations from Louis XVI's reign, especially the Fontaine fables in Mme Serbat's bed-room, the superb tapestries, and the bed in which Napoleon slept the night after Waterloo when he had fled to Maubert Fontaine. I bet he didn't sleep very well. The furnishings and treasures came from the last three houses of the Serbat family and that is what the château still looks like – the family home of a rich man of good taste. (Open daily 1 July to 30 September; Saturday, Sunday 1 March to 30 June.)

TOURIST INFORMATION Mairie (in season –
59.38.50.17)

HOTEL
Boste, rue Léon Bérard (59.38.50.62). Almost a local institution. Traditional regional dishes and grills over wood. Delicious. ROOMS A–C. MEALS B–C. Shut 1 October–15 November; Sunday evening, Monday 1 September–30 June.

SAUVETERRE-DE-GUYENNE
[GIRONDE]

Typical bastide built in 1281 by Edward I of England, it still has four fortified gates, somewhat disfigured, and a big sloping centre square, surrounded by stone arcades. It is in Entre-Deux-Mers country, where D670 from St Émilion over the Dordogne meets D230, which later becomes D672 down to St Macaire on the Garonne. Though the original low arcades still stand, the houses above them have been greatly altered over the centuries, no doubt to the advantage of the people living in them.

Sauveterre's market day is very lively and its wine festival to celebrate the bringing in of the vintage is famous even in Gironde. People bring out their tables and load them with food, the wine barrels are placed around the square and the music and dancing continues for hours.

MARKET Tuesday

HOTEL
Guyenne (56.71.54.92). ROOMS A–C. MEALS A–C. Open all year.

SIMORRE
[GERS]

This attractive little hamlet on the D12, 17km SW of Lombez has a heavily fortified brick church of 1304, once part of a Benedictine monastery. It has been called 'the most beautiful fortified church in Gascony', which may be so but it is far from original. Viollet-le-Duc, the architect-'restorer' of last century, did some great jobs, such as restoring Notre-Dame in Paris, Amiens and Laon cathedrals and virtually rebuilding Carcassonne. But sometimes his enthusiasm ran away with him and with this church he 'feudalized' it considerably. However, it has some splendid stained glass and stalls carvings.

SOLFERINO
[LANDES]

Napoleon III was an enthusiastic experimental agriculturist and regenerator of land. He ran model farms on his land and tried various experiments. One was here on an ancient estate on D44 just east of where it crosses N10 in the heart of Les Landes. The soil was cleaned and improved, irrigation was introduced, new trees planted, seed sown to grow maize and other crops. I suppose that now he would have been accused of meddling with a natural habitat! But it wasn't the original habitat anyway, for

pines had been planted a century before, and the Landes peasants needed new crops to survive. It must have been a success,
for it still grows 4856 hectares of maize and strawberries. There
is a museum in the old mairie, but although part is devoted to
the history of Les Landes it is mostly about the 'Imperial Family'.

HOTEL

Vieux Logis (58.07.21.01). Logis de France. ROOMS B–C. MEALS
C–E. Shut February school holidays; Saturday, Sunday evening
low season.

SORDE-L'ABBAYE
[LANDES]

Old pilgrim stop-over between Peyrehorade (*see* page 205) and
Salies-de-Béarn (*see* page 233) on D29, beside a pleasant stretch
of Gave d'Oloron. A ramparted small town with a fine twelfth-
century abbey church. Archaeological finds have included a
Roman villa with mosaics and thermal baths. Interesting abbey

Mosaic detail from abbey at Sorde

remains include a long underground gallery next to a stream, once used as a cellar and fish pond, and a sixteenth-century abbot's house with a polygonal turret. Fine views from here of several rivers with the Pyrenees in the distance.

SOULAC-SUR-MER
[GIRONDE]

This beach resort near to Pointe de Grave, the south point of the Gironde estuary, was an important port from Roman times until the end of the Hundred Years War, when English troops were landed on its estuary side to try to save Bordeaux. It has a fine safe beach and caters well for the Bordelais who drive the 94km for a day out or a weekend.

The beautiful twelfth-century Benedictine abbey church of Notre-Dame-de-la-Fin-des-Terres has a remarkable story. The drifting sands gradually covered it and it was abandoned in 1757. But it was uncovered during the Landes reclamation, cleaned up and is back in use. There is a *son et lumière* telling its story during July.

A small museum in Fondation Soulac-Medoc, rue Ausone near the casino is devoted to Aquitaine artists and sculptors.

TOURIST INFORMATION place du Marché (56.59.85.56)
FESTIVAL August – Music Festival

HOTELS

Molière, 22 rue F. Lafargue (56.09.82.69). Simple. ROOMS B–D. MEALS A–C. Open 1 April–1 October.
Pins, L'Amélie-sur-Mer, 4km SW (56.09.08.01). ROOMS C–E. MEALS A–F. Shut January, February; Friday, Sunday evening in winter.

SOUSTONS
[Landes]

'South Town' the English called this bastide when they built it in the fourteenth century, and the French version is not far out. A busy centre these days for plastics, cork and wood, and centre of an agricultural region known for maize, chickens and asparagus. It is 10½km inland but only a drive shaded with plane trees away from Étang de Soustons – a lake fringed with rushes but known for sailing and fishing. This lake is joined by waterways to Vieux-Boucau on the coast.

Tourist Information Grange de Labouyrie
(58.41.52.62)
Market Monday

HOTELS

Pavillon Landais, 26 avenue du Lac (58.41.14.49). On the lakeside, opposite Latché, the domaine belonging to President Mitterand. Superb cooking of regional ingredients. Rooms D–E. Meals D–F. Shut 20 December–1 March; Sunday evening, Monday in winter.

Hostellerie du Marensin, place Sterling (58.41.15.16). Rooms C. Meals A–D. Shut November; Saturday.

TARBES
[Hautes-Pyrénées]

An animated large industrial town on the Adour river 19km NE of Lourdes and commercial capital of the Hautes-Pyrénées department. Tarbes started to grow at the beginning of the nineteenth century because of its important fairs and markets, and became an industrial centre after the opening of the Midi railway in the 1870s. Now it uses mountain-generated electricity for engineering and chemicals. Rich valley land is used for pasture and wheat. Tarbes, today, is also a canoeing centre.

Its earlier history was particularly disastrous and bloody,

from the Hundred Years War through the Wars of Religion, when it was devastated by three big Protestant attacks, to the attempted stand by a French army against some of Wellington's columns in 1814.

Napoleon set up a national stud (Haras) in 1806 for breeding cavalry horses from a cross between local, Moorish and English strains. The stud still flourishes as a breeding centre for show-jumping and eventing horses, which are known as Tarbais.

In the Musée Massey, in a villa within the Massey gardens, a floor is devoted to the horses and to the history of Light Cavalry – Hussards in French, Hussars in English – from the first formation in Hungary in 1474, to their adoption by 34 countries in Europe and Latin America. There are over 100 models of cavalrymen meticulously equipped and dressed. You can visit the Haras on afternoons from early July to the end of February and the museum daily except Monday and Tuesday. They are both within easy walking distance of place Verdun, the town centre where the information office is located. The other half of the Massey museum has an extensive and interesting collection of paintings of French, Flemish, Italian and Spanish schools of the fifteenth and nineteenth centuries. The museum tower gives a lovely view over the Adour valley to the Pyrenees. It is in a delightful park (Jardin Massey) to which the remains of a fifteenth-century abbey cloisters have been moved for décor. The park was laid out by Placide Massey (1777–1853), a director at Versailles, for his own pleasure.

The twelfth-century cathedral has been much altered.

You can see the birthplace of Marshal Foch, the first ever Allied Commander-in-Chief and a name known to almost every household in the world from the First World War until his generation died out recently.

Ferdinand Foch, born in 1851, became a teacher at the École de Guerre and France's greatest strategist. Unfortunately he did not always agree with the British Expeditionary Force Commander Field Marshal Douglas Haig, who believed in mobile warfare. Haig was in fact a Hussar officer! It was obvious by 1917 that the Allies were at cross-purposes and needed a single commander. The French morale was deteriorating after the defeat of their Nivelle offensive. The normally obdurate Scot, Haig, surprised everyone by suddenly announcing that 'if Marshal Foch cares to make known his wishes, I shall do my best to follow them'. Foch became Commander-in-Chief, Allied Forces. As you can see from the museum in his birthplace, he received as many medals and honours as any soldier in modern history. He was even given great artistic and civilian honours, being made a member of the Académie Française and the most prestigious British honour, the Order of Merit. He died in 1929. (Museum closed Tuesday, Wednesday.)

TOURIST INFORMATION place Verdun (62.93.36.62); Hautes-Pyrénées department, 6 rue Eugéne-Ténot (62.93.03.30)

MARKET Thursday

FESTIVALS January – week of Café-Théâtre; March – Occitan Folk Festival; August – Horse-races; September – Fête du Cheval; November – Floralies

HOTELS

Président, route Lourdes, N21 (62.93.98.40). Modern Grand Hotel. Ninth-floor restaurant Toit de Bigorre with mountain views. Pool. ROOMS E. MEALS B–F. Open all year.

Aragon, at Juillan, route Lourdes, 5km SW (62.93.99.33). Cosy chalet-like hotel with excellent cooking. ROOMS D–E. MEALS A–G. Shut 2–7 January; Sunday evening, Monday October–Easter.

Ferme de St Ferréol, at Chis, 9km NE on N21 (62.36.22.15). In country facing Pyrenees. Fresh family cooking. Logis. ROOMS B–E. MEALS A–F. Shut Friday, Sunday off season. Restaurant shut Sunday evening except July, August.

RESTAURANTS

Amphitryon, 38 rue Larrey (62.34.08.99). Famous restaurant of Pyrenees, long known for regional cooking, has gone modern. A pity! MEALS D–F. Shut 4–20 August; Saturday lunch, Sunday.

Toup' Ty, 86 ave Barère (62.93.32.08). New favourite with locals. Bourgeoise house; good, sensible cooking. MEALS A–F. Shut 10 July–10 August; Sunday evening, Monday.

URRUGNE
[Pyrénées-Atlantiques]

Poor Urrugne, already on the N10, has almost been run over recently by the A63 motorway. But it has not yet been overrun by St Jean-de-Luz. Anyway, it is used to such invasions. In 1813 Soult's French Armies took it over on their retreat from Spain; then a few days later Wellington's forces overran the French in a battle just outside the village, and took it. Urrugne has kept its Basque traditions and is a very pleasant place, a walk from St Jean-de-Luz and 8km from Hendaye.

The village hugs a small hill topped by a tenth-century church, fortified with strong outer walls pierced with loopholes for shooting arrows through. The main side door still has the marks of French and English bullets from 1813. Fitting, perhaps, that the inscription on the clock in the sixteenth-century belfry reads: *Vulnerant Omnes, Ultima Necat* – All wound, the last one kills. Inside are the standard Basque three galleries in oak, some fine stained glass, and bas reliefs which include *The Fall of Man*. By the church is the pelota court and an attractive seventeenth-century town hall with stone arcades.

It has three family-run, one-star hotels.

A tree-lined avenue leads to Château d'Urtubie, in a little park below the N10. Built originally in 1380 for Edward III of England, it is now mainly eighteenth century, though the two round towers at the entrance have survived from the original. Marshal Soult stayed in it before the battle in 1813, and Wellington moved in the day after the battle. It contains a fine collection of seventeenth-century Flanders tapestries.

A lane from Urrugne takes you to the pilgrims' chapel of Notre-Dame-de-Socorri in a shady cemetery-close with views to the hill of La Rhune.

HOTEL
Chez Maïté, place Mairie (59.54.30.27). Simple but comfortable and welcoming Logis. ROOMS B–D. MEALS C. Shut January; Sunday evening, Monday.

VALENCE-SUR-BAÏSE
[Gers]

A hamlet of only 200 people due S of Condom on the D930 but worth visiting. A bastide founded by the Count of Armagnac for the English in 1274, it still has its small main square with arcades, fourteenth-century church with octagonal towers, and town hall, town gates and tower du Guardes. It was a Roman site called Glezia and there are mosaics, coins, pottery and Roman weights and measures in the museum, which is in the splendid old Abbey of Flaran. This Cistercian abbey is set in woods and has a large fine formal garden. The Order of Citeaux built the Romanesque church and cloisters in 1151. It was damaged in the Hundred Years War, the Religious Wars and in the French Revolution. But it has been carefully and successfully restored and is open to visitors every day except Tuesday.

HOTEL

Ferme de Flaran, route de Condom (62.28.58.22). Peaceful. Swimming-pool. Very good regional cooking. Good value. ROOMS C. MEALS B–F.

VAYRES
[Gironde]

9km W of Libourne by N89 and D242, a small town with a medieval château altered in the sixteenth century by Louis de Foix, who had the Phare de Cordouan built, the famous lighthouse. It has a lovely arcaded courtyard. The façade facing the Dordogne from the seventeenth century is approached by an elegant double staircase and a bridge over the moat. Some of the attractive rooms are used for receptions (open afternoons July, August; Sunday and holidays rest of the year).

VERDELAIS
[Gironde]

At this small village in the Entre-Deux-Mers countryside, just N of the Garonne river, François Mauriac, the great modern novelist, lived in retreat from Paris to do much of his writing, and Toulouse-Lautrec, the painter, was buried here in 1901.

Henri Toulouse-Lautrec's mother, the Countess of Toulouse-Lautrec-Monfa, lived in Château Malromé, 6km NE of Verdelais at St André-du-Bois. When her son came out of a sanatorium where he had been treated for alcoholism, she brought him here away from his Paris life on the Left Bank hoping that the country air and rest from the life he led around the Paris cabarets would restore his health. Alas, he died here at the age of thirty-seven, not from alcoholism but from a paralytic stroke brought on by venereal disease. He is buried in Verdelais cemetery. His grave is marked with a plain tomb. You can visit Château Malromé on afternoons in summer and Sunday the rest of the year except that it's closed from early November to the end of March. In the room where he died are drawings and reproductions of his work. The château was built in the twelfth to fifteenth centuries for the Counts of Béarn.

One of Toulouse-Lautrec's most unusual works is in the pleasant Hostellerie Saint-Pierre in Verdelais. Here he used to sit drinking and sketching while his mother was in church. A panel on which he had sketched himself is in the hotel hall. It was discovered by accident. While you are there looking at it, try Jean-Paul Decriteau's genuine *cassoulet Landais* with goose confit.

On the hill above the cemetery is a rather spectacular calvary reached by a wide stone staircase with angels guarding it at the bottom and views from the top of the Garonne and Landes forest. ½km away begins the estate of Malagar, which has been owned by the Mauriac family from 1843, and still is. The writer François Mauriac, who was born in Bordeaux, inherited the fine stone mansion in 1918. Until his death, he spent each spring and autumn there and said that it was the one place where he knew himself. His son Claude and family still use Malagar for holidays but I am told that it is being made ready to open as a museum.

There are views across the Garonne to Château d'Yquem and the estate produces a Premières Côtes de Bordeaux called Château Malagar.

Verdelais was an important place of pilgrimage from the fourteenth century, and the walls of the basilica of Notre-Dame are almost covered in ex-voto plaques. Paralytics in particular come to pray beneath a fourteenth-century wooden statue of the Virgin.

HOTEL

Saint-Pierre (56.62.02.03). Very good regional cooking with Bordeaux wines at sensible prices (including Malagar). ROOMS A–B. MEALS A–E.

VERDON-SUR-MER
[GIRONDE]

This little seaside resort has grown since the 1960s into an important port and industrial zone. The deep water has allowed for a container and petrol tanker terminal to be built (opened 1976) and petrol tanks have been installed. It was being built up before the war but the Germans wrecked it.

VIC-FÉZENSAC
[GERS]

Busy and pleasant market town among rich farming lands 30km NW of Auch on the important N124. It still has a few old arcades and houses. But now it is known for Armagnac brandy, horse breeding and fêtes and fairs, including a renowned corrida (bullfight) at Whitsun. They play rugby here too, and hold horse-races.

HOTEL

D'Artagnan, 3 cours Delom (62.06.31.37). Known for Gascon cooking. Simple Logis de France. ROOMS A–C. MEALS A–E.

VIEUX-BOUCAU-PORT-D'ALBRET
[LANDES]

Once an important port at the mouth of the Adour river, which changed its course from flowing to Capbreton in the fourteenth century. Then in 1578 the river was artificially deviated to run out near Bayonne, and Vieux-Boucau wasted away. Now it is becoming increasingly popular as a holiday resort and is known often as Vieux-Boucau-les-Bains, although a new Port d'Albret for pleasure boats is being built up. Vieux-Boucau has a little canal running through the centre. Modern holiday villages have been built with plenty of sport and other outdoor entertainments. Le Mail, the paved pedestrian promenade, is attractive, especially when lit at night in season. The resort is on the north bank of a lagoon, between the beach and pines. A canalized conduit feeds the harbour from this lake, which is joined to the Étang de Soustons, where there is more holiday sporting activity (*see* page 241). This lake is joined to Étang Blanc (*see* Penon, page 205). The whole ensemble makes a very pleasant holiday area.

Vieux-Boucau's modern arena holds 4000 spectators for corridas and Courses Landaises. Its pelota fronton is one of the best in Les Landes and there are weekly matches from June to September. The lake is known particularly for sailing.

TOURIST INFORMATION Port d'Albret (58.48.13.47)
MARKET Soustons: Monday
FESTIVALS 15 August – Lake Festival with fireworks;
mid-September – Courses Landaises

HOTELS

Côte d'Argent, rue Principale (58.48.13.17). One of four Logis de France in the resort. ROOMS B–D. MEALS C–G. Shut 1 October–15 November; Monday in winter.

Maremne, ave de la Plage (58.48.12.70). Cheap, good value. ROOMS B–C. MEALS A–E. Open 20 March–1 November.

VILLANDRAUT
[GIRONDE]

Little town on the edge of the Landes forest 14km SW of Langon, Villandraut was the birthplace of Bertrand de Goth who became Pope Clément V (1264–1314), the controversial pope who disbanded the corrupt Knights Templars and moved the Papacy from Rome to Avignon, thus at least bequeathing us Châteauneuf-du-Pape wine!

As soon as he was Pope, he built himself a massive moated castle in his home town, rectangular, with six towers, and altogether grandiose. It was fifty-two metres long and forty-three metres deep. Clément was notorious for spending the Papal wealth. Now it is a massive ruin, mirrored in the slow-running waters of the river Ciron. The six towers give the ruins a splendid silhouette. Clément is buried in a white marble tomb in the large Gothic church at Uzeste, 5km SE.

HOTEL
Goth (56.25.31.25). ROOMS B–D. MEALS A–E. Restaurant shut 15 November–15 January; Saturday.

VILLENEUVE-DE-MARSAN
[LANDES]

Although pleasant, nothing very exciting about this village 17km E of Mont-de-Marsan except for two really outstanding restaurants.

At his self-named Relais et Châteaux hotel, Francis Darroze offers what he calls 'traditional family cuisine'. Traditional, perhaps, to the Darroze family, who sprinkle their talents generously around Gascony. Few families could rival it.

Robert Garrapit at the Europe is renowned as a local personality, as a chef and as a connoisseur of Armagnac brandy. He buys everything possible from local farms, especially ducks, chickens and geese.

TOURIST INFORMATION Town Hall (58.45.22.68)

HOTELS

Francis Darroze, Grande-Rue (58.45.20.07). See text. Relais et Châteaux. Totally renovated inside. ROOMS F–G. MEALS G. Shut January; Sunday evening, Monday October–June.

Europe, place Boiterie (58.45.20.08). See text. ROOMS A–D. MEALS B–F. Shut 15 November–8 December.

YQUEM, CHÂTEAU D'
[GIRONDE]

The Château d'Yquem is a fine fortress standing on a hill just off the D8 in the heart of the Sauternais S of Pregnac. There are splendid views across its vineyards to Mont-Ste-Croix across the river. Built in the early Renaissance, it was remodelled in the seventeenth century. The Lur-Saluces family have lived there since 1785 (*see* Vineyards, page 50). The present owner Comte Alexandre de Lur-Saluces took over from his father in 1970 and is totally dedicated to the magnificent sweet wine which since 1855 has been the only wine in Sauternes and Barsac with the Premier Grand Cru accolade. The local people of the five Sauternais villages have wisely chosen him to be their mayor.

It was in his mayoral capacity that he told me that the best time to drink a nice chilled glass of Sauternes was at 11a.m. as the first drink of the day. It happened to be 11a.m. at the time. He poured me a glass of Château d'Yquem. Presumably at 11p.m. the best time to drink it would be as a nightcap! He says that you can drink it right through a meal and that it brings good health and long life.

You can visit the vineyards and the courtyard of Château d'Yquem but you won't get a peep of wine being made unless you are in the wine business and have influence. You certainly will not be offered a tasting. This nectar is far too valuable to be offered to passing tourists. Only three quarters of the vines are actually producing Château d'Yquem wines. The rest are young vines.

Picking is done only by skilled workers, mostly working full time on the estate. To pick the grapes at exactly the right moment of 'noble rot' (overripe Botrytized grapes), the workers go through the vineyard four to eleven times picking individual grapes. Harvesting can last two months from mid-September to mid-November. The wine matures in cask for three years before bottling.

The wine is made from 80 per cent Sémillon and almost 20 per cent Sauvignon with a little Muscat. The 100 hectares of vines produce about 65,000 bottles a year. Each vine produces only about one glass of wine per year! A sweet d'Yquem must be kept ten years and will usually last fifty years – but not in my house!

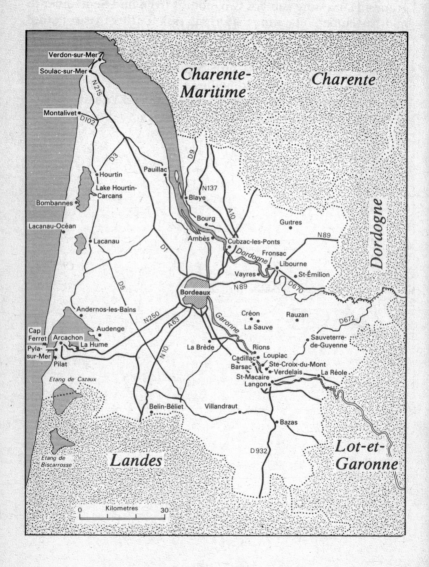

2 *Gironde*

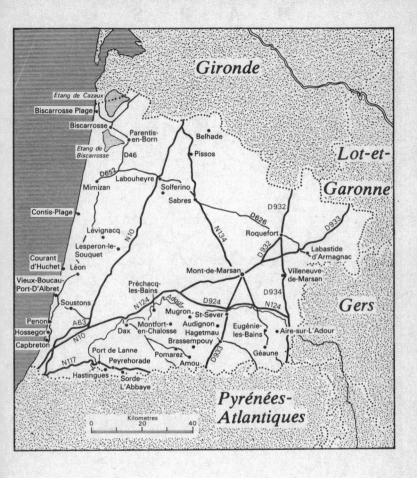

Gironde

Etang de Cazaux

Biscarrosse Plage

Biscarrosse

Parentis-en-Born

Belhade

Etang de Biscarrosse

D46

Pissos

Lot-et-

D652

Labouheyre

Garonne

Mimizan

Solferino

Sabres

D932

Contis-Plage

D626

Lévignacq

N10

Roquefort

Lesperon-le-Souquet

D932

D933

Labastide-d'Armagnac

Courant d'Huchet

Léon

N134

Mont-de-Marsan

Villeneuve-de-Marsan

Vieux-Boucau-Port-D'Albret

Préchacq-les-Bains

Gers

Soustons

N124

Adour

D924

D934

N124

Penon

A63

Mugron

St-Sever

Eugénie-les-Bains

Aire-sur-L'Adour

Hossegor

N10

Dax

Montfort-en-Chalosse

Audignon

Hagetmau

Capbreton

Brassempouy

Port de Lanne

Pomarez

D933

Géaune

N117

Peyrehorade

Amou

Hastingues

Sorde L'Abbaye

Pyrénées-Atlantiques

Kilometres
0   20   40

3 *Landes*

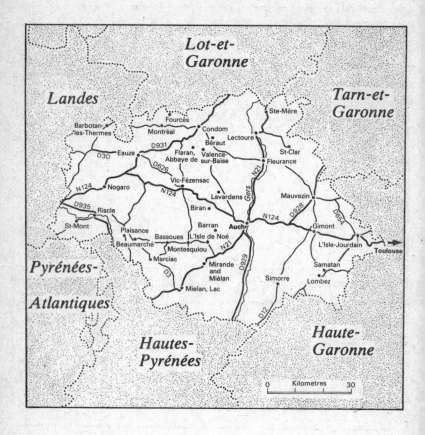

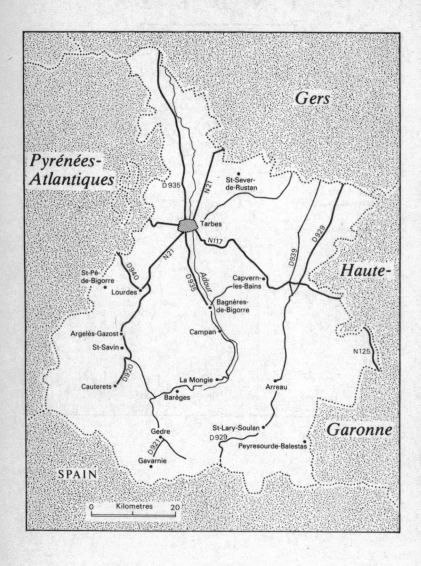

6   *Hautes-Pyrénées*

INDEX

For names of hotels and restaurants see under individual entries